REMEMBERING THE MEMPHIS MASSACRE

REMEMBERING THE MEMPHIS MASSACRE

An American Story

Edited by BEVERLY GREENE BOND *and* SUSAN EVA O'DONOVAN

The University of Georgia Press
Athens

© 2020 by the University of Georgia Press
Athens, Georgia 30602
www.ugapress.org
All rights reserved
Designed by Melissa Bugbee Buchanan
Set in Alegreya

Most University of Georgia Press titles are
available from popular e-book vendors.

Printed digitally

Library of Congress Cataloging-in-Publication Data

Names: Bond, Beverly G., editor. | O'Donovan, Susan E., editor.
Title: Remembering the Memphis Massacre : an American story /
edited by Beverly Greene Bond and Susan Eva O'Donovan.
Description: Athens : The University of Georgia Press, [2020] |
Includes bibliographical references and index.
Identifiers: LCCN 2019044400 | ISBN 9780820356501 (hardback) |
ISBN 9780820356518 (paperback) | ISBN 9780820356495 (ebook)
Subjects: LCSH: Memphis Race Riot, Memphis, Tenn., 1866. | Race riots—
Tennessee—Memphis—History—19th century. | African Americans—Violence
against—Tennessee—Memphis—History—19th century. | Memphis (Tenn.)—
Race relations—History—19th century.
Classification: LCC F444.M557 R46 2020 | DDC 305.896/07307681909034—dc23
LC record available at https://lccn.loc.gov/2019044400

CONTENTS

vii
List of Illustrations

ix
Foreword: Remembering Memphis,
Remembering Reconstruction
GREGORY P. DOWNS

1
Introduction
SUSAN EVA O'DONOVAN AND BEVERLY GREENE BOND

11
The Cotton Economy and the Rebirth of American Slavery
JOSHUA D. ROTHMAN

27
"Cash for Slaves": The African American Trail of Tears
CALVIN SCHERMERHORN

37
Black Soldiers and Sailors and the Defense of Freedpeople's Rights
JOSEPH P. REIDY

53
"Thank God That the Tyrants Rod Has Been Broken":
The Abolition of Slavery in Tennessee
JOHN C. RODRIGUE

68
Structural Violence: The Humanitarian
Crisis before the Memphis Massacre
JIM DOWNS

77
Urban Battlegrounds: Reconstruction in Southern Cities
KATE MASUR

89
Christianity and Race in the Memphis Massacre of 1866
ELIZABETH L. JEMISON

102
Words of Resistance: African American Women's Testimony
about Sexual Violence during the Memphis Massacre
HANNAH ROSEN

120
On Duty in Memphis: Fort Pickering's African American Soldiers
ANDREW L. SLAP

132
Black Organizing Traditions after Slavery
JULIE SAVILLE

149
Black Constitutionalism and the Making of the Fourteenth Amendment
TIMOTHY S. HUEBNER

166
"The Violent Bear It Away": White Responses to
Black Political Mobilization during Reconstruction
CAROLE EMBERTON

178
"I Have Had to Pass through Blood and Fire":
Henry McNeal Turner and the Rhetorical Legacy of Reconstruction
ANDRE E. JOHNSON

190
Memory Battles: History, Memory,
and the Meanings of Reconstruction
K. STEPHEN PRINCE

205
Acknowledgments

207
Contributors

211
Index

ILLUSTRATIONS

3
Memphis Massacre marker

18
Front Street, Memphis, 1845

20
Distribution of the enslaved population, 1860

30
Peter, 1863

31
Nathan Bedford Forrest slave trading advertisement, 1857

42
Hubbard Pryor before his enlistment, 1864

43
Hubbard Pryor after his enlistment, 1864

55
Levee at Memphis, 1862

71
Unidentified wartime refugee

79
Memphis refugee camp, 1862

80
Celebrating abolition in Washington, D.C., 1866

82
"The Irrepressible Conflict," 1866

84
"First Municipal Election in Richmond," 1870

103
Scenes of the Memphis Massacre, 1866

105
Memphis Colored Orphan Asylum, 1866

129
David Warrington

142
African American men cast their first vote, 1867

171
Hunting black men in West Tennessee, 1874

179
Henry McNeal Turner, 1863

200
Nathan Bedford Forrest monument, 1905

FOREWORD

Remembering Memphis, Remembering Reconstruction

GREGORY P. DOWNS

A week after federal troops finally put an end to the three-day pogrom in Memphis in 1866, Republican congressional leader Thaddeus Stevens waved an account of the massacre on the floor of the House of Representatives to prove that Republicans needed to disenfranchise high-ranking Confederates in a proposed version of the Fourteenth Amendment. "I hear several gentlemen say, that these men should be admitted as equal brethren," Stevens said scornfully. "Let not these friends of secession sing to me their siren song of peace and good will until they can stop my ears to the screams and groans of the dying victims at Memphis." The massacre was "more horrible in its atrocity, although not to the same extent, than the massacre at Jamaica. Tell me Tennessee or any other State is loyal of whom such things are proved!"[1] General Ulysses S. Grant called the attacks in Memphis a "massacre" and used them to lobby for an increase in the size and budget of the regular army.[2] After a special congressional committee investigated the massacre, producing some of the extraordinarily painful testimony quoted in this volume's chapters, Republicans printed extra copies of the report to distribute to the country as proof of the "*animus* and the spirit of the people in the South" and to motivate citizens to vote against Democrats.[3] By August, a generally moderate military newspaper used the Memphis Massacre and a later one in New Orleans to prove the need for "strongly garrisoning the subjugated portions of the Union.... Some people persistently shut their eyes to this fact; but the riots, let us hope, will now open them."[4]

The pogrom in Memphis may well have saved Reconstruction and thus, in some crucial way, the United States. In May 1866, when the massacre began, all federal power seemed at risk in the Confederate states. On the very first day of the massacre, President Andrew Johnson had ordered the army not to try civilians in front of military commissions in places where civil courts were open. As a result of Johnson's order and the Supreme Court's decision in *Ex parte Mil-*

ligan, it seemed likely that occupation—and with it the hope of a new order in the South or at least minimal protection for freedpeople—would disappear.⁵

Propelled by the "screams and groans of the dying victims at Memphis," Congress responded. At unspeakable cost, the 1866 massacres at Memphis and New Orleans did open the eyes of some Republicans and enough northern voters to save Reconstruction in the 1866 midterm elections. That outcome buoyed Republicans to put ten of the rebel states (except, ironically, Tennessee) back under military supervision, and commanding generals were charged with overseeing the first-ever mass registration of black men—including hundreds of thousands of formerly enslaved people—as the country sought to remake state constitutions and the foundations of southern society. For a time, years even, actual equality seemed conceivable. For a bit longer—decades—African Americans claimed political power even when their calls for equality were denied. Those opened doors were in part the legacy of the moans of the dying in Memphis. So, too, was the Fourteenth Amendment, which Stevens championed as a response to the massacre. The very words that created birthright citizenship, equal protection, and due process for all Americans are a tribute to and a product of the martyrs of Memphis. In some ways, not just Tennessee history or southern history but U.S. history changed in response to the blood that was spilled in that city.

Even as the Memphis Massacre shaped debates on the floor of Congress and editorials in the nation's leading newspapers, it was also something too perilously easy to forget or to brush aside. In time, as some dreams of Reconstruction were crushed in the Jim Crow world of the 1890s, white southerners and their allies turned what Grant and congressmen called a "massacre" into a "race riot," as if the fault—and the blood—were on the hands of freedpeople. For a century and a half, the city of Memphis covered up the places where freedpeople screamed for help and died and the spots where they gathered and fought back. Even as the city commemorated slave trader and Ku Klux Klan leader Nathan Bedford Forrest and Confederate president Jefferson Davis, and even in the late twentieth century when it drew in tourists in search of Beale Street and the city's legendary African American musical and cultural history, and even with the creation of a museum at the Lorraine Motel, the site of the assassination of Dr. Martin Luther King Jr., the Memphis Massacre was untold on the very streets where it had occurred. History had happened there, and revisionists of the worst kind—propagandists and guilty amnesiacs—covered it up.

This wonderful book is evidence that those cover-ups did not prevail, that the truth has not been forgotten. The authors in this volume draw from earlier historians who wrote the events into the broader story of Reconstruction and the long history of Memphis and Tennessee. Heroic Memphians kept the past alive and worked against forgetting. In the chapters in this volume, we discover—or, more properly, rediscover—both the groans of the dying and the heroic testimony of those who lived and were determined to see that the crimes were prosecuted and the victims' voices heard. We have learned a great deal about Memphis's role in the growth of the slave system on the Mississippi River and about white Tennesseans' violent efforts to sustain as much of slavery as they could in the years after emancipation. We have also learned about the world that black Memphians made during the Civil War: the accomplishments and communities that the murderers hoped to destroy. We have learned about the soldiers who moved from Fort Pickering into the city and about the families and formerly enslaved people who joined them in what must have been an extraordinary, vibrant world.

The silence around the Memphis Massacre was only one aspect of the silence around Reconstruction more broadly, and breaking the silence around Memphis is a part of the pressing contemporary need to break that larger silence. During the twentieth century, as the country dedicated dozens of Civil War national parks and monuments, there were none dedicated to Reconstruction and emancipation. The amnesia and propaganda that buried Memphis under misnamings and myths buried, too, an important moment in the country's history: when four million people claimed their freedom, when the nation debated in the most profound terms the rights of citizens and the possibility of an equal society, and when white southerners led campaigns of terror and intimidation to overthrow those gains and impose Jim Crow segregation. For at least a half century, this approach successfully convinced many white Americans to think of Reconstruction with shame, as a tragic era of corruption. Since the mid-twentieth century, historians have almost completely undone that propaganda, and scholars have extended early work by former slave John Lynch and by former Reconstruction judge Albion Tourgée and, especially, W. E. B. Du Bois's 1935 *Black Reconstruction in America*. This history, capped by Eric Foner's still-remarkable *Reconstruction: America's Unfinished Revolution* and Steven Hahn's *A Nation under Our Feet*, has inspired hundreds of monographs and articles that have excavated a deeper, more accurate picture of Reconstruction across the South.

But this new scholarly vision of Reconstruction is too little known beyond the academy. Where once nonacademics knew the propaganda of Reconstruction, now younger people seem to know almost nothing about it at all, neither good nor bad. Historians have been more successful thus far at driving bad history from the public sphere than in replacing it, despite heroic work by hundreds of valiant practitioners, including the stellar scholars in this volume.

To reach the people, we need to go to the people, as Beverly Bond and Susan O'Donovan have worked to do with their programming and this book. The parallel effort to establish historically accurate markers in Memphis is one crucial step, which I hope will lead to further public explorations of both the massacre and the broader history of African Americans in the city. It is crucial that we undo the propaganda of the past, as Memphis has already worked to do in removing memorials to white supremacy. But it is even more important, in my view, to produce and promulgate better histories, else we risk replacing propaganda with a new kind of amnesia. Memphis, where freedpeople built social, religious, educational, economic, and political communities even before the Civil War ended, now has a chance to once again be a beacon and a guide in the way we as a nation remember both those communities and the violent efforts to destroy them. It is important, as these chapters show, that we see freedpeople not only as victims—though in May 1866 many of them were—but also as family members, as churchgoers, as business owners, as veterans, as schoolchildren, as painters, as musicians, as seamstresses, as people not just making do but making life. Only then will we be able to show the true impact of the violence that aimed to destroy not just individuals but a whole world, and we will also show the resilience of a people who would not be destroyed.

It would be gracious to end this foreword at this point. To say, well done. But let's do more. Now, we have historical markers on the streets of Memphis and a national park site dedicated to Reconstruction in Beaufort, South Carolina. We are getting somewhere. And yet I cannot resist using these last few words to remind us that Memphis, despite all it represents, does not represent the entirety of the South. Nor, for that matter, does the town of Beaufort or the city of New Orleans. It is possible to overstate how unique Memphis was, to make it and New Orleans the dual beacons of the suffering of freedpeople in the South in 1866.

In fact, Congress did not need to look solely at Memphis or New Orleans to see this suffering. In one of the most extraordinary sets of testimony in American history, the U.S. Congress heard from more than 140 witnesses called before the Joint Committee on Reconstruction, many of whom described bloodshed and mayhem on plantations, in small towns, and in places unknown to modern maps. In the weeks after the Memphis Massacre, in the weeks after he brandished the report from Memphis on the floor of Congress, Thaddeus Stevens received other letters, including one especially vivid description of the hanging of twenty-four freedpeople in Pine Bluff, Arkansas.[6] Stevens and other Republicans read reports from across the South of thousands of assaults, of two to three murdered freedpeople a day in Mississippi, of efforts to "entirely extirpate" the freedpeople "from the face of the earth."[7] In graphic—

sometimes, arguably pornographic—detail, these reports described horrors that would be unspeakable except for the need to speak about them aloud, lest the suffering be forgotten.

These attacks, the daily assaults on rural freedpeople, were hard for northerners to picture even as they responded powerfully to the stories from Memphis and New Orleans. It was all too easy to let single, extraordinary urban events eclipse the mundane atrocities out in the countryside. It was all too hard—perhaps too horrifying—to picture the ongoing daily violence in the South's plantation districts. Toward the end of the nineteenth century, a congressman estimated that more than fifty thousand African Americans were murdered between 1863 and 1888.[8] As we honor the fallen in Memphis—and those who carried on—it is crucial that the events in Memphis and New Orleans not overshadow the vast majority of freedpeople who lived in rural farming and plantation regions, whose stories did not frequently make northern newspapers or the halls of Congress, whose struggles and successes and suffering are as yet less known, even to historians.

In Montgomery, Alabama, the Equal Justice Initiative directed by Bryan Stevenson has compiled a list of lynching victims and memorialized them there. We should take this awe-inspiring project as a challenge—almost as a dare to fulfill our professional obligations—to try together to recover the names and stories of as many as we can of those fifty thousand and of the millions more who carried on and struggled, survived, and sometimes thrived, and who, in the process, kept alive not only their communities but hopes for a better and more just nation. Only when the South—no, the nation—is full of memorials and monuments to them and their lives will we have fulfilled our mission as historians and as human beings. When people cannot drive through the South without seeing markers of the true past, when they cannot walk its sidewalks without pausing at tributes to the fallen and the risen, when they cannot look over the farmland without seeing the blood in the soil, then we will have made progress on the great task remaining before us. The great work in Memphis—and in this volume—should be not a moment for congratulation but for inspiration, to go forth and make it multiply.

NOTES

1. *Congressional Globe*, 39th Cong., 1st sess., 2544.

2. *Army and Navy Journal*, May 26, 1866, 636; Brooks D. Simpson, *Let Us Have Peace: The Politics of War and Reconstruction, 1861–1868* (Chapel Hill: University of North Carolina Press, 1991), 136–37; John Y. Simon, ed., *The Papers of Ulysses S. Grant*, vol. 16: 1866 (Carbondale: Southern Illinois University Press, 1988), 257–59.

3. *Congressional Globe*, 39th Cong., 1st sess., 4266.

4. *Army and Navy Journal*, August 11, 1866, 812.

5. Ex parte Milligan, 71 U.S. 2 (1866).

6. Wm. P. Mallet to Thaddeus Stevens, May 28, 1866, box 3, Stevens Papers, Library of Congress, Washington, D.C.

7. *Report of the Joint Committee on Reconstruction, at the First Session, Thirty-Ninth Congress* (Washington, D.C.: Government Printing Office, 1866), 2:16–17.

8. Douglas R. Egerton, *The Wars of Reconstruction: The Brief, Violent History of America's Most Progressive Era* (New York: Bloomsbury, 2014), 296, 304.

REMEMBERING THE MEMPHIS MASSACRE

INTRODUCTION

SUSAN EVA O'DONOVAN AND
BEVERLY GREENE BOND

The trouble started late on April 30, 1866. Sparked by verbal sparring between white city police officers and a group of black men recently mustered out of the Union army, a wave of violence erupted, escalating within hours to mass murder and mayhem. For three terrible days, mobs of white men, many of whom would never be identified, roamed the streets of South Memphis, leaving blood, rubble, and terror in their wake. Their chief targets were African Americans: soldiers and civilians; men, women, and children; young and old. By the time the streets cleared on May 3, at least forty-six African American men, women, and children and two white men lay dead. A few white people who had been closely associated with the city's growing population of black residents also felt the anger of the terroristic gangs. An unknown number of black Memphians, many of whom were recent arrivals who had sought sanctuary in the city during the war, had fled for their lives, some never to return. White missionaries who had come to educate the newly freed people also fled. Every African American church and schoolhouse was destroyed, hundreds of homes and businesses were burglarized and burned, and white assailants raped at least five black women. Although contemporaries and some historians termed these three days of violence a "race riot," not one white person died at a black person's hand. As a federal commander noted in the days following the event, "what [was] called the 'riot'" was "in reality [a] massacre" of extended proportions.[1]

News of the massacre shocked a still war-weary nation. Erupting a year after the Confederate surrender at Appomattox Court House, Virginia, the bloody events at Memphis lent new urgency to ongoing debates about the meaning of freedom, the rights of citizens, and the role of Congress in defining and then protecting both. The aftermath of the massacre also revealed black southerners as a powerful political force. Appearing before military and congressional investigators to denounce the actions of the mob, black women and men took the opportunity to articulate their own often more inclusive vision of freedom, one in which black southerners would enjoy the same rights and privileges that the nation had automatically extended for decades to white citizens. In so doing, black Memphians joined forces with formerly enslaved people across the South to help guide the nation toward a more fully realized version of democracy in which freedom would be the birthright of all Americans.

The nation changed in the months and years following the massacre. Seizing control of Reconstruction policy from a conciliatory President Andrew Johnson, Congress passed and the states ratified the Fourteenth and Fifteenth Amendments along with a host of supporting legislation. An upsurge of grassroots activism led to the expansion and repopulation of the American political universe. Black men appeared alongside white men at polling places, on juries, and at every level of civic engagement from local police forces to the U.S. Senate. Black southerners, women and men alike, found in freedom new opportunities to enter into professions long closed to people of African descent, and they took up a wide range of skilled and entrepreneurial professions. Many became shopkeepers, teachers, doctors, lawyers, police officers, and ministers. Although their numbers remained small, some even became landowners, farmers, and planters. Working within a political structure that most had known only from the outside under slavery, black southerners participated in the writing and passing of new laws, helping to lay the legal, political, social, and economic foundations for who we would become as a people and as a nation.

Yet as Gregory P. Downs notes in his foreword and as Carole Emberton and K. Stephen Prince explain in their contributions to this volume, this dynamic and biracial history was within a few generations quickly and deliberately "forgotten," swept aside by a rising tide of white supremacy. A sectional reconciliation was bought at the price of black people's part in American history. The African American involvement in Reconstruction, if admitted at all, came to be enfolded in a history decried as a "tragic era." First coined by historian Claude G. Bowers and then adopted by a wide swath of white Americans, northern and southern, the phrase "tragic era" was meant to convince the nation that the years following the end of the Civil War had been a terrible aberration, a period in which the country had been turned topsy-turvy, the bottom rail replacing the top.[2] This narrative was captured and conveyed in popular culture too, most notably by D. W. Griffith in his 1915 blockbuster silent film, *The Birth of a Nation*, and by Margaret Mitchell's 1936 novel, *Gone with the Wind*, and the film adaptation that followed three years later. Any discussion of the period's emancipatory, progressive, and transformative history was generally confined to African American circles. As a nation, we publicly shunned both the prom-

The Memphis Massacre marker at Army-Navy Park, Memphis, Tennessee, was erected on May 1, 2016. Photo by authors.

ises and black people's foundational role in reshaping American civil, political, and social life. Even as commemorations of Civil War battles and the men who fought them proliferated—at Gettysburg, Antietam, Shiloh, Vicksburg, and elsewhere—nothing equivalent emerged to offer public recognition of Reconstruction's history, never mind an acknowledgment of the black women and men who had made so much of that history. For most Americans, the end of the Civil War became the end of the story.

However, that began to change by the 1960s. Encouraged by a surging academic interest in the African American past, an interest galvanized initially by the civil rights movement, which illuminated both the oppressions of Jim Crow and a black America that was anything but passive, historians have spent the past fifty years rethinking and rewriting Reconstruction's history. The story they tell is no longer one of national travesty but rather one of national promise. Reconstruction was an "unfinished revolution," announced historian Eric Foner in his 1988 book.[3]

As historians have reconsidered Reconstruction and the many revolutions it unleashed, their insights and explanations have gained important footholds in college curricula, textbooks, and scholarly monographs. Historians simultaneously have reconsidered the Civil War, its causes, and its combatants. This has resulted in reinterpreted museum exhibits, public commemorations of black soldiers, and productions like Hollywood's 1989 blockbuster film, *Glory*, and Ken Burns's 1990 documentary series, *The Civil War*. But although the nation has embraced a more inclusive Civil War history, we have not been as quick to publicly engage with Reconstruction's arguably darker and more troubled history. Even now, a century and a half after the Civil War ended, Americans have continued to stubbornly rebuff the combined efforts of scholars and the National Park Service to develop new historical sites that would bring those years of post-emancipation racial reckoning to public attention.[4]

By the second decade of the twenty-first century, however, it became all too obvious that Americans had no choice but to face that past head on. Spurred by savage outbreaks of racial violence in Ferguson, Missouri; Baltimore, Maryland; and Charleston, South Carolina; and by heated debates over the public display of Confederate symbols and the rise of the Black Lives Matter movement, many of us acknowledged that to move forward we had to look back. Black history has come to matter to a degree and depth never before experienced in this country, and interest in this history has ignited curiosity about deeper, darker aspects, such as Reconstruction. In an era of public and often painful reckonings with racism and its legacies, Americans are coming to realize that we can no longer afford to hide from the hard parts of our past. We need to acknowledge and understand our racial histories in all their many dimensions.[5]

In West Tennessee, the Memphis Massacre Project stepped into this fraught arena of historical memory.[6] With the sesquicentennial of the Civil War behind us and that of Reconstruction upon us, a diverse group of historians, lawyers, educators, church leaders, archivists, librarians, students, and community leaders came together to commemorate the more than forty people who lost their lives in the 1866 Memphis Massacre. We knew it would not be easy work. In a city dominated by the towering marble figures of Jefferson Davis and Nathan Bedford Forrest (the former the president of a failed nation, the other a murderous slave trader), few citizens were aware of the violence that had swept their city a century and a half earlier. Even fewer had any inkling of the social, legal, and constitutional consequences of those three terrible days. Any reasonable accounting of the massacre needed careful contextualization. The violence did not take place in a vacuum. Understanding the who, what, when, where, and why of the event meant that we and the audience we wanted to reach had no choice but to delve into the histories of slavery and the Civil War. No understanding of the Memphis Massacre would be complete without taking that wider history into account. Likewise, any attempt to understand the consequences and legacies of those terrible three days in May 1866 required looking beyond them to consider what the massacre meant for a nation that was still coming to terms with four years of war and the emancipation of four million people. We needed to convey the message that what happened in Memphis was a national story and how—in many respects—it remains an ongoing story.

The Memphis Massacre Project formally launched on February 1, 2016. Over the next five months, we conducted a flurry of public events and organized lectures, book talks, teachers workshops, and seminars. We met on the campuses of LeMoyne-Owen College (whose institutional roots reach back to the post–Civil War era and the Memphis Massacre), Rhodes College, and the University of Memphis. We sponsored events at the Memphis Public Library, at the National Civil Rights Museum, in churches, in classrooms, and at the historic Orange Mound community in South Memphis. Local and national press and other media picked up and broadcast our message. When we launched, few people outside of academia had ever heard of the Memphis Massacre. Before we held our closing event, the 1866 murders of dozens of black Memphians by white mobs had become national news. The ugly history of Reconstruction had surfaced at last.

One hundred and fifty years of silence does not break easily or cleanly. The chapters in this volume continue the work we started in 2016. Based on the papers presented at the two-day symposium that capped the semester-long sequence of public events, these chapters strive to embed the Memphis Massacre within the larger historical and experiential landscape of the U.S. story. Our goal is to help readers understand how and why the Memphis Massacre matters and why, more than ever, Reconstruction's hard histories demand our collective respect and attention.

Historical events are inexplicable without careful reference to the circumstances that shaped them and from which they emerged. This is why the chapters that follow start with slavery and not freedom. How and why people came to the Mississippi Valley and the roles they played in a quickly developing cotton economy helped set the stage for what would follow. Cotton brought wealth, ambition, settlement, and enslaved people by the hundreds of thousands, many of whom landed in West Tennessee. Likewise, the Civil War, especially in the Mississippi Valley, mattered significantly to the violence that rattled Memphis in 1866. Thus after Joshua Rothman and Calvin Schermerhorn in the first two chapters of this book lay out the antebellum story of cotton's rise and its utter dependence on the labor of enslaved people, the next three chapters, contributed by Joseph Reidy, John Rodrigue, and Jim Downs, guide us through four years of a war that was simultaneously liberating and destructive. Emancipation was a fraught and dangerous process, a point made explicitly by Downs and reiterated by Julie Saville in her chapter on black organizing traditions. While there was little inevitable about emancipation, and full freedom in the form of a constitutional amendment was not a given either, the war still unleashed great change. Before hostilities ended, Abraham Lincoln's government had recruited nearly 180,000 black men to military service, 20,000 of whom came out of Tennessee; thousands of people had been displaced from the countryside and moved into Memphis and its nearby refugee camps; and an ever-larger chorus of voices had joined a growing debate over the place of black southerners in a postslavery nation. Black people—many of them Union soldiers and even more of them refugees struggling to stay alive while war raged around them—weighed in alongside white politicians, newspaper editors, and other citizens. They pressed for equal rights, fair treatment, and the removal of barriers based on race or prior condition. The country had begun to change under the cover of war.

The Confederate surrender in April 1865 and the ratification of the Thirteenth Amendment eight months later lent even greater urgency to the debate over freedom's meanings. With slavery abolished and four million black southerners now free, the nation—including West Tennessee and the city of Memphis—had to figure out what needed to come next. The laws and customs of slavery no longer applied. With staple agriculture still the region's chief economic engine, black and white southerners faced the daunting project of restoring the cotton economy on a free-labor basis even as they faced the equally daunting project of imbuing the word "freedom" with substance and meaning. These dilemmas raised a host of deceptively simple, profoundly important questions about the nation's future and about where people of color should or could fit in. Who should work, at what, for how long, and on what terms? Were civil and political rights birthrights or privileges that people needed to earn? Were black soldiers to be accorded the same rights that automatically accrued to white soldiers? Were black bodies now sacrosanct, or would they remain subject to white people's whims? But most pressing of all was the larger question of who had the right to decide on these issues. White southerners generally thought that the privilege of decision-making lay with those who had always been free. Formerly enslaved people, including black women, thought otherwise. They insisted that it was their future too, and they claimed front-row seats in any debate about what freedom should mean.

None of the questions that arose as a consequence of the Confederate defeat were easy to answer, and they often became flash points for heated and occasionally violent engagement. Conversations loud and soft, fierce and fair unfolded on farms and plantations, in legislative halls, in schoolrooms, and in country stores; they took place along public roads, in workplaces, in barnyards, and in kitchens. Indeed, debates about the future of America's formerly enslaved people arose wherever people chanced to meet, and cities and streets, fields and farms were sites of social, political, and cultural struggle. As Kate Masur explains in her chapter about the urban battlegrounds of the post–Civil War South, cities were especially combustible places. As Elizabeth Jemison explains, so too were churches, where a black Christianity that abhorred human bondage collided with a southern white Christianity that had long rested its defense of slavery on a selective reading of scripture.

In May 1866, Memphis exploded against this superheated backdrop of urban overcrowding, confusion, fear, hope, and ambition. The pressure had been building for decades, but war and emancipation sent long-standing racial, economic, cultural, class, and gender tensions rocketing to new heights. Like so much of human history, the murderous eruption of a white mob was both unexpected and perfectly logical. As Hannah Rosen and Andrew Slap show in their chapters, the Memphis Massacre was no accident. It grew out of long-standing and intensifying tensions between black and white, free and enslaved, women and men. Yet as is the case with so much of human history, the outcome was not inevitable. The white mob acted out of pent-up frustrations about the Union victory and wartime disruptions coupled with deep fears for the future, but the aggressors did not get what they wanted. Rosen and Slap remind us that black Memphians refused to back down; instead, they stood up, stepped forward, and in testimony presented to congressional and military investigations, countered the mob's vision of a strictly limited freedom with those of their own. Indeed, black Memphians so forcefully rejected a conservative construction of the South's future that they helped to push the nation in a much more radical direction. In this sense, Memphis served as a catalyst for even more radical changes to the nation's social, political, and legal institutions.

By galvanizing the nation to more forcefully protect black freedom, the Memphis Massacre also helped to intensify and accelerate a grassroots insurgency. Tapping into long-standing strands of what Timothy Huebner in his chapter describes as a black constitutionalism and Julie Saville explains as an organizing tradition, an African American movement for social, civic, and political justice swept the post–Civil War South. Its leaders were many: former black soldiers, black women made angry by continued assaults on their persons by white men, workers who demanded that they be paid for the labor that slaveholders stole, and ministers, such as the tireless Henry McNeal Turner of Georgia, of whose rhetorical power Andre Johnson writes in his chapter. As Saville reminds us, it was also a wider New World project, as formerly enslaved people throughout the nineteenth-century Americas shrugged off centuries of slavery's weight and labored collectively to give substance and form to black liberation.

But as many of the contributors demonstrate, making freedom real was a dangerous proposition, made so by white southerners (and eventually more than a few white northerners) who yearned for the pre–Civil War racial order, in which black Americans knew and kept to a subordinate place. To a certain extent, the success of black activism can be measured by the intensity of white people's resistance, and as the massacre at Memphis and subsequent events demonstrated, white resistance to black freedom was fierce. It was also relentless, and slowly, battle by battle, blow by blow, death by death, former slaveholders and their allies retook much of the ground that had been "lost" to emancipation. By the mid-1870s and increasingly thereafter, white supremacists' counterrevolution gained an oppressive momentum, slowing the changes that the Civil War and black liberation had unleashed. The backlash was ruthless, making its presence and politics felt in a surge of discriminatory laws, in the organization of extralegal associations like the paramilitary night riders of whom Carole Emberton writes in her chapter, in a rising tide of lynching, and eventually in the proliferation of towering monuments to white supremacy and Confederate heroes. The goal, K. Stephen Prince tells us in the closing chapter, was to eradicate "the last vestiges of black civil equality and political participation."

But not even the heaviest of granite or marble edifices nor the regular outbursts of anti-black terror has ever entirely suppressed either African Americans' dreams of full freedom or their organizing tradition. Despite the bruising weight of disenfranchisement, Jim Crow, and white supremacy, flickers of Reconstruction's black insurgency survived. We witnessed their dogged presence in the organization in 1909 of the National Association for the Advancement of Colored People (NAACP) and in an outpouring of scholarship from black intellectuals like W. E. B. Du Bois, Carter G. Woodson (the father of what has become Black History Month and founder of the *Journal of African American History*), and John Hope Franklin (the author of a still widely assigned textbook on African American history).[7] We especially saw their power resurface in the sit-ins, marches, and voter registration drives that led to the Civil Rights Act of 1964 and the Voting Rights Act of 1965. We saw it in Memphis during the 1968 sanitation workers strike. And now, at the close of the second decade of the twenty-first century, we see the same quest for full and equal treatment in the rise of the Black Lives Matter movement and in the frank and open debates about the lingering presence of Confederate symbols on our public landscapes.

This latest line of engagement has been especially visible in Memphis. In conjunction with the Memphis Massacre Project, the National Park Service worked with the Memphis chapter of the NAACP to unveil a first-of-its-kind memorial to black victims of Reconstruction. That in itself was a history-making event. But Memphis refused to stop there. On December 20, 2017, the statues of Jefferson Davis and Nathan Bedford Forrest came down, ending nearly a century-long reign over downtown. Four months later, a marker describing Forrest's hand in the buying and selling of slaves went up, stating publicly for the first time Forrest's role in what Schermerhorn decries as the African American Trail of Tears.[8] We may be a century and a half late, but Memphians of all classes and colors are coming together with like-minded people from across the country to write a new history that foretells a new future. This history does not flinch away from the hardest and darkest parts of our past; it no longer subscribes to white supremacy's deliberate omissions; and it seeks to tell a more complete, unvarnished, and inclusive story about slavery, freedom, and the struggle for equal rights. This volume is a small part of that process.

NOTES

1. "Memphis Riots and Massacres," *U.S. Serial Set*, no. 1274, House Report 101, 39th Cong., 1st sess., 5. For a book-length treatment of the massacre, see Stephen V. Ash, *A Massacre in Memphis: The Race Riot That Shook the Nation One Year after the Civil War* (New York: Hill and Wang, 2013).

2. Claude G. Bowers, *The Tragic Era: The Revolution after Lincoln* (New York: Houghton Mifflin, 1929).

3. Eric Foner, *Reconstruction: America's Unfinished Revolution* (New York: Harper and Row, 1988).

4. In addition to K. Stephen Prince's contribution to this volume, see David W. Blight, *Race and Reunion: The Civil War in American Memory* (Cambridge, Mass.: Belknap, 2001), and Cecilia Elizabeth O'Leary, *To Die For: The Paradox of American Patriotism* (Princeton, N.J.: Princeton University Press, 1999).

5. Gregory P. Downs and Kate Masur, "There's No National Site Devoted to Reconstruction—Yet," *Atlantic*, April 29, 2015.

6. See https://www.memphis.edu/memphis-massacre.

7. W. E. B. Du Bois, *Black Reconstruction: An Essay toward a History of the Part Which Black Folk Played in the Attempt to Reconstruct Democracy in America, 1860–1880* (New York: Harcourt Brace, 1935); Carter G. Woodson, *Negro Makers of History* (Washington, D.C.: Associated Publishers, 1928); and John Hope Franklin, *From Slavery to Freedom: A History of African Americans* (New York: Knopf, 1947).

8. "Memphis Removes Confederate Statues from Downtown Parks," *USA Today Network*, December 20, 2017; "Memphis's Novel Strategy for Tearing Down Confederate Statues," *Atlantic*, December 21, 2017; "New Historical Marker to Tell the Truth of Nathan Bedford Forrest, Slave Trade in Memphis," *Commercial Appeal* (Memphis), March 5, 2018.

The Cotton Economy and the Rebirth of American Slavery

JOSHUA D. ROTHMAN

In the fall of 1834, a steamboat carried author Joseph Holt Ingraham up the Mississippi River from New Orleans, through the sugar parishes of southern Louisiana, and on to the city of Natchez, Mississippi. As he toured the adjacent plantation districts of southwestern Mississippi, Ingraham was struck by how dramatically the agricultural foundation of the state had changed in the fifty years or so that preceded his visit. "When this state was first settled," he observed, "tobacco was exclusively cultivated as the grand staple." But by the 1830s, tobacco had been entirely displaced. Instead, Ingraham continued, "planters have no room for anything but their cotton, and corn, on their plantations, and scarcely are they willing to make room even for the latter." After all, given the money to be made from cotton, wasting space to grow corn that might be bought from somewhere else seemed absurd.[1]

The truth was that "planters" did not actually produce cotton at all; the enslaved people they held captive did. The white men who owned those people and the land they worked were entirely aware of this fact, and by the time of Ingraham's visit, they understood that maximizing the annual crop came down to a fairly straightforward equation: the more enslaved people a white man could force to labor in the fields, the more bales of cotton he was likely to see at the end of a season. From what Ingraham saw and heard on his travels, the economic imperatives for white landowners in Mississippi were clear and consuming. Ingraham wrote, "To sell cotton in order to buy negroes—to make more cotton to buy more negroes, 'ad infinitum,' is the aim and direct tendency of all the operations of the thorough-going cotton planter; his whole soul is wrapped up in the pursuit."[2]

What Ingraham witnessed in Mississippi was part of the steady, lockstep expansion of cotton and slavery across the landscape of North America in the first half of the nineteenth century, which would not halt until the Civil War broke out in 1861. By that point, there were four million enslaved people living in fifteen states plus the District of Columbia, which gave the United States the largest enslaved population in the world. When the U.S. Constitution was ratified in 1789, however, few people would have imagined such a future for the country, and slavery seemed to lose momentum in the early years of the republic. Rather than a planned development, the explosive growth of slavery in the nineteenth-century United States emerged from a series of ideological, diplomatic, military, political, economic, and technological factors, which all converged and overlapped within a matter of decades. Resulting in a phenomenon that some scholars refer to as the "second slavery," most of those factors were linked to the desire to exploit cotton as a cash crop. In the early republic, as cotton became the most vital commodity on earth, invigorated the national economy, and gave rise to the manufacturing of the early Industrial Revolution, it also made human bondage an immensely powerful force in American life.[3]

The American Revolution and its aftermath left the leaders of the new United States feeling deep collective ambivalence about the institution of slavery. Before them was the task of maintaining a union that included people inspired by the rhetoric of freedom and liberty that had suffused the revolution and others who were thoroughly committed to using slave labor. Indeed, some individuals, none more famous than Thomas Jefferson, claimed and vocalized the rhetoric of freedom while maintaining their commitments to slavery at the same time.[4]

The irresolution arising from this array of competing interests and ideologies was embedded in the Constitution itself. Numerous constitutional provisions folded slavery directly into the framework of the national government and put the power of the federal state behind it. Most notorious and important was the clause providing that an enslaved person would be enumerated as three-fifths of a free person for the purposes of congressional representation and federal taxation. That formulation layered a structural political incentive for slavery on top of preexisting economic incentives. It effectively encouraged slaveholders to enlarge the enslaved populations of their respective states because slavery provided those states with national clout well beyond the numbers of white citizens living in them. In the federal Congress that gathered in the spring of 1789, for instance, South Carolina and Connecticut had the same number of elected representatives even though the latter had nearly 100,000 more free white residents than the former. Slaveholding also provided federal executive power alongside such legislative bonuses. It was not merely a matter of unusually strong leadership nor was it a coincidence that four of the first five U.S. presidents came from Virginia, the state with the largest enslaved population by far in the early republic. Rather, this result was, at least in part, a consequence of the overrepresentation of slave states in the electoral college.[5]

The Constitution also committed the federal government to the use of military force to assist in putting down slave insurrections. It contained a clause providing for the return of enslaved people who fled from slaveholding states to non-slaveholding states, thus making it impossible for a legally enslaved person to be truly free anywhere in the country. And it forbade Congress from taking any action with respect to the transatlantic slave trade until 1808, thereby at least temporarily acquiescing to the trade and sacrificing an entire generation of Africans to the horrors that trade entailed.[6]

Yet even though these federal endorsements were real and significant, the framers of the Constitution purposefully avoided explicit mentions of enslaved people or slavery in the document. For example, in three different places where straightforward references to "slaves" might have appeared, the Constitution's authors turned to obfuscations instead and alluded to "other persons," "such persons," and "person[s] held to service or labour."[7] They wished neither to refer directly to slavery in what was intended as a permanent national charter, nor to offend individuals who opposed slavery. But they were also unable to ignore slavery's economic prominence and political significance. Thus delegates to the Constitutional Convention simply sidestepped the linguistic challenge with which they were presented by being evasive and using euphemisms.[8]

No one was fooled by such equivocations, of course, and constitutional coyness had little operational impact on slavery in the early republic. But it pointed toward the possibility that the compromises with slavery written into the Constitution might be temporary ones on a road toward slavery's disappearance. And there were signals after 1776 that slavery was weakening as an institution. Many white people of conscience believed that either it might wane on its own and die a natural death or, more likely, that it would fade to the point where it became an insignificant oddity on the American landscape. The latter path would do little for those who remained enslaved, but an enervated slavery was one that opponents of the institution felt could feasibly be dealt with in the future.[9]

The signs of slavery's decline were numerous as the eighteenth century wound down. It generally was understood that Congress would act to ban the transatlantic slave trade as soon as the Constitution allowed it in 1808, and the body passed laws in 1794 and 1800 that barred the building or outfitting of American ships for use in the trade and prohibited U.S. citizens from investing in or working on ships that carried enslaved people across the Atlantic. Indeed, by the early years of the nineteenth century, only South Carolina allowed the foreign slave trade at all. Every other state had outlawed it between the 1770s and the 1790s.[10]

Moreover, slavery everywhere north of the Chesapeake region appeared to be headed toward extinction or significant degeneration. In 1787, the Northwest Ordinance provided that slavery would always be illegal in the Northwest Territory, which lay above the Ohio River between Pennsylvania's western boundary and the Mississippi River and out of which would eventually emerge seven free states. Northern states, meanwhile, began phasing out slavery and outlawing it within their borders. Pennsylvania, Massachusetts, New Hampshire, Connecticut, and Rhode Island, in fact, had at least edged toward the systematic emancipation of enslaved people even before the ratification of the Constitution. By 1804, every state north of the Mason-Dixon Line had either banned slavery outright or instituted a plan for the gradual emancipation of their enslaved populations.[11]

Even the states of the Upper South made provisions that might, in time, have pushed them toward similar kinds of emancipation plans. In 1782, Virginia instituted a liberal manumission law that enabled slaveholders to free enslaved people they owned without the burdens of what had been cumbersome and expensive legal measures. Maryland followed suit with a similar law in 1796, and in 1797 Delaware passed legislation that declared any enslaved person sold out of state to be automatically free. In these states, the liberative ideals of the revolution had made significant inroads among elites, and the tobacco economy that had made slavery indispensable to them in the colonial period had long since entered a period of stagnation. The mixed economy of livestock, grain, and other crops coming to replace tobacco was not nearly so labor intensive, and so by the turn of the nineteenth century, slavery in the Upper South became in the eyes of many white people both morally questionable and economically unsustainable.[12]

In 1776, only 5 percent of the black population in the United States was free. By 1790, that number had risen to 8 percent, and by 1800 it was 11 percent. At that point, nearly one-fifth of Maryland's black population was free, more than half of Delaware's was, and the number of free black people in Virginia had increased by more than 50 percent in the preceding decade alone. These were relatively small steps, but had matters continued trending in this direction, one can imagine an alternate universe in which slavery became so morally repugnant, so economically unprofitable, and so effectively useless that it would eventually have been found only in places like South Carolina and Georgia. In such a universe, grappling with the economic and political implications of abolition still might have been difficult but could perhaps have been entirely manageable. Shortly before leaving the White House in 1801, John Adams wrote to two Quaker abolitionists expressing his support for gradual emancipation and his sense that "the practice of slavery is fast diminishing." He believed himself to be making an honest assessment of the future.[13]

There was always a certain element of denial in prognostications like this because the overall numeric population of enslaved people in the early republic never actually stopped growing. The enslaved population increased by nearly 30 percent during the 1790s, and in 1800 nearly 900,000 people lived in bondage in the United States. In addition, over the course of the initial decades of the nineteenth century, it became clear that most white Americans had stopped even their wishful thinking about a future without slavery. Instead, slavery was reborn and given new life. The population of enslaved people in the United States increased by hundreds of thousands during every single decade between 1800 and 1860, and slavery in the nineteenth century became far more important to the nation, its white citizens, and its economy than it had ever been in the colonial era.[14]

In part, this departure from the road toward universal black freedom was a response to ideological changes, as the idealism of the revolutionary era ebbed and was replaced by a nasty backlash against that freedom. Rooted in a reaction to black people's violent resistance to slavery, such as the Haitian Revolution in the Caribbean in the 1790s and Gabriel's Rebellion in Virginia in 1800, this backlash led growing numbers of whites to reconsider the notion that all people were entitled to liberty simply by being human. Rather, they concluded that liberty for people of African descent was dangerous, that perhaps it had gone too far, and that the security of white lives required that black people be strictly controlled, subordinated, and enslaved. Demonstrating some of the practical implications of this ideological reversal was the policy of Virginia, which in 1806 undid its liberal manumission law from 1782 and instituted in its place a law that forced enslaved people who managed to attain freedom after its passage to leave the state within a year or face the prospect of re-enslavement.[15]

Compounding this turnabout in mind-set when it came to black people was an advance of a new set of ideas in the early republic that suggested that true freedom for white people required their expansion across the continent, where yeoman farmers would lay claim to the bounty of North America and fulfill their aspirations as independent people. There was no greater exponent for this vision of the destiny of the United States than Thomas Jefferson, and diplomatically no one did more than Jefferson to create the conditions for putting that vision into practice. When Jefferson assumed the presidency in 1801, European control over the city of New Orleans threatened to compromise the access of growing numbers of trans-Appalachian American farmers to the Gulf of

Mexico and thus to global markets. By acquiring the Louisiana Territory from France in 1803, Jefferson doubled the size of the United States overnight and gained tens of millions of acres of land onto which Americans might extend white settlement. He also secured New Orleans as a western port and thus effectively reinvigorated the prospects for agricultural production in the American interior. Slavery would underpin the realization of those prospects in short order.[16]

Of course, simply laying claim to territory in which slavery might take root did not in and of itself clear a path for its doing so. Even after the Louisiana Purchase, British efforts to undermine the stability of the United States along its northern and western borders remained a threat, as did any number of indigenous nations that inhabited the land onto which white people wished to move. But the might of the American military enabled the expansion of slavery as well, and if Jefferson was responsible for much of the necessary ideological vision and diplomatic negotiation to make that happen, Andrew Jackson provided the muscle.

Jackson became nationally famous during the War of 1812 for thwarting a British assault on New Orleans late in 1814. Even though technically the war had ended by then, Jackson's triumph at the battle put to rest any lingering sentiment among the British that invading the United States was worth expending their resources. When it came to indigenous people, meanwhile, Jackson spent more than twenty years fighting, killing, cheating, buying out, and treating with "Indians," whom he considered savages, inferior to white people, and lacking understanding about how to make a sophisticated economy function. He defeated the Red Stick Creeks in Alabama in 1814 and imposed a treaty that extracted from the Creek Nation more than twenty million acres of land in Georgia and Alabama. He led a campaign against the Seminoles in Georgia and Florida beginning in 1818, and shortly after becoming president in 1829, Jackson called for and received authorization to engineer the wholesale removal of Native people from the eastern United States. That policy resulted in numerous treaties, mostly executed under some form of duress or chicanery, which American troops implemented by forcibly exiling more than a half dozen indigenous nations from their homelands and across the Mississippi River. Within a year of Jackson's leaving office in 1837, the southeastern United States had been largely cleared for the development of a white agricultural slaveholding empire.[17]

Cotton was the key to it all. Cotton was the reason so many white people wanted what had been indigenous people's land in the Southeast. Cotton was the foundation of the "civilized" economy envisioned by Andrew Jackson and his allies. And cotton was the crop that stimulated slavery anew in the United

States. As white Americans forced Native people off the landscape of the Deep South, they replaced them with cotton fields and imported legions of enslaved black people to labor there.

It had never been a secret that cotton grew bountifully in the soil of the Deep South, nor was it surprising that white farmers would use slave labor to grow it. What made the cotton economy of the nineteenth century a new and powerful engine for American expansion was not only the availability and security of the land itself for white settlement, but also the technological advances that made cotton more profitable than anyone would have considered possible before. Most significant in this regard, of course, was the cotton gin. Most Americans learn in grade school of Connecticut teacher Eli Whitney, the supposed lone genius inventor who came up with the idea for the cotton gin after a visit to a Georgia plantation. Although this story is vastly oversimplified, Whitney's 1793 design for a basic machine that used a series of mesh grids, combs, and spiked gears to separate cotton fibers from cotton seeds did break through the processing bottleneck that had long made short-staple cotton an inefficient and unprofitable crop to grow in large quantities. It typically took one person an entire day to clean the seeds from one pound of cotton fiber by hand, but Whitney's design enabled that same person to clean fifty pounds per day. Scaling up and modifying Whitney's design, as many manufacturers did, only increased that productivity.[18]

Had there been no market for southern cotton, the innovations of Whitney and his successors might not have mattered much, but theirs were hardly the only technological breakthroughs that enabled the cotton bonanza of the nineteenth century. No less important were spinning, carding, and weaving machines, which made the early Industrial Revolution in both England and the United States. First powered by waterwheels and then by steam, textile machinery helped to feed a seemingly insatiable demand for raw cotton that could be turned into thread and cloth. Cotton cloth was lightweight and easier to dye than wool and other fabrics. Once machines made the cloth cheap to produce, the consumer market for it was immense. By the 1810s, it seemed that no matter how much cotton farmers and planters of the American South could force their laborers to supply, there would be both foreign and domestic manufacturers who wanted it. This boom would have dramatic moments of bust, such as those that sent the American economy into deep tailspins in 1819 and 1837. But overall, southern cotton commandeered the attention of producers, consumers, shippers, bankers, and merchants for nearly three-quarters of a century, and it propelled capitalist development in the Western world.[19]

As these advances in machinery and production joined forces with the innovation of the steamboat, which could move cotton to market predictably and

Front Street, Memphis, Tennessee, 1845. Photograph Collection, Memphis and Shelby County Room, Memphis Public Library.

in volume, white men flocked by the hundreds of thousands to Alabama, Mississippi, northern Louisiana, western Georgia, South Carolina, and West Tennessee. Beginning in earnest in the 1810s, they abandoned older parts of the eastern states with the hopes of becoming wealthy by growing cotton on the western frontier. Southern output of the crop increased accordingly. In 1792, the year before Whitney invented his cotton gin, the South produced roughly 3 million pounds of raw cotton. In 1801, it produced nearly 50 million pounds. By 1820, the figure was 160 million pounds. By 1840, southern output hit around 830 million pounds, and in 1860, the cotton crop that white southerners seceded in part to defend yielded 2.2 billion pounds.[20]

For the enslaved population of the United States, the consequences of the mass migration of white people to the cotton frontier were dramatic and dreadful. No more would slaveholders in the Upper South worry about what they might do with their "surplus" laborers. Fewer let their moral qualms about slavery keep them up at night, nor would very many consider either manumitting the black people they enslaved or sending them to Liberia, the West African colony founded in 1822 by reformers who imagined it as a way to get rid of slavery while also limiting the growth of an American population of free black people. Instead, Upper South slaveholders who decided not to leave for the cotton frontier with their enslaved people could simply sell them to those who did. A domestic slave trade filled the niche left by the closing of the transatlantic trade. Sent into the work environment of the Deep South, which everyone understood to be cruel, violent, and hellish, enslaved people lost their communities and their families so that Maryland and Virginia farmers might have a little extra money in their pockets, slave traders might have a business opportunity, cotton planters could have a steady labor supply, textile manufacturers could have raw materials, and consumers around the world could wear inexpensive and comfortable clothing.[21]

Between 1810 and 1840, the enslaved population of Alabama rose from 2,600 to 253,000; Mississippi's went from 14,000 to 195,000; Louisiana's from 34,000 to 168,000; and Tennessee's from 44,000 to 183,000. By 1860, those four states alone held roughly 1.5 million people in bondage, nearly 40 percent of the entire American enslaved population. Those four states also produced nearly 70 percent of the cotton crop of the United States, whose value by 1860 amounted to almost 60 percent of all American exports. By the middle of the nineteenth century, cotton had become the economic analogue of what oil would become in the twentieth century, and the United States was the cotton economy's Saudi Arabia. It made roughly two-thirds of all the cotton in the world, and by the outbreak of the Civil War large swaths of the Deep South had essentially become a series of slave labor camps designed solely to put cotton onto global markets.[22]

The rebirth of slavery in the United States in the decades before the Civil War was not an unfortunate accident of history. It was not something created by individual actors who simply made their choices in response to the demands of a free market, and neither was it something that happened despite the intentions of the nation's founders and despite the efforts of the U.S. government and its leaders. On the contrary, the expansion of slavery in the United States happened entirely under the aegis of both state governments and the federal government. Over the course of the nineteenth century, white southerners whined loudly about the supposed interference of the federal government with slavery and about the supposed unfairness with which the government treated them. In truth, the federal government provided the state and market protections and infrastructure without which the expansion of slavery and the growth of the cotton economy almost certainly would have been impossible.

Nowhere was this more evident than in the domestic slave trade, without which cotton farmers might well have been unable to furnish their enterprises with a sufficient number of forced laborers. The same federal law that banned the transatlantic slave trade after 1808, for example, also provided regulations for shipping enslaved people domestically, and thus it both licensed and

MAP
SHOWING THE DISTRIBUTION
OF THE
SLAVE POPULATION
OF THE
SOUTHERN STATES
OF THE
UNITED STATES
Compiled from the
CENSUS OF
1860.

Washington, September 1861.

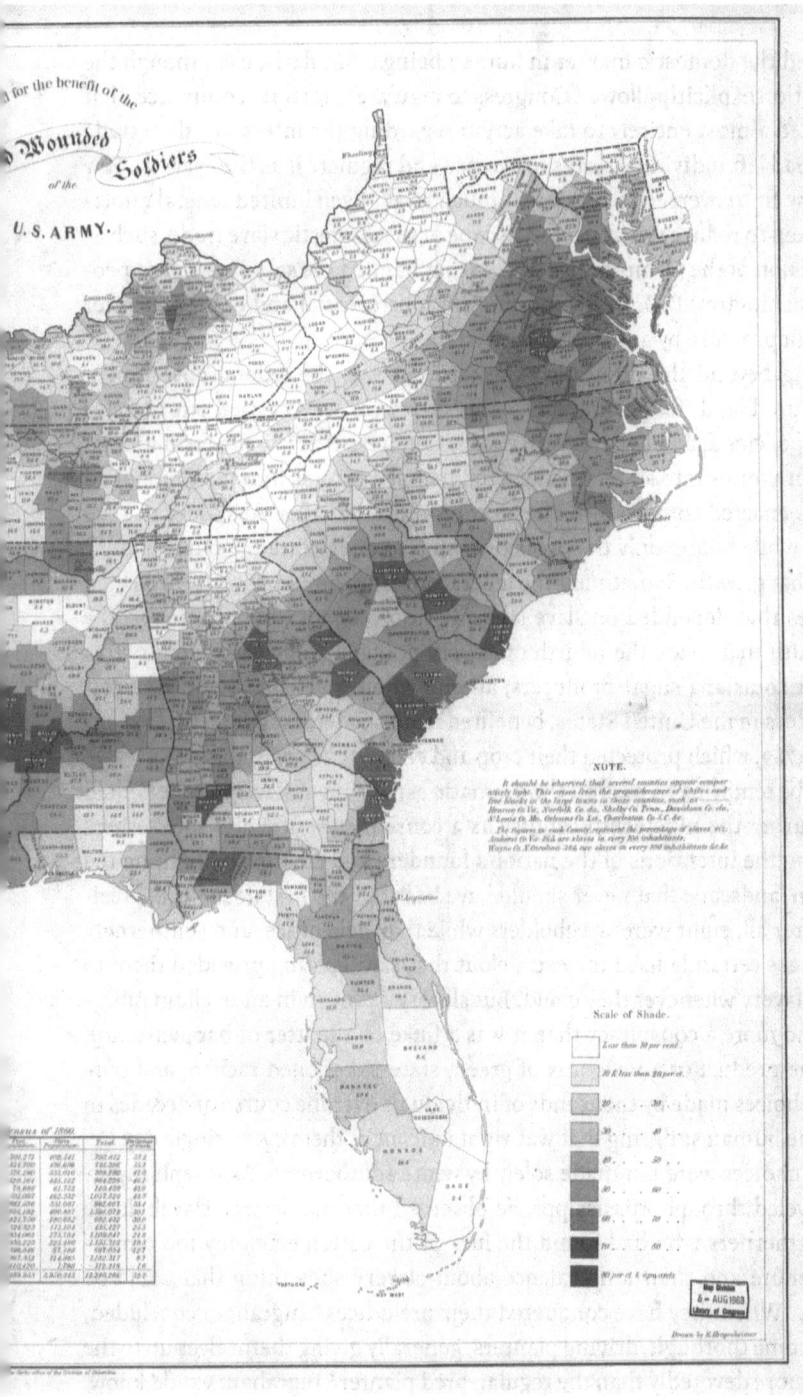

Distribution of the enslaved population, 1860. Geography and Map Division, Library of Congress, Washington, D.C.

structured the domestic market in human beings. Similarly, even though the Constitution explicitly allowed Congress to regulate interstate commerce, that body failed almost entirely to take action regarding the interstate slave trade and instead left individual states to oversee and regulate it as they saw fit. Few states saw fit to oversee or regulate it much at all. Even limited federal efforts undertaken to reduce the impact and scope of the domestic slave trade, such as the provision of the Compromise of 1850 that banned the sale of enslaved people in Washington, D.C., were enormously controversial and came only after decades of pressure by antislavery activists.[23]

Looking beyond the domestic slave trade, it was the federal government that acquired land, fought wars, negotiated treaties, and carried out coercive eviction policies against Native Americans. Congress oversaw the formation of federal territories into states and ushered new slave states into the Union, and Congress enacted compromise after compromise that allowed slavery to keep growing while taking only the occasional step to demarcate the outer boundaries of that growth. Sometimes, the federal government even overtly protected industries that depended on slave labor. Cotton was not the only crop in the Deep South that made the rebirth of slavery possible. Sugar was vital to it as well, and Louisiana sugar producers, among whom were many of the largest slaveholders in the United States, benefited from a federal sugar tariff, first enacted in 1789, which protected their crop and ensured its profitability.[24]

It can be tempting to pass off the dramatic expansion of slavery in the United States during the nineteenth century as a consequence of white southerners perverting the intentions of the nation's founders and creating a blight on the American landscape that never should have been. Of the first dozen U.S. presidents, after all, eight were slaveholders while they held office, and southerners in Congress certainly used the extra clout that slaveholding provided them to protect slavery whenever they could. But slavery's growth in antebellum America was no more a conspiracy than it was a fluke or a matter of happenstance. It was the product of a toxic mix of greed, state-sanctioned racism, and purposeful choices made by thousands of individuals over the course of decades to ignore the human suffering that was right in front of them every single day.

Those choices were not made solely by white southerners. As Joseph Ingraham traveled through Mississippi, he observed that many large slaveholders were northerners who had found the lure of the cotton economy too tempting to ignore and their ambivalence about slavery something that could be resolved. "When they have conquered their prejudices," Ingraham concluded, "they become thorough, driving planters, generally giving themselves up to the pursuit more devotedly than the regular-bred planter." Ingraham would know. Born in Maine, he married the daughter of a large slaveholder from Natchez in the 1840s. He died in that city in 1860.[25]

NOTES

1. Joseph Holt Ingraham, *The South-West, by a Yankee* (New York, 1835), 2:89.
2. Ibid., 2:91.
3. The term "second slavery" refers in part to the fact that the institution of slavery was reinvigorated and became geographically more expansive not only in the southern United States but also throughout the Atlantic world in the nineteenth century. See, for example, Anthony E. Kaye, "The Second Slavery: Modernity in the Nineteenth-Century South and the Atlantic World," *Journal of Southern History* 75 (August 2009): 627–50; Dale W. Tomich, *Through the Prism of Slavery: Labor, Capital, and World Economy* (Lanham, Md.: Rowman and Littlefield, 2003); and Dale Tomich and Michael Zeuske, "Introduction: The Second Slavery: Mass Slavery, World-Economy, and Comparative Microhistories," *Review: A Journal of the Fernand Braudel Center* 31, no. 2 (2008): 91–100. On the expansion of slavery and the development of the cotton economy in nineteenth-century America, see Edward E. Baptist, *The Half Has Never Been Told: Slavery and the Making of American Capitalism* (New York: Basic, 2014); Sven Beckert, *Empire of Cotton: A Global History* (New York: Knopf, 2014), esp. chap. 5; Daniel S. DuPre, *Transforming the Cotton Frontier: Madison County, Alabama, 1800–1840* (Baton Rouge: Louisiana State University Press, 1997); Walter Johnson, *River of Dark Dreams: Slavery and Empire in the Cotton Kingdom* (Cambridge, Mass.: Belknap, 2013); John Hebron Moore, *The Emergence of the Cotton Kingdom in the Old Southwest: Mississippi, 1770–1860* (Baton Rouge: Louisiana State University Press, 1988); and Adam Rothman, *Slave Country: American Expansion and the Origins of the Deep South* (Cambridge, Mass.: Harvard University Press, 2005).
4. The literature on the approach of the political leaders of the revolutionary generation to slavery is vast. A provocative but decent overview is Paul Finkelman, *Slavery and the Founders: Race and Liberty in the Age of Jefferson*, 2nd ed. (Armonk, N.Y.: Sharpe, 2001). Also see Duncan J. MacLeod, *Slavery, Race and the American Revolution* (New York: Cambridge University Press, 1974); Gary B. Nash, *Race and Revolution* (Lanham, Md.: Rowman and Littlefield, 1990); and Donald L. Robinson, *Slavery in the Structure of American Politics, 1765–1820* (New York: Harcourt Brace Jovanovich, 1971), esp. chap. 2. An older but still useful starting point for the views of Jefferson in particular is John Chester Miller, *The Wolf by the Ears: Thomas Jefferson and Slavery* (New York: Free Press, 1977).
5. Twenty-first-century works dealing with the role of slavery in the framing of the Constitution include David Waldstreicher, *Slavery's Constitution: From Revolution to Ratification* (New York: Hill and Wang, 2009); Lawrence Goldstone, *Dark Bargain: Slavery, Profits, and the Struggle for the Constitution* (New York: Walker, 2005); and George William Van Cleve, *A Slaveholders' Union: Slavery, Politics, and the Constitution in the Early American Republic* (Chicago: University of Chicago Press, 2010). For a list of members of the first Congress, see Fergus M. Bordewich, *The First Congress: How James Madison, George Washington, and a Group of Extraordinary Men Invented the Government* (New York: Simon and Schuster, 2016), xiii–xv. On the inflated role of slave states in the electoral college, see Akhil Reed Amar, "The Troubling Reason the Electoral College Exists," *Time*, November

8, 2016, http://time.com/4558510/electoral-college-history-slavery. The "three-fifths clause" of the U.S. Constitution is contained in article 1, section 2.

6. The U.S. Constitution provided military support for squashing insurrections in article 1, section 8; provided for the return of fugitive slaves in article 4, section 2; and barred action with regard to the transatlantic slave trade in article 1, section 9. A more expansive view of the Constitution's protections for slavery appears in Finkelman, *Slavery and the Founders*, 6–10.

7. This language appears in article 1, section 2; article 1, section 9; and article 4, section 2, respectively.

8. Nash, *Race and Revolution*, 14; Gary J. Kornblith, *Slavery and Sectional Strife in the Early American Republic, 1776–1821* (Lanham, Md.: Rowman and Littlefield, 2010), 34; Finkelman, *Slavery and the Founders*, 6.

9. On optimism about the prospects for slavery's disappearance, see Matthew Mason, *Slavery and Politics in the Early American Republic* (Chapel Hill: University of North Carolina Press, 2006), chap. 1; Nash, *Race and Revolution*, chap. 1; and David Brion Davis, *The Problem of Slavery in the Age of Revolution, 1770–1823* (Ithaca, N.Y.: Cornell University Press, 1975), chaps. 6 and 7.

10. An Act to Prohibit the Carrying on the Slave Trade from the United States to Any Foreign Place or Country, *United States Statutes at Large*, 3rd Cong., 1st sess., 347–49, approved March 22, 1794; An Act in Addition to the Act Entitled "An Act to Prohibit the Carrying on the Slave Trade from the United States to Any Foreign Place or Country," *United States Statutes at Large*, 6th Cong., 1st sess., 70–71, approved May 10, 1800. In 1785, South Carolina had instituted a temporary but renewable ban on the importation of captive people from Africa, only to suspend the ban and reopen the trade in 1803. On Congress and the transatlantic slave trade in the early republic, see Don E. Fehrenbacher, *The Slaveholding Republic: An Account of the United States Government's Relations to Slavery*, completed and edited by Ward M. McAfee (New York: Oxford University Press, 2001), esp. chap. 5; Robinson, *Slavery in the Structure*, chap. 8; MacLeod, *Slavery, Race and the American Revolution*, 31–47.

11. On slavery and the Northwest Ordinance, see Finkelman, *Slavery and the Founders*, chap. 2; Robinson, *Slavery in the Structure*, 379–86; David Brion Davis, "The Significance of Excluding Slavery from the Old Northwest in 1787," *Indiana Magazine of History* 84 (March 1988): 75–89; and John Craig Hammond, *Slavery, Freedom, and Expansion in the Early American West* (Charlottesville: University of Virginia Press, 2007), chaps. 6 and 7. On the abolition of slavery in the North, see Ira Berlin, *Many Thousands Gone: The First Two Centuries of Slavery in North America* (Cambridge, Mass.: Harvard University Press, 1998), chap. 9; Arthur Zilversmit, *The First Emancipation: The Abolition of Slavery in the North* (Chicago: University of Chicago Press, 1967); Joanne Pope Melish, *Disowning Slavery: Gradual Emancipation and "Race" in New England, 1780–1860* (Ithaca, N.Y.: Cornell University Press, 1998); Gary B. Nash and Jean R. Soderlund, *Freedom by Degrees:*

Emancipation and Its Aftermath in Pennsylvania (New York: Oxford University Press, 1991); Shane White, *Somewhat More Independent: The End of Slavery in New York City, 1770–1810* (Athens: University of Georgia Press, 1991); and Edgar J. McManus, *Black Bondage in the North* (Syracuse, N.Y.: Syracuse University Press, 1991).

12. On the evolution of slavery in the Upper South in the early republic, see Berlin, *Many Thousands Gone*, chap. 10; Robert McColley, *Slavery and Jeffersonian Virginia* (Urbana: University of Illinois Press, 1964); Eva Sheppard Wolf, *Race and Liberty in the New Nation: Emancipation in Virginia from the Revolution to Nat Turner's Rebellion* (Baton Rouge: Louisiana State University Press, 2006); Alan Taylor, *The Internal Enemy: Slavery and War in Virginia, 1772–1832* (New York: Norton, 2013); T. Stephen Whitman, *The Price of Freedom: Slavery and Manumission in Baltimore and Early National Maryland* (Lexington: University Press of Kentucky, 1997); Barbara Jeanne Fields, *Slavery and Freedom on the Middle Ground: Maryland during the Nineteenth Century* (New Haven, Conn.: Yale University Press, 1985); Christopher Phillips, *Freedom's Port: The African American Community of Baltimore, 1790–1860* (Urbana: University of Illinois Press, 1997); Max Grivno, *Gleanings of Freedom: Free and Slave Labor along the Mason-Dixon Line, 1790–1860* (Urbana: University of Illinois Press, 2011); Patience Essah, *A House Divided: Slavery and Emancipation in Delaware, 1638–1865* (Charlottesville: University Press of Virginia, 1996); and William H. Williams, *Slavery and Freedom in Delaware, 1639–1865* (Wilmington, Del.: Scholarly Resources, 1996).

13. Ira Berlin, *Slaves without Masters: The Free Negro in the Antebellum South* (New York: Pantheon, 1974), 46–47; John Adams to George Churchman and Jacob Lindley, January 24, 1801, in *The Works of John Adams*, ed. Charles Francis Adams (Boston, 1854), 9:92.

14. Berlin, *Slaves without Masters*, 396–97.

15. Douglas R. Egerton, *Gabriel's Rebellion: The Virginia Slave Conspiracies of 1800 and 1802* (Chapel Hill: University of North Carolina Press, 1993); James Sidbury, *Ploughshares into Swords: Race, Rebellion, and Identity in Gabriel's Virginia, 1730–1810* (Cambridge: Cambridge University Press, 1997); Wolf, *Race and Liberty in the New Nation*, chap. 3; David P. Geggus, ed., *The Impact of the Haitian Revolution in the Atlantic World* (Columbia: University of South Carolina Press, 2002); Gordon S. Brown, *Toussaint's Clause: The Founding Fathers and the Haitian Revolution* (Jackson: University of Mississippi Press, 2005); Laurent Dubois, *Avengers of the New World: The Story of the Haitian Revolution* (Cambridge, Mass.: Belknap, 2005); *An Act to Amend the Several Laws Concerning Slaves*, in *The Statutes at Large of Virginia, from October Session, 1792, to December Session, 1806*, ed. Samuel Shepherd (Richmond, Va., 1836), 3:251–53.

16. Peter J. Kastor, *The Nation's Crucible: The Louisiana Purchase and the Creation of America* (New Haven, Conn.: Yale University Press, 2004); Roger G. Kennedy, *Mr. Jefferson's Lost Cause: Land, Farmers, Slavery, and the Louisiana Purchase* (New York: Oxford University Press, 2003); Jon Kukla, *A Wilderness So Immense: The Louisiana Purchase and the Destiny of America* (New York: Anchor, 2003); Drew R. McCoy, *The Elusive Republic: Political*

Economy in Jeffersonian America (Chapel Hill: University of North Carolina Press, 1980), esp. chap. 8; Peter S. Onuf, *Jefferson's Empire: The Language of American Nationhood* (Charlottesville: University of Virginia Press, 2000); James Ronda, ed., *Thomas Jefferson and the Changing West: From Conquest to Conservation* (Albuquerque: University of New Mexico Press, 1997); Rothman, *Slave Country*, chap. 1.

17. David S. Heidler and Jeanne T. Heidler, *Old Hickory's War: Andrew Jackson and the Quest for Empire* (Mechanicsburg, Pa.: Stackpole, 1996); Robert V. Remini, *Andrew Jackson and His Indian Wars* (New York: Penguin, 2001); Rothman, *Slave Country*, chap. 4; Anthony F. C. Wallace, *The Long, Bitter Trail: Andrew Jackson and the Indians* (New York: Hill and Wang, 1993).

18. Angela Lakwete, *Inventing the Cotton Gin: Machine and Myth in Antebellum America* (Baltimore, Md.: Johns Hopkins University Press, 2003).

19. Beckert, *Empire of Cotton*, esp. chaps. 3–8.

20. Robert H. Gudmestad, *Steamboats and the Rise of the Cotton Kingdom* (Baton Rouge: Louisiana State University Press, 2011); Joan E. Cashin, *A Family Venture: Men and Women on the Southern Frontier* (Baltimore, Md.: Johns Hopkins University Press, 1991); Stuart Bruchey, *Cotton and the Growth of the American Economy, 1790–1860* (New York: Harcourt, Brace, and World, 1967), 14–17.

21. Baptist, *Half Has Never Been Told*; Calvin Schermerhorn, *The Business of Slavery and the Rise of American Capitalism, 1815–1860* (New Haven, Conn.: Yale University Press, 2015); Steven Deyle, *Carry Me Back: The Domestic Slave Trade in American Life* (New York: Oxford University Press, 2005).

22. *A Century of Population Growth, from the First Census of the United States to the Twelfth, 1790–1900* (Washington, D.C., 1909), 133; Bruchey, *Cotton and the Growth*, 7, 18, 19, 22.

23. An Act to Prohibit the Importation of Slaves into Any Port or Place within the Jurisdiction of the United States, from and after the First Day of January, in the Year of Our Lord One Thousand Eight Hundred and Eight, *United States Statutes at Large*, 9th Cong., 2nd sess., 426–30, approved March 2, 1807; Lacy K. Ford, *Deliver Us from Evil: The Slavery Question in the Old South* (New York: Oxford University Press, 2009), 447–60; David L. Lightner, *Slavery and the Commerce Power: How the Struggle against the Interstate Slave Trade Led to the Civil War* (New Haven, Conn.: Yale University Press, 2006).

24. An Act for Laying a Duty on Goods, Wares, and Merchandises Imported into the United States, *United States Statutes at Large*, 1st Cong., 1st sess., 24–27, approved July 4, 1789; Rothman, *Slave Country*, 171–72, 178–79; Richard Follett, *The Sugar Masters: Planters and Slaves in Louisiana's Cane World, 1820–1860* (Baton Rouge: Louisiana State University Press, 2005), chap. 1.

25. Ingraham, *South-West, by a Yankee*, 2:92.

"Cash for Slaves"
The African American Trail of Tears

CALVIN SCHERMERHORN

Forced migration was the central event in the lives of most enslaved Americans, and for many it was a tragic prelude to the Memphis Massacre of 1866 and a false start to freedom. Between 1790 and 1860, 1.1 million enslaved people were moved out of the Upper South and into the Deep South as planters and slave traders surged to the new cotton frontier. That was African Americans' own Trail of Tears. In the antebellum republic, this social upheaval was signposted in a quotidian way. "Cash for slaves," barked newspaper advertisements offering banknotes for black bodies. These ads were common in Maryland and Virginia, like "cash for gold" or "cash for houses" today.[1] B. M. and Walter L. Campbell's ads were splashed across Maryland newspapers: "Negroes Wanted," they said, assuring that "all who have slaves to sell will be sure to get the highest price, when the negroes are young and likely" and pointing customers to their private jail on Pratt Street in Baltimore (now the site of the Baltimore Convention Center).[2] The Campbells wanted the young, the able, and the resilient. And Maryland slavers answered.

Hannah Robinson was just eighteen when a Maryland slaver sold her to the Campbells in 1848. Maybe her owner was broke. Maybe he wanted to punish her. Most likely he wanted to cash in on rising prices. Whatever the motive, Robinson's world splintered. After her sale, the dark-skinned teenager who stood only five feet tall was jailed in B. M. Campbell's Baltimore City compound, warehoused along with other African Americans being forced to wait for a ship that would take them beyond the reach of their loved ones. Some historians have called it the "Second Middle Passage," an American sequel to the transatlantic Middle Passage of 12.5 million Africans.[3] Like during the Middle Passage, slave traders calculated that Robinson would have to be sold far away from her home if they were going to profit. Bondspeople were selling for about 60 percent more in New Orleans than in the Chesapeake.

So in October 1848, Robinson was consigned to the slave ship *Kirkwood*, which was sailing for New Orleans. She was among 147 captives in the hold of the three-masted wooden vessel. After a terrifying nineteen-day sea passage among strangers, she was jailed again and then sold in New Orleans. Slavers staking their bondspeople's health and lives on cotton returns bought young workers like Robinson. The Campbells had a wide and distinguished clientele, including the general and future president Zachary Taylor.[4] Most slave traders demanded cash, but big and successful ones like the Campbells sold also on credit.

Slavers took it as their right to inflict violence on nonwhite people. Hannah Robinson landed on the Mississippi cotton frontier in Yalobusha County. Misery was washing over the land. Less than two decades before, the Treaty of Dancing Rabbit Creek had been the pretext for the Choctaw Trail of Tears. Army personnel and contractors removed the Choctaw people from their own land; a fifth of them died from starvation, exposure, and diseases such as cholera, smallpox, and whooping cough. Removals of Creeks, Cherokees, and Seminoles followed. The land's new white owners moved in African Americans, who cleared the woodlands to feed steamboats and planted cotton to fatten slavers' margins. While misery swelled so did slavers' ambitions.[5]

Hannah Robinson had spent nearly seventeen years in slavery before she sought freedom in Memphis in July 1863. She fled war to what seemed like safety and a place of opportunity among other refugees. Three years later, Robinson was tending her sick daughter on May 2, 1866, when twenty men, including some she recognized as policemen, broke into her rented house on Gayoso Street. Robinson's son and husband were also there, along with five female neighbors taking refuge. One week later, Robinson's daughter died. Robinson attributed the death to the men who had assaulted her daughter in her sickbed during the massacre.[6] Slavery's culture of impunity had not disappeared but had been transformed into a new kind of coercion and terror, which affected many black Americans in Memphis and beyond.

Mary Jordan was about seventeen when she was taken from her family in North Carolina and packed aboard the merchant sailing ship *Phoenix* in Petersburg, Virginia, bound for New Orleans. Like Robinson, Jordan had been stolen from relatives. Many enslaved people recalled their sales as theft or kidnapping. The men who bought and sold Jordan were some of the most active slave traders of the 1840s.[7] They took her north from her native North Carolina before shipping her south. Twenty years later, Mary Jordan was living in Memphis. She was a newly widowed mother of three daughters when a mob set ablaze the saloon adjacent to her house and locked her and her daughters in their own home as it caught fire. She had survived slavery and civil war only to see her world go up in flames once more. Although her oldest daughter feared that they would be shot if they tried to flee the burning house, Jordan risked the bullets to escape. But she was stopped by a white man who held a gun to her chest while rain poured on the sick baby in her arms. A few weeks later, her seven-month-old daughter died of exposure. However, this tiny victim was not counted in the official death toll of the Memphis Massacre. After losing everything except her two surviving daughters, Mary Jordan moved to Fayette County, Tennessee.[8] As so many others had also experienced, slavers had stolen her from family in North Carolina, and explosive racist hatred took almost everything else.

In the 1830s, one in seven enslaved African Americans was carried by force across state lines. By the 1840s and 1850s, the ratio was one in thirteen. These forced migrations disrupted families; in the Virginia Tidewater region, one in five enslaved people was stolen from an intact family. For every individual sold, jailed, and bound away, a parent lost a son or daughter. A sibling lost a sibling. The process tore loved ones from loved ones, generation from generation.[9] Those caught up in the slave trade were disinherited from social capital and their ancestors' wisdom, forced to reconstitute a family life under new and often terrifying conditions.

Like Hannah Robinson and Mary Jordan, Albert Harris experienced this process of serial, intergenerational theft. In his case too, forced migration eventually brought him to a neighborhood in South Memphis. Harris's path was similar to that of Solomon Northup, who published a narrative of his experiences, *Twelve Years a Slave*, in 1853. Harris testified to a congressional committee investigating the Memphis Massacre that he was "born and raised in Virginia" but was forced to say good-bye to his family and other loved ones and travel a thousand miles to the strange land of the Lower Mississippi River valley.[10]

Harris may have been the same Albert Harris who at eighteen years old was shipped out of Petersburg, Virginia, by the notorious Richmond jailer and slave trader Bacon Tait, who made a fortune on the African American Trail of Tears. In 1859, Tait's credit report estimated his worth at $400,000 (the equivalent of $152 million today). His corner of Richmond was known as "the devil's half acre" and included Lumpkin's Jail with its "whipping room," where inmates were shackled to the floor and tortured.[11] Slavers used brutal disciplinary measures, and those who fell into the hands of slave traders were subjected to arbitrary violence, torture, rape, incarceration, and sudden jarring movements aboard ships, in railroad cars, and on rough trails.

Albert Harris was among 197 African-descended captives aboard the merchant sloop *Hark Away*, which docked in New Orleans in mid-November 1838.

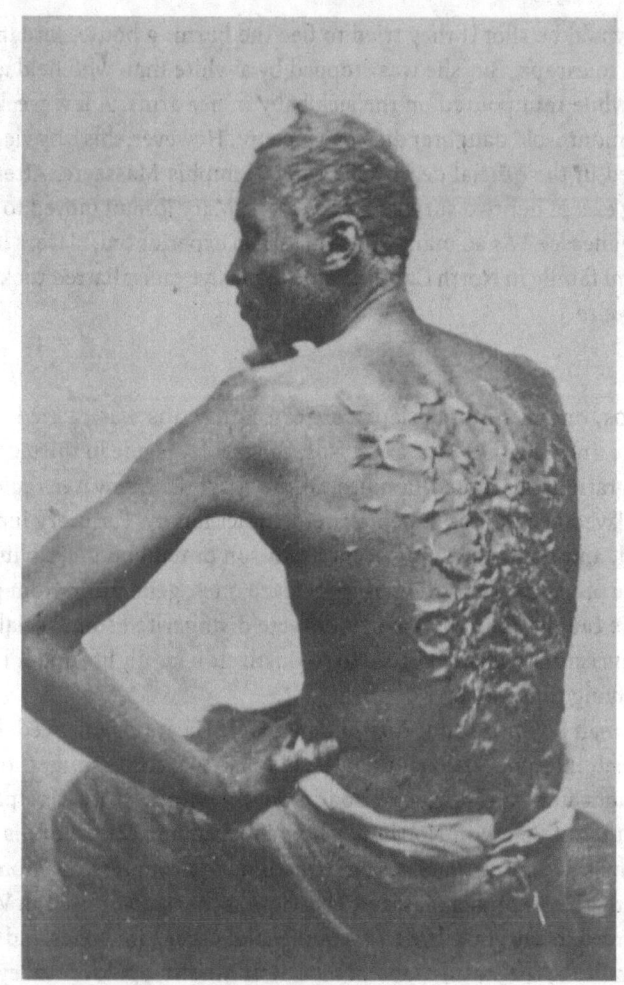

Slave traders were not the only ones to leave deep and abiding scars on black people's bodies and souls. On escaping to Union lines, Peter's body bore testimony to the horrors that had been inflicted by an overseer's whip. Photograph taken April 2, 1863. From Joseph H. Taylor Album, ca. 1861–ca. 1865, RG 165: Records of the War Department General and Special Staffs, 1860–1952, National Archives and Records Administration, Washington, D.C.

> **N. B. FOREST,**
> **DEALER IN SLAVES,**
> **No. 87 Adams-st, Memphis, Ten.,**
> HAS just received from North Carolina, twenty-five likely young negroes, to which he desires to call the attention of purchasers. He will be in the regular receipt of negroes from North and South Carolina every month. His Negro Depot is one of the most complete and commodious establishments of the kind in the Southern country, and his regulations exact and systematic, cleanliness, neatness and comfort being strictly observed and enforced His aim is to furnish to customers A. 1 servants and field hands, sound and perfect in body and mind. Negroes taken on commission. jan21

Slave traders, like Nathan Bedford Forrest, routinely took out advertisements in southern newspapers, advertising their human wares alongside advertisements for wagons, land, seed, groceries, and other commodities. *Memphis Daily Appeal*, June 14, 1857, in Chronicling America: Historical American Newspapers, Library of Congress, Washington, D.C.

Two enslaved shipmates died on the passage, and one newborn, who was not listed on the initial manifest, survived. When Harris arrived in New Orleans, he was taken up by slave trader Thomas Boudar and sold to the highest bidder. As one of the city's leading slave traders, Boudar auctioned scores of bondspeople at a time, sometimes under the majestic domes of the St. Charles Hotel or the St. Louis Hotel in the Crescent City, both known as the "Exchange."[12]

Slave markets in New Orleans and Memphis were conspicuous and part of active markets that reflected each city's growing economy. Between jail, ship, and auction, Harris's slavers incorporated him into a thousand-mile labor supply chain that serviced the interests of different sections of the American South. Deep South slavers wanted bound workers. Upper South slavers wanted the cash they could pocket for selling their human property. Most Deep South slavers were deeply in debt, and a vast supply of borrowed wealth traveled north by northeast as the African American Trail of Tears led south by southwest. The domestic slave trade also fit into a larger and more expansive commercial network—the great cotton chain or cotton triangle. Albert Harris's forced journey represented one leg of that vast network of global trade. After Harris disembarked at the port of New Orleans, his place aboard the cargo ship was filled with bales of slave-made lint bound for Liverpool and England's booming textile industry. There, workers and merchants refilled the ship's hold a third time, packing it with finished goods and English commodities, such as coal and iron, items that would find an eager market in New York City. Then the ship would begin its transoceanic circuit once again: moving enslaved people south, cotton east, and commodities west in roughly that order.[13]

Harris's ordeal was part of a nineteenth-century version of the globalization evident in contemporary supply chains. These processes conceal the conditions under which so many consumer goods (including electronics) and foods are produced today—the slave-caught seafood that goes into pet food, the tasty shrimp, the smartphones, the fast fashion, and the sumptuous chocolate that most of us enjoy. All of these products are caught, peeled, farmed, mined, sewed, or grown under conditions that are illegal in the United States.[14] Today's globalization has antecedents in the nineteenth century, when Britons and Americans in free territories and free states bought cheap cotton cloth, sugar, tobacco, coffee, or cocoa produced by enslaved people. It was a time when New Yorkers and Londoners could actually buy bonds backed by the flesh and bones of enslaved people, all while breathing free air.[15] That commerce propelled the African American Trail of Tears.

Slavery was big business. Enslaved people were second only to land in terms of total monetary worth in the United States. In 1840, for instance, the bodies of enslaved people like Hannah Robinson, Mary Jordan, and Albert Harris made up more than 19 percent of U.S. wealth. In 1860, enslaved people were worth more than $3 billion to their owners. In today's economy, that would be equivalent to $12.1 trillion or 67 percent of the 2015 U.S. gross domestic product. Enslaved people were slaveholders' most readily available form of collateral too, and slavers regularly took out mortgages on enslaved people in order to buy land, seed, tools, and often more people.[16] Simultaneously seen as laborers, commodities, and valuable collateral, African Americans bore more than the weight of a slaveholder's whip; they bore the burden of a fast-growing economy.

Despite these circumstances, enslaved people formed families under slavery's severe constraints. They risked separations when they fell in love and promised themselves to one another. After Harris was stolen from his family in Virginia and forcibly removed to Louisiana, he met and married Annie, a Georgia native—only to be separated from her when he was sold up the Mississippi River to Memphis, where from the early 1850s until 1863 he was owned by a sawmill, J. B. Griffing and Company.[17] The Civil War and emancipation ended his enslavement and also his separation from Annie. The two reunited in Memphis, where Harris worked as a shoemaker in North Memphis, just south of where I-40 passes St. Jude Children's Hospital today.

But the trauma of being black people in the American South was not yet over. In May 1866, Albert and Annie Harris experienced the Memphis Massacre. Several white men burst into their home and robbed them of more than $300 and a shotgun; their house was spared burning because a fire would have threatened a neighboring white-owned grocery. After the massacre, the Harrises left Memphis for DeSoto County, Mississippi, where they purchased a small farm. They had realized in May 1866 that the Civil War was not really over and that emancipation was not final if their home could be invaded without consequence to the attackers. In fact, none of the white assailants were tried for their crimes in that atmosphere of reaction and terror against freedpeople.

Like the Harrises, Mathilda Howley was freed from slavery only to confront new forms of terror. A witness to the Memphis Massacre, Howley recalled of her early life that she "was stolen after I got to be a big girl." Like so many African Americans, Howley understood slavery as stealing, robbery, human larceny. She did not recall exactly when her owner, Welland Jones, moved her from her birthplace in Christian County, Kentucky, to Marshall County, Mississippi, but she never forgot how she felt when it happened. Enslaved people who were moved overland were often in chains, men bound together by the wrists, handcuffed, or shackled, and women tied with rope. Children and disabled, sick, or elderly people often rode in wagons. All bivouacked along the rough roads tying the South together. In fact, so many people were moved that between 1800 and 1860, the geographic center of slavery in the United States moved with them, six hundred miles from Petersburg, Virginia, to the western border of Georgia.[18]

Like the Native American Trails of Tears, the African American Trail of Tears was legal, deliberate, and coordinated. The U.S. government created the conditions for a national slave market when it banned the African slave trade in 1808 but refused to throw up roadblocks to the internal trade, leaving the question of regulation up to the individual states. This did not go over well with abolitionist Henry Stanton, who in 1839 demanded that Congress use its commerce power to arrest the process. The "internal slave trade is the great jugular vein of slavery; and if Congress will take the same weapon with which they cut off the foreign trade, and cut this vein, slavery would die of starvation in the southern, and of apoplexy in the northern slave states," he argued. But Congress, which was dominated by slaveholding interests, refused to act.[19] Thus while states like Mississippi and Louisiana periodically prohibited slave traders from bringing captives across state lines for sale, slavers circumvented rules like Louisiana's strict requirement that captives entering the state bear certificates of good character by manufacturing fake certificates. Mississippi banned the interstate slave trade in its 1832 constitution, but the legislature never got around to enforcing the ban by statute. Tennessee prohibited the interstate slave trade from 1827 to 1855 but like its neighbor to the south never got around to enforcing the ban.[20]

African Americans paid the price. Looking back on his life as a bondsperson, William (Billy) Coe said that the Memphis Massacre marked "four times I lost everything I had." He was a long-time city resident who had been forcibly moved from Virginia. About one-third of bondspeople moved with their owners, usually along the dirt roads meandering west by southwest through the Appalachians and into the Tennessee and Mississippi River bottoms. When interviewed about the night when his shop was burned, Coe did not know how old he was at the time or what became of his family.[21] That was not uncommon. About half of all enslaved children lost parents, usually their fathers, to sale and removal.

Forced migration and the Civil War had tragic consequences, highlighted by the bloody events of early May 1866. The ordeals of Billy Coe, Hannah Robinson, Mary Jordan, and Albert Harris are the individual parts of a process that removed more than 1.1 million African Americans out of the Upper South and into the cotton fields of the Lower South. The internal slave trade affected nearly every black family in the antebellum republic. Their forced migration built the South into a place of enormous capital growth and staggering economic development. The unpaid fruits of their labors created an interest so strong that between 1861 and 1865, Confederate leaders staked hundreds of thousands of lives and the future of their civilization on it. And when the Confederate cause was lost, its adherents picked up the pieces of slavery and rearranged them into a new regime of forced labor, racial terrorism, and political exclusion. That intention was announced unambiguously by the 1866 massacres in Memphis and then only weeks later in New Orleans and in the rise of a white supremacist political insurgency. The Ku Klux Klan, the Knights of the White Camelia, the White League, and other white paramilitaries forged common cause on the landscape of the African American Trail of Tears.

NOTES

1. *Daily National Intelligencer* (Washington, D.C.), May 30, 1826, 4; *Baltimore (Md.) Republican*, June 16, 1829, 3; *Alexandria (Va.) Phenix Gazette*, October 25, 1825, 1; Steven Deyle, *Carry Me Back: The Domestic Slave Trade in American Life* (New York: Oxford University Press, 2005), app. A.

2. *Easton (Md.) Star*, August 1, 1848, 3.

3. Ira Berlin, *Generations of Captivity: A History of African-American Slaves* (Cambridge, Mass.: Harvard University Press, 2003), 14.

4. Inward Slave Manifest (*Kirkwood*), New Orleans, October 14, 1848, microfilm 1895, roll 12, image 132, National Archives and Records Administration, Washington, D.C. (hereinafter NARA); *Cash for Blood: The Baltimore to New Orleans Domestic Slave Trade*

(Bowie, Md.: Heritage Books, 2002), 632; N. H. Blanchard, *Sketch of the Life and Character of Gen. Zachary Taylor* (New York, 1847), 27.

5. Joshua D. Rothman, *Flush Times and Fever Dreams: A Story of Capitalism and Slavery in the Age of Jackson* (Athens: University of Georgia Press, 2012); Adam Rothman, *Slave Country: American Expansion and the Origins of the Deep South* (Cambridge, Mass.: Harvard University Press, 2005); Walter Johnson, *River of Dark Dreams: Slavery and Empire in the Cotton Kingdom* (Cambridge, Mass.: Belknap, 2013), chap. 1.

6. Testimony of Hannah Robinson, "Memphis Riots and Massacres," *U.S. Serial Set*, no. 1274, House Report 101, 39th Cong., 1st sess., 193.

7. Inward Slave Manifest (*Phoenix*), New Orleans, October 24, 1846, microfilm 1895, roll 11, images 646–47, NARA; Edward E. Baptist, "'Stol' an' Fetched Here': Enslaved Migration, Ex-Slave Narratives, and Vernacular History," in *New Studies in the History of American Slavery*, ed. Edward E. Baptist and Stephanie M. H. Camp (Athens: University of Georgia Press, 2006), 243–74.

8. Testimony of Mary Jordan, "Memphis Riots and Massacres," 234–35; 1880 U.S. Census, Fayette County, Tennessee, District 9, 29.

9. Robert H. Gudmestad, *A Troublesome Commerce: The Transformation of the Interstate Slave Trade* (Baton Rouge: Louisiana State University Press, 2003), chap. 1; Susan Eva O'Donovan, "Universities of Social and Political Change: Slaves in Jail in Antebellum America," in *Buried Lives: Incarcerated in Early America*, ed. Michele Lise Tarter and Richard Bell (Athens: University of Georgia Press, 2012), 124–48.

10. Testimony of Albert Harris, "Memphis Riots and Massacres," 62; Calvin Schermerhorn, *The Business of Slavery and the Rise of American Capitalism, 1815–1860* (New Haven, Conn.: Yale University Press, 2015), chap. 6.

11. Abigail Tucker, "Digging Up the Past at a Richmond Jail," *Smithsonian* (March 2009), http://www.smithsonianmag.com/history/digging-up-the-past-at-a-richmond-jail-50642859/?no-ist.

12. Inward Slave Manifest (*Hark Away*), New Orleans, October 17, 1838, microfilm 1895, roll 8, images 300–304, NARA; Maurie D. McInnis, *Slaves Waiting for Sale: Abolitionist Art and the American Slave Trade* (Chicago: University of Chicago Press, 2011), 166–67.

13. Levy's Letter Sheet Price-Current (New Orleans), February 16, 1839, 2; *New York Commercial Advertiser*, May 8, 1839, 2.

14. Kevin Bales, *Blood and Earth: Modern Slavery, Ecocide, and the Secret to Saving the World* (New York: Random House, 2016).

15. Edward E. Baptist, *The Half Has Never Been Told: Slavery and the Making of American Capitalism* (New York: Basic, 2014), chap. 7.

16. Ibid., 246.

17. John L. Mitchell, *Tennessee State Gazette and Business Directory for 1860–61* (Nashville, Tenn.: John L. Mitchell, 1860), 469.

18. Testimony of Mathilda Howley, "Memphis Riots and Massacres," 189; Calvin

Schermerhorn, *Money over Mastery, Family over Freedom: Slavery in the Antebellum South* (Baltimore, Md.: Johns Hopkins University Press, 2011), 15.

19. H. B. Stanton, "Mr. Stanton's Speech at the Anniversary of the American Anti-Slavery Society" (May 7, 1839), *Massachusetts Abolitionist*, May 23, 1839, 14, cited in David L. Lightner, *Slavery and the Commerce Power: How the Struggle against the Interstate Slave Trade Led to the Civil War* (New Haven, Conn.: Yale University Press, 2006), 102.

20. Deyle, *Carry Me Back*, chap. 2.

21. Testimony of William (Billy) Coe, "Memphis Riots and Massacres," 102.

Black Soldiers and Sailors and the Defense of Freedpeople's Rights

JOSEPH P. REIDY

The violence in Memphis in May 1866 occurred during a period of drastic change set loose by the Civil War. Tennessee's exemption from President Abraham Lincoln's Emancipation Proclamation had not prevented the collapse of slavery as the organizing principle of southern society. In areas of the state under the influence of federal armed forces, enslaved people began to act as though they were free, although both rebel and Unionist slaveholders alike continued to consider them as property. In much of the countryside, and often right under the noses of Union troops in the garrison towns, people of African ancestry continued to be held in bondage. The end of the war and the ratification of the Thirteenth Amendment guaranteed the formal end of slavery, but Confederate sympathizers and Unionists who opposed emancipation aimed to keep black people in a condition of subservience.

These efforts did not go uncontested. On the one hand, federal military authorities and the garrisons at the Union's Fort Pickering, including the Third U.S. Colored Heavy Artillery, a full regiment of black artillerymen, and officials of the Bureau of Refugees, Freedmen and Abandoned Lands (commonly known as the Freedmen's Bureau), aimed to safeguard the freedom and rights of freedpeople. Many black veterans of the U.S. Navy and the U.S. Army also resided in Memphis. What is more, the large population of black soldiers and veterans, many of whom lived with their families in South Memphis in the vicinity of Fort Pickering, had developed a distinct view of the rights that they expected military authorities to protect. Having fought to defeat the Confederate rebellion, they refused to be treated as slaves, which made them all the more objectionable to the foes of emancipation. In the spring of 1866, as the Third U.S. Colored Heavy Artillery was being mustered out of service, the predominantly Irish police of Memphis took it upon themselves to try to keep black people in their subordinate place. Then the explosion—what *Harper's*

Weekly characterized in May 1866 as the "riotous proceedings" that constituted "a disgrace to civilization"—occurred.[1]

Modest in size, Memphis ranked thirty-eighth among all U.S. cities in 1860. The population was nearly twenty-three thousand, of whom roughly three thousand were enslaved people and just shy of two hundred were free people of color.[2] Memphis served as the key commercial center in the thriving cotton-growing region of West Tennessee, northern Mississippi, and eastern Arkansas. The plantation system was brutal, and many of its enslaved victims had only recently been relocated there from points farther east. Although wealthy planters, merchants, and slave traders predominated economically and socially in the city, commercial development preceding the war had also given rise to a laboring class of more than four thousand Irish immigrants and native-born workers. The city's politics reflected these changes. Although the secession crisis temporarily muzzled much of the traditional Unionist sentiment, the restoration of federal control over the city in June 1862 drew it to the surface once again. But as slavery disintegrated, anti-emancipation Unionists joined Confederate sympathizers in scapegoating the black population for every social, economic, or political challenge that arose.

Amid the uncertainty of war, black residents of Memphis acted much as their counterparts did in other southern cities that federal forces had liberated from the Confederates. After first establishing their freedom, they aimed to strengthen it by stabilizing their families and reinforcing ties to the churches and benevolent and fraternal associations that black southerners had organized in slavery. The Sons of Ham was one such association. Founded in 1859, it provided social, spiritual, and material assistance to people in need.[3] The city's transportation links (which included the Mississippi River and the railroads heading south to Mississippi, east to South Carolina, and northeast to Ohio) had made it an attractive destination for freedom seekers even before the arrival of the Yankees. Louis and Matilda Hughes, for instance, who were enslaved in northern Mississippi, tried without success on several occasions to escape to Memphis, hoping to use it as a way station to points farther north.[4]

The quest for freedom took forms other than ill-starred attempts at escape. The enslaved man William Webb, for instance, became energized by the campaign of the first Republican presidential candidate, John C. Frémont, in 1856. As his owner's family moved from one place to another in Mississippi, Tennessee, Louisiana, and Kentucky during the late 1850s, Webb made contact with enslaved communities at each stop, advising them that the end of slavery was near, that "we expected to be free," and that they must prepare accordingly.[5] The well-known slave insurrection threat of 1856, which was largely centered in Tennessee, reflected this sense of expectation of major change in the offing among Webb and countless other enslaved men and women on the western cotton frontier.⁶

Lincoln's election, secession, and the start of the war brought tensions to a head. Confederate strategists knew the importance of Memphis to the defense of the rebel heartland. The Union general-in-chief Winfield Scott's much-ridiculed but prescient Anaconda Plan contained two major components: a naval blockade of the Atlantic and Gulf coasts and joint military and naval operations along the Mississippi River. Accordingly, Confederate engineers began constructing fortifications at Memphis and other strategic points, such as Fort Pillow, forty miles upriver. In September 1861, a correspondent from a Detroit newspaper observed black men armed with axes and shovels being marched through the city to work on the fortifications, and he remarked sardonically that such work amounted to "riveting their chains" more tightly in place.⁷ What he did not realize at the time was the extent to which the mobilization of black men increased their awareness about the war, its potential impact on slavery, and the likely spots where the northerners might attack.

When federal forces retook control of Memphis in 1862, the tables turned. Taking a page from the Confederate playbook, Union military officials employed black laborers to transform the city into a staging area for operations farther to the south, particularly against Vicksburg. Pro-Confederate planters abandoned West Tennessee, setting in motion a flow of enslaved people into Memphis, first as a trickle and then as a torrent. (By early 1865, the black population would exceed sixteen thousand.)⁸ In short order, the U.S. Army's engineer, quartermaster, and commissary departments came to employ thousands of men. They and their families lived in such quarters as they could find in the city or in so-called contraband camps, which began to take shape in the southern suburbs of the city near Fort Pickering. In the fall of 1862, the Confederate counteroffensive in Mississippi forced the relocation of Camp Holly Springs and its inhabitants to Memphis. According to James Yeatman of the Western Sanitary Commission, who visited the camp in 1863, its "clean and airy" dwellings consisted of "four rows of good log huts . . . with small plots for gardens in front. The streets and alleys were all clean and well swept, having good drainage and excellent police arrangements." A similar site, Camp Shiloh, which laborers of the engineer's department had constructed using tents furnished by federal authorities and building materials they had scavenged from around the city, boasted its own school and church. Eventually, federal officials also opened a camp on President's Island to absorb the newcomers and put them to work chopping wood for government transport vessels.⁹

The Union's military buildup inevitably drew in black men as soldiers. Although the army did not begin accepting black recruits until after Lincoln issued the Emancipation Proclamation, the navy had never completely excluded black men; at the start of the war, they constituted approximately 5 percent of its enlisted force. During the war's first summer, the captains of ships operating in Virginia's waters repeatedly encountered enslaved men who sought freedom and protection aboard naval vessels and offered their services in return. In September 1861, navy secretary Gideon Welles advised the flag officers of each squadron to enlist as many contrabands as their needs required. Commanders of vessels in the Mississippi Squadron tapped into the reserve of black men with experience on the rivers. As operations extended farther along the Cumberland and Tennessee Rivers, those commanders, too, enlisted men who were fleeing from slavery. By the spring of 1863, black sailors were a sizable and growing presence on the vessels involved in operations against Vicksburg.[10]

On May 27, 1863, Confederate fire from the Vicksburg batteries sank the U.S.S. *Cincinnati*. Among the fourteen men who died on board, four were contraband sailors. As the summer advanced, many white sailors fell victim to disease, and flag officer David D. Porter reiterated navy secretary Welles's earlier endorsement of black enlistment as a way to meet the manpower needs of his squadron. Convinced that "white men can not stand the southern sun," Porter was confident that black men could, and he issued orders accordingly.[11] As a result of these directives, black men comprised increasingly larger numbers of crewmen on the vessels of the Mississippi Squadron. By the spring of 1864, they were fully one-third of its enlisted force—by far the highest percentage of all the U.S. Navy's Civil War squadrons—and they served on nearly every vessel. During the summer of 1864 on the U.S.S. *General Price*, they made up 37 percent of the crew and on the U.S.S. *Rattler* approximately 60 percent. Of the roughly 18,000 men of African ancestry who served in the U.S. Navy during the Civil War, approximately 600 were natives of Tennessee.[12] Not atypical was Andrew Minter who, following his discharge, settled in Memphis and purchased a home with the $500 final pay he received.[13] Another 1,000 black sailors had been born in Mississippi. Some portion of the 2,800 sailors who were born in Virginia had been relocated to Tennessee and Mississippi before the war.

When the U.S. government began enlisting black men as soldiers in the spring of 1863, the number of recruits from West Tennessee and the states to the south that bordered the Mississippi River increased dramatically. By the end of the war, the total number of soldiers credited to these states was Tennessee, 20,000; Mississippi, 18,000; Arkansas, 5,500; and Louisiana, 24,000.[14] Among the Tennesseans were more than 1,100 men who in June 1863 had begun enlisting at Fort Pickering in the First Tennessee Heavy Artillery (African Descent), which later became the Third U.S. Colored Heavy Artillery. In April 1864, Sergeant William J. Brown penned a remarkable letter to Secretary of

War Edwin M. Stanton. A free-born man who claimed to be the first to enlist in the regiment, Brown wished to lay before Stanton certain grievances, insisting that "we have never had our Just Rights." He drew particular attention to their low pay, the result of a War Department decision to pay black soldiers $10 per month minus $3 for clothing rather than the customary $13 per month plus a clothing allowance paid to white soldiers. This had an adverse impact on the black men's ability to support their families; moreover, it placed them in the awkward position of earning less than the contracted contraband laborers who worked alongside them improving the defenses of Fort Pickering. On behalf of the men in the regiment, he demanded equality with white soldiers.[15]

Regardless of the pay they earned, black soldiers and sailors experienced a life-altering transformation when they entered federal service. They became free despite Tennessee's exemption from the Emancipation Proclamation, and, just as important, they were treated as free men with the expectation that they would conduct themselves accordingly, as the photographs of Private Hubbard Pryor, who enlisted in the Forty-Fourth U.S. Colored Infantry at Chattanooga, illustrate. Black men in uniform fought to save the Union, to abolish slavery, and to claim the rights enjoyed by citizens of the American republic. By the end of the war, this expectation included the right of men's suffrage. The soldiers' and sailors' quest for freedom and full citizenship radiated throughout black communities in the North as well as the South.

This spirit was on full display in January 1865, when the black citizens of Memphis held a parade to commemorate the second anniversary of the Emancipation Proclamation. First came the printers with a printing press turning out fresh copies of the proclamation, then came "Shoemakers, Carpenters, Blacksmiths, Whitewashers, Bricklayers, Sewing Machine Operators, and Barbers." Following the fraternal and benevolent societies (including the Sons and Daughters of Ham and the Odd Fellows' Benevolent Society) came the draymen, wood dealers, and hawkers. The banners that parade participants proudly carried revealed the community's loyalty to the national government as well as its awareness of important national events. They saluted "America, the Home of the Brave and the Free" as well as Generals Ulysses S. Grant, William T. Sherman, and George H. Thomas. They pronounced 1863 "The Year of Jubilee" and rejoiced in "Two Years of Liberty." Proclaiming "Liberty or Death," they declared "We are Marching On, No Compromise" to achieve "Liberty, Education, and the Right of Suffrage."[16] Days later, black leaders in Nashville forwarded a remarkable petition to the state's Union convention also requesting "the privilege of citizenship," fully embracing "the obligations imposed by it," and bolstering their case by noting that "near 200,000 of our brethren" then served in the Union army.[17]

Hubbard Pryor before his enlistment in the Forty-Fourth U.S. Colored Troops, October 1864. Letters Received, 1863–1888, microfilm 750, CT 1864, RG 94: Records of the Adjutant General's Office, National Archives and Records Administration, Washington, D.C.

Around the same time, Louis and Matilda Hughes were making their way home to Panola County, Mississippi, from the Confederate saltworks at Mobile, Alabama. They had been leased to the facility, but a threatened raid by Union troops had forced its closure. After reaching home, they "longed for freedom" but had to content themselves with "hoping and praying for the coming of the day." "After we came back from Alabama," Louis Hughes later explained, "we were held with a tighter rein than ever. We were not allowed to go outside of the premises." But the signs of impending change were everywhere. Later that spring, members of their owner's family traveled to Memphis and encountered a black soldier serving as a picket guard whom they recognized as the former slave of an uncle. Upon hearing an account of this meeting, the couple's owner groused that he would have died before stopping for the former-slave-turned-soldier.[18]

Hubbard Pryor after his enlistment in the Forty-Fourth U.S. Colored Troops, October 1864. Letters Received, 1863–1888, microfilm 750, CT 1864, RG 94: Records of the Adjutant General's Office, National Archives and Records Administration, Washington, D.C.

Only in the summer of 1865 did the Hugheses succeed in making their way safely to Memphis and freedom. Louis Hughes and a companion had gone to the city in June to seek the assistance of federal military authorities. The officer with whom they spoke advised them that soldiers would be willing to help for a fee. Hughes and his companion arranged for an escort of two men, who accompanied them home, kept their former owners at bay, and then traveled with the Hugheses, other family members, and friends back to Memphis. They reached the city and claimed their freedom on July 4.[19] Their arrival on the anniversary of the nation's birth underscored the unsettled state of black people's freedom fully three months after the Confederate surrender. Slavery died hard in Mississippi and West Tennessee. Indeed, Memphis resident Ann George testified that she was held in slavery until December 1865.[20]

Although the end of the Civil War meant an end to the Confederacy and slavery, many questions had yet to be resolved. Two of the most serious ones concerned the contours of the new labor system that would take the place of slavery and the extent to which formerly enslaved people would have access to the full array of rights and privileges that white citizens enjoyed. The presence of the large federal force in Memphis, which included well over a thousand black soldiers, set West Tennessee apart from other regions of the former Confederacy. Since their families lived in camps adjacent to Fort Pickering and scattered through the city, these soldiers had deep and personal ties to the local black community. Black women in the settlements, such as Lucy Hunt, found employment at the fort, cooking and washing clothing for the soldiers.[21] Even soldiers without families frequented the churches, small businesses, and night spots near the fort, where they reinforced their ties with the community. All served as champions of formerly enslaved people's rights.[22]

They did not act alone in this work. At the end of the war, federal military officials assumed authority over freedmen's affairs pending the restoration of civil authority under the auspices of reconstructed governments in the former Confederate states. The Freedmen's Bureau, which Congress had created within the War Department the month before Lincoln's assassination, assumed that responsibility. General Clinton B. Fisk, the bureau's assistant commissioner for Kentucky and Tennessee, maintained his headquarters in Nashville. Memphis was a regional administrative center for West Tennessee.

During the summer and fall of 1865, Freedmen's Bureau commissioner Oliver Otis Howard in Washington, D.C., identified as a key objective the creation of a system of compensated labor guided by formal contracts to take the place of slavery. Throughout the South, bureau agents dutifully vetted proposed contracts and collected copies of documents they approved, often having to overcome skepticism on the part of laborers and landowners along the way. The officials then fielded complaints of noncompliance and attempted to resolve disagreements. Employers typically faulted freedpeople for unauthorized absences, disobedience, or insubordination. Workers complained chiefly of ill treatment; failure to furnish agreed-upon housing, rations, and medical care; and nonpayment of wages.[23] As Brigadier General Benjamin P. Runkle, superintendent of the District of Memphis during 1866, reported, people who left the city for employment on Mississippi plantations faced particularly grim conditions, but those who worked in Memphis and elsewhere in West Tennessee often fared little better. The problem was that employers applauded the bureau's efforts to make "the negro do his duty" and work faithfully, but they detested the agents' interventions on behalf of protecting "the negro in his rights."[24]

Urban settings posed opportunities and challenges similar to yet distinct from those of rural areas. Garrison cities like Memphis and Nashville had served as beacons that attracted black migrants from the earliest days of the federal military presence in the spring of 1862. Such places offered employment as well as protection. The end of hostilities brought demobilization and, with that, declining prospects for regular employment, although men and women with skills fared better than the unskilled. The shoemaker Albert Harris, a fifty-three-year-old Virginia native who had lived in Memphis for more than a decade, opened a shoemaking shop in his home during the war and had managed to save about $350 by the time the Memphis Massacre erupted in 1866. Andrew Minter, the navy veteran who had purchased a home in Memphis, found work "running on the river," earning $50 per month, roughly five times what a plantation laborer generally received. His wife, a seamstress, was busy making dresses "all the time." The blacksmith William Coe also managed to find regular employment, but he did not mince words in characterizing the difficulties associated with doing so. Employers had treated him "pretty rash all the time," much more so after the war than before, and they were particularly careless about paying him. "I didn't get one-third of what was due me," yet his requests for settlement fell on deaf ears. "Everybody seems to try to get the advantage of me," he concluded, "and not against me alone, but against every colored person."[25]

In August 1865, General Davis Tillson, the bureau's superintendent of the subdistrict of Memphis, envisioned a plan for providing "comfortable homes" with "fair wages and kind treatment" to black people who lacked "sufficient means" to support themselves or who could not demonstrate permanent employment enabling them to "provide for their own wants and necessities." The caveat was that they would have to leave the city and accept work on farms and plantations in the countryside. Officials reserved the right to use military force when necessary to persuade the recalcitrant to accept relocation.[26] The plan created considerable confusion in the city, particularly when long-term residents fell victim to the dragnet along with recent migrants. Assistant Commissioner Fisk approved the relocation scheme and even enlisted the support of black community leaders, such as Warner Madison, to promote cooperation. "It is important that the colored people demonstrate beyond doubt, that they can appreciate the real value of liberty," Fisk explained, "by well ordered lives, and industrious habits." He counseled that "the enemies of freedom, rejoice when they can point to circumstances where large numbers of colored people are idling away their time."[27]

In correspondence with Fisk, Madison at first charged that soldiers were receiving payments from prospective employers for able-bodied people delivered for work on plantations. In time, however, Madison (and other members of the committee appointed by the August 1865 State Convention of Colored

Men to "look after the interests of our people" in Shelby County) applauded Fisk's effort to promote industry and avert destitution.[28] Another member of the Shelby County committee, Anthony Motley, objected vigorously to the bureau's initiative, however, labeling it emphatically as the revival of "the great Slave trade."[29] Notwithstanding the opposition expressed by "the most respectable & intelligent portion of the colored citizens" of Memphis, as an official characterized them, the relocations continued. For good measure, federal authorities also banned the black residents of the city from holding "public entertainments, balls, and parties."[30]

Apart from causing divisions in the black community—pitting long-time residents against newcomers, the fully employed against the irregularly employed and the unemployed, and those who supported the Freedmen's Bureau's policies against those who did not—the relocation program also fed the fires of racial tension between the city's black and white residents. With the bureau acting so vigorously against the perceived vagrancy of black residents, white residents felt vindicated.

Although Madison and other members of the oversight committee took the part of the Freedmen's Bureau in its efforts to resettle unemployed urban residents to the countryside, they also pressed the case for equal civic and political rights. The service of black men in the army and navy undergirded this claim. Soldiers and sailors knew that their actions had helped to save the Union from destruction, but there was more. Their experience under arms helped develop traits of discipline and loyalty beginning with their comrades, embracing their families and communities, and extending to the nation. They understood that the discipline honed through daily interactions with officers and peers would prove useful in civilian pursuits, particularly as they began independent lives as freedmen. By working hard and behaving responsibly, they believed, they would achieve much more than economic self-sufficiency; they would also earn the respect of their fellow citizens, white and black. The Memphis Massacre exposed the fragility of these assumptions.

By early 1866, tensions between black and white residents of South Memphis began to boil over, due in no small measure to the growing animus of the Irish police toward freedpeople in general and black soldiers in particular. Apart from the general uncertainty brought on by the destruction of slavery, the growing national obsession over the reconstruction of the former Confederate states also manifested locally. As former Confederates clamored for restitution of their political rights and President Andrew Johnson sparred with congressional Radicals for control over Reconstruction policy—with Johnson pointedly vetoing the bills that guaranteed the civil rights of all citizens and reauthorized the Freedmen's Bureau in March—freedpeople and Irish residents alike pressed for guarantees of their rights. The Memphis electorate had placed Irishmen in every key post in the city and in a majority of the seats on the city council. The Irish saw black soldiers neither as contributors to the Union's victory nor as legitimate advocates for the rights of their people, but as "black sons of bitches" who "were fighting here against our rights."[31] What is more, native-born Confederate sympathizers viewed black veterans both as contributors to the defeat of the rebellion and as objectionable symbols of black freedom and manhood. One elderly black victim of police violence testified that he had encouraged his son, a veteran of the Union army, to go "into the country to work" because the Irish had "disturbed a great many who were discharged from the army." Another black veteran knew that his army-issued blue clothing made him a marked man.[32]

Because black regiments generally lacked seniority compared to the white volunteer units, they remained in service for months after the end of the war. When the members of the Third U.S. Colored Heavy Artillery were discharged in April 1866, they were instructed to remain in Memphis until they received their final pay. The married men joined their families, and the single men pitched a camp adjacent to Fort Pickering. They continued to enjoy access to the fort, but the government-issued weapons that they had relinquished at muster-out remained under lock and key. Some men did possess pistols, shotguns, and other firearms of their own. As days of waiting for the paymaster turned into weeks, some of the men became restive.[33]

In the circumstances, black soldiers sought strength in numbers. The discharged artilleryman Tony Cherry later reported that some of the men had been in the habit of frequenting "several saloons in the neighborhood where they got liquor," one of which was operated by two sergeants of his company. On May 1, 1866—the first day of the violence—they "had been drinking right smartly," and some began "hallooing 'Hurrah for Abe Lincoln'" as they exchanged taunts and insults with the police. Both sides soon replaced words with bullets, and the melee began. By the next day, most of the soldiers—many with their families—had taken refuge in the fort although some sallied out to engage the police and rioters with pistols and shotguns. "They were killing our boys everywhere," Cherry explained. "We saw them shot down like beasts, and it was pretty hard to remain quiet, for those who had arms, without trying to do something to stop it." When he realized how events were unfolding, he decided to remain inside the fort, where he and his comrades kept up small-arms fire with their personal weapons, having been denied access to the ordnance locker and its cache of rifles and ammunition by the officers. When the rioters threatened to attack the fort, however, the officers and men executed a defensive plan, loading the artillery pieces and preparing to open fire, if necessary, to repel the mob.[34]

As the experience of the naval veteran Andrew Minter and his wife illustrated, the riot turned their world upside down, exploding their pathway to the rewards of their hard work and to enjoyment of the respect of their fellow citizens, black and white. Thanks to what he earned working on the river, Minter reported, he had purchased more than $100 in provisions from an Irish grocer named John Callahan, who had "always appeared very friendly to me." But once the riot began, Callahan abandoned that persona. With several accomplices, he broke into the Minters' home, shot Andrew Minter in the hand, and tore into a trunk in search of the "good clothes" he knew his customer possessed. The robbers also stole the Minters' money and provisions, and then Callahan set fire to their prized possession, their home. Minter later estimated that he and his wife lost $1,000 worth of property altogether.[35] Their loss of confidence in the promise of freedom was incalculable.

During the year between April 1865 and May 1, 1866, black Tennesseans made great strides toward leaving the rubble of slavery behind, just as their counterparts in other former slave states had done. Soldiers and sailors returned home and rejoined their families in the work of Reconstruction. They found employment, and some opened businesses of their own. They settled into homes where they began to raise families. They strengthened the institutions that had assisted them in the struggle against slavery—particularly the church and various benevolent associations—and they took advantage of the benefits that federal occupation also inaugurated, specifically access to schools and to the interventions of the Freedmen's Bureau in addressing injustice and adjudicating disputes with former owners and other white citizens. Yet despite all the slights and insults they had endured before and after the Confederate surrender, they scarcely could have foreseen the violence that exploded on May 1, 1866.

When it did, black soldiers used the weapons at their disposal until resistance proved futile or they exhausted their ammunition. In a narrow sense, they and the other black victims of the white mob's violence were fighting for their lives. But just as important, they were upholding the freedom that their wartime service and sacrifices should have guaranteed. They desired to enjoy the fruits of their labor and to go about their peaceful pursuits unmolested. With talk of a national civil rights bill in the air, they also looked to a future in which they would enjoy the fruits of equal citizenship—perhaps one day even exercising the right of suffrage—that would place them fully on a par with white citizens. Though their losses were often irreplaceable, the death and destruction they endured in early May 1866 helped launch the next chapter in the nation's long and still-unfinished encounter with the legacy of slavery, Radical Reconstruction, when the hope of better days again brightened the horizon.[36]

NOTES

1. "The Memphis Riots," *Harper's Weekly*, May 26, 1866, 321. *Harper's* published a follow-up report in the next issue: "The Late Riot at Memphis," June 2, 1866, 339.

2. *Population of the United States in 1860; as Compiled from the Original Returns of the Eighth Census, under the Direction of the Secretary of the Interior, by Joseph C. G. Kennedy, Superintendent of Census* (Washington, D.C.: Government Printing Office, 1864), xxxi–xxxii, 467.

3. "Emancipation Celebration in Memphis," *Anglo-African* (New York), January 28, 1865, 4.

4. Louis Hughes, *Thirty Years a Slave: The Institution of Slavery as Seen on the Plantation and in the Home of the Planter* (Milwaukee, Wis.: South Side Printing, 1897), 80–90, 94–100.

5. William Webb, *The History of William Webb, Composed by Himself* (Detroit, Mich.: Egbert Hoekstra, Printer, 1873), 13–30, 18 (quotation).

6. Harvey Wish, "The Slave Insurrection Panic of 1856," *Journal of Southern History* 5, no. 2 (1939): 206–22; Herbert Aptheker, *American Negro Slave Revolts* (1943; rpt., New York: International Publishers, 1969), 84–85.

7. "Slaves Riveting Their Chains," reprinted in *Anglo-African* (New York), September 21, 1861, 3.

8. John Cimprich, *Slavery's End in Tennessee, 1861–1865* (Tuscaloosa: University of Alabama Press, 1985), 31, 53; James Gilbert Ryan, "The Memphis Riots of 1866: Terror in a Black Community during Reconstruction," *Journal of Negro History* 62, no. 3 (1977): 244. During the summer of 1865, a census conducted under the auspices of the Freedmen's Bureau counted 15,828 freedpeople in the city of Memphis and another 681 on President's Island. See Steven Hahn et al., eds., *Freedom: A Documentary History of Emancipation, 1861–1867*, ser. 3, vol. 1, *Land and Labor, 1865* (Chapel Hill: University of North Carolina Press, 2008), 267n1.

9. James Yeatman, *A Report on the Condition of the Freedmen of the Mississippi, Presented to the Western Sanitary Commission, December 17th, 1863* (St. Louis, Mo.: Western Sanitary Commission Rooms, 1864), 1–2. In the spring of 1863, Colonel John Eaton Jr., the general superintendent of contrabands in the Department of the Tennessee, prepared a comprehensive report on conditions among black refugees in the department for the benefit of the American Freedmen's Inquiry Commission, an advisory body that war secretary Edwin Stanton had recently established. See John Eaton to Jno. A. Rawlins, April 29, 1863, O-328 1863, Letters Received, ser. 12, Records of the Adjutant General's

Office, RG 94, National Archives and Records Administration, Washington, D.C. A portion of the report is reproduced in Ira Berlin et al., eds., *Freedom: A Documentary History of Emancipation, 1861–1867*, ser. 1, vol. 3: *The Wartime Genesis of Free Labor: The Lower South* (Cambridge: Cambridge University Press, 1990), 684–98.

10. Gideon Welles to Captain Thomas T. Craven, September 25, 1861, as published in U.S. Naval War Records Office, *Official Records of the Union and Confederate Navies in the War of the Rebellion*, ser. 1 (Washington, D.C.: Government Printing Office, 1894–1922), 4:692; Gideon Welles to Flag-Officer C. H. Davis, April 30, 1862, ibid., 23:80–81. See also Joseph P. Reidy, "Black Men in Navy Blue during the Civil War," *Prologue: Quarterly of the National Archives and Records Administration* 33, no. 3 (2001): 155–67, esp. 156–58; David L. Valuska, *The African American in the Union Navy, 1861–1865* (New York: Garland, 1993); Steven J. Ramold, *Slaves, Sailors, Citizens: African Americans in the Union Navy* (DeKalb: Northern Illinois University Press, 2002); and Thomas C. Buchanan, *Black Life on the Mississippi: Slaves, Free Blacks, and the Western Steamboat World* (Chapel Hill: University of North Carolina Press, 2004).

11. Lt. George M. Bache to [Adm. David D. Porter], May 29, 1863, as published in U.S. Naval War Records Office, *Official Records of the Union and Confederate Navies*, ser. 1, 25:42–43; General Orders 76, Mississippi Squadron, July 23, 1863, ibid., 25:327–28. See also Reidy, "Black Men in Navy Blue."

12. Reidy, "Black Men in Navy Blue," 156–58. Estimates regarding the racial composition of the crews of naval vessels and the nativity of black sailors derive from research conducted at Howard University in collaboration with the U.S. Department of the Navy and the U.S. National Park Service. Some results of this work may be explored at https://www.nps.gov/civilwar/search-sailors.htm.

13. Testimony of Andrew Minter, "Memphis Riots and Massacres," *U.S. Serial Set*, no. 1274, House Report 101, 39th Cong., 1st sess., 171–72.

14. *Freedom: A Documentary History of Emancipation, 1861–1867*, ser. 2: *The Black Military Experience*, ed. Ira Berlin et al. (Cambridge: Cambridge University Press, 1982), 12.

15. Wm. J. Brown to Honourable Secretary of War, April 27, 1864, in Berlin et al., *Black Military Experience*, 377–78.

16. "Emancipation Celebration in Memphis," *Anglo-African* (New York), January 28, 1865, 4. See also Alrutheus Ambush Taylor, *The Negro in Tennessee, 1865–1889* (Washington, D.C.: Associated Publishers, 1941), 85–88; Armstead L. Robinson, "'Plans Dat Comed from God': Institution Building and the Emergence of Black Leadership in Reconstruction Memphis," in *Toward a New South? Studies in Post–Civil War Southern Communities*, ed. Orville Vernon Burton and Robert C. McMath Jr. (Westport, Conn.: Greenwood, 1982), 71–102; Cimprich, *Slavery's End in Tennessee*, 72–80; and Stephen V. Ash, *A Massacre in Memphis: The Race Riot That Shook the Nation One Year after the Civil War* (New York: Hill and Wang, 2013), esp. chap. 4.

17. Andrew Tait et al. to the Union Convention of Tennessee, January 9, 1865, in Berlin et al., *Black Military Experience*, 811–14.

18. Hughes, *Thirty Years a Slave*, 169–71.

19. Ibid., 176–87.

20. Testimony of Ann George, "Memphis Riots and Massacres," 258.

21. Testimony of Lucy Hunt, "Memphis Riots and Massacres," 17, 200–201.

22. The testimony of officers of the Third U.S. Colored Heavy Artillery corroborates these ties. See, for instance, that of Lt. Frederick Hastings and Capt. A. W. Allyn, "Memphis Riots and Massacres," 205, 245.

23. For the most comprehensive treatment of this subject, see Hahn et al., *Land and Labor*, 1–70, 71–85, 170–97, 309–31, 392–413, 494–510, 598–614, 681–96, 746–56, 796–808, 910–27.

24. Testimony of Bvt. Brig. Gen. Benjamin P. Runkle, "Memphis Riots and Massacres," 279.

25. Testimony of Albert Harris, Andrew Minter, and William Coe, "Memphis Riots and Massacres," 62–63, 171–72, 102–3.

26. Circular 5, Office Supt R. F. and A. L. [Refugees, Freedmen and Abandoned Lands] Subdist Memphis, August 28, 1865, in Hahn et al., *Land and Labor*, 268–69.

27. Clinton B. Fisk to Warner Madison et al., October 7, 1865, quoted in Hahn et al., *Land and Labor*, 276n1.

28. Warner Madison to General C. B. Fisk, September 13, 1865, 269–70; and Madison to Fisk, October 13, 1865, 275–76, both in Hahn et al., *Land and Labor*. On the state convention and its charge to the delegates representing each county, see *Proceedings of the State Convention of Colored Men of the State of Tennessee . . . Held at Nashville, Tenn., August 7th, 8th, 9th and 10th, 1865* (Nashville, Tenn.: Daily Press and Times Job Office, 1865), 18.

29. Anthony Motley to Gen[era]l Fisk, September 28, 1865, in Hahn et al., *Land and Labor*, 271.

30. Bvt. Brig. Gen. N. A. M. Dudley to Capt. Clarke, September 30, 1865, in Hahn et al., *Land and Labor*, 273. The order prohibiting parties is quoted at 274–75n4.

31. Testimony of Allen Summers, "Memphis Riots and Massacres," 171. The congressional investigators characterized the Irish predominance in local politics in this way: "The city government was utterly and completely Irish in nearly all its branches: the mayor was an Irishman; the recorder was an Irishman; nine out of sixteen [members] of the city council were Irish; and out of one hundred and eighty members of the police force, one hundred and sixty-three were Irish, and all the members of the police committee were Irish. The fire department was nearly all Irish." See "Report" in "Memphis Riots and Massacres," 23.

32. Testimony of Primus Lane and Frank Williams, "Memphis Riots and Massacres," 97, 179.

33. Testimony of Lt. Frederick Hastings, "Memphis Riots and Massacres," 205.
34. Testimony of Tony Cherry, "Memphis Riots and Massacres," 182–86. Lt. Frederick Hastings estimated that a hundred families of soldiers took refuge in Fort Pickering. "Memphis Riots and Massacres," 207.
35. Testimony of Andrew Minter, "Memphis Riots and Massacres," 172.
36. See Eric Foner, *Reconstruction: America's Unfinished Revolution, 1863–1877* (New York: Harper and Row, 1988).

"Thank God That the Tyrants Rod Has Been Broken"

The Abolition of Slavery in Tennessee

JOHN C. RODRIGUE

Writing from Nashville on January 13, 1865, even as Republican leaders in the U.S. House of Representatives were postponing a vote on the Thirteenth Amendment for lack of the necessary votes, Tennessee's military governor and the vice president elect, Andrew Johnson, informed Abraham Lincoln of the action of a state constitutional convention then in progress. "The Convention composed of more than five hundred delegates from all parts of the State have unanimously adopted an amendment to the Constitution forever abolishing Slavery in this State and denying the power of the Legislature passing any law creating property in man," Johnson wrote. "Thank God that the tyrants rod has been broken." The amendment to the Tennessee constitution would go before the people on February 22, and Johnson confidently predicted "the state will be redeemed and the foul blot of Slavery erased from her escutcheon." Tennessee voters indeed approved this amendment to the state constitution, ending slavery in Tennessee three years after federal military forces began making inroads into the Lower Mississippi Valley and, in the process, emancipating enslaved people.[1]

In this chapter I provide an overview of slavery's formal abolition in Tennessee. This work is part of a larger project on the destruction of slavery in the Lower Mississippi Valley, covering the period from the secession crisis through final ratification of the Thirteenth Amendment in December 1865 and encompassing the four insurgent states along the Mississippi River that joined the Confederacy: Tennessee, Mississippi, Arkansas, and Louisiana. Viewing this region as a distinct geopolitical entity, I examine the myriad ways that slavery was brought to an end in it. Of these states, only Mississippi did not abolish slavery during the war. While integrating military developments, political developments in the states and in Washington, and the disintegration of slavery on the plantations into a chronological narrative, this project is also linked together by three overarching themes. The first is to demonstrate the multidimensional process of emancipation and abolition in the Lower Mississippi Valley. The second is to revise the standard "war-for-Union to war-for-freedom" narrative of the Civil War. And the third is to argue that wartime Reconstruction in the states of the Lower Mississippi Valley (except Mississippi) was central to transforming the Emancipation Proclamation into the abolition of slavery. Understanding abolition in Tennessee requires a brief elaboration of these three themes.

The Lower Mississippi Valley experienced all five major dimensions of wartime emancipation and abolition, which can be said of no other geographical region of the Confederacy. First, parts of all four states experienced the emancipation of enslaved people—or "military emancipation"—under federal antislavery measures prior to the Emancipation Proclamation. Second, universal military emancipation under the Emancipation Proclamation occurred in all of Arkansas and Mississippi and most of Louisiana. Third, there were exclusions from the proclamation, including all of Tennessee and southern Louisiana. Fourth, state-level abolition took place in Arkansas and Louisiana in 1864 and Tennessee in early 1865. Finally, Mississippi essentially abolished slavery under federal authority after the war ended. Federal power, in the guise of the Thirteenth Amendment, also ensured that no state could ever reintroduce slavery.

The second theme offers a revision of the "war-for-Union to war-for-freedom" narrative, which focuses overwhelmingly on the Emancipation Proclamation, almost relegating the abolition of slavery to an afterthought. Although historians have recognized that the proclamation freed slaves but did not abolish slavery, they have not fully appreciated the difficulty—or the political significance—of translating military emancipation into constitutional abolition. Republicans were firmly committed to the abolition of slavery after January 1863 (many were committed well before that), but it was not clear how that goal would be achieved. Antislavery thought had long held that the states, with federal assistance, would abolish slavery. Congress had dealt with the problem of Reconstruction almost from the start of the war, but it never enacted legislation specifying the conditions for states' readmission. Even the Thirteenth Amendment, as Michael Vorenberg has shown, was originally intended to work in conjunction with Reconstruction legislation, and few antislavery advocates, ironically, placed much stock in the Thirteenth Amendment when it was introduced in Congress in December 1863. Thus, the transformation of the Civil War into a war for freedom was not a one-step process but rather a two-step process: war-for-Union to Emancipation Proclamation, and Emancipation Proclamation to constitutional abolition. The second step of this process was every bit as essential to the eradication of slavery as the first, even though the first receives greater attention.[2]

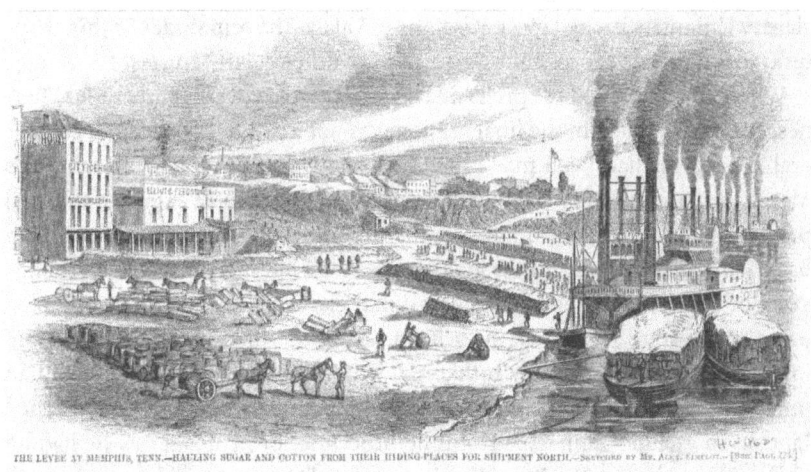

The Union occupation of Memphis ended the trade blockade, releasing stores of cotton and other crops for shipment north. Sketch by Alex Simplot, *Harper's Weekly*, 1862. Prints and Photographs Division, Library of Congress, Washington, D.C.

This leads to the project's third theme: the Lower Mississippi Valley as the crucible within which military emancipation became constitutional abolition. The issue of abolishing slavery as a condition for a state's restoration to the Union arose as a direct result of Union military success in 1862 in the Lower Mississippi Valley. Following the federal military conquest and occupation of western and central Tennessee and southern Louisiana (and eastern Arkansas and parts of Mississippi) by mid-1862, amorphous Unionist movements emerged in both states that included slaveholders and antislavery advocates as well as "conditional Unionists" and former secessionists. The Emancipation Proclamation precipitated the split among southern Unionists into proslavery and antislavery factions, especially in Louisiana and Tennessee, and for the next two years these groups tussled over the state restoration process. Free-state forces attempted to organize new governments that would abolish slavery, while "conservative Unionists" undertook various efforts to hold elections under the states' antebellum constitutions and restore their states to the Union with slavery intact. The possibility of the states that had seceded returning to the Union while retaining slavery may seem remote in hindsight, but at the time it worried slavery's opponents and motivated its advocates. Transforming the Emancipation Proclamation into the constitutional abolition of slavery resulted from various factors, but an essential one—the significance of which has not been fully appreciated—was the contest between free-state and proslavery Unionists in the Lower Mississippi Valley. The remainder of this chapter traces how this process of transformation unfolded in Tennessee.[3]

When Lincoln issued the preliminary proclamation in September 1862, Tennessee's exclusion from the final version was not a given, even though considerable progress had been made in cultivating Unionism following Johnson's March 1862 appointment as military governor. Many people expected the final proclamation to include Tennessee. The preliminary proclamation sparked a backlash against Unionism throughout the state, but it also created a groundswell of support for holding congressional elections in the Union-occupied parts of the state so as to gain exclusion from the final proclamation. More important, when some forty influential Unionists—including men who had previously been or would later become bitter political opponents—petitioned Lincoln to exclude Tennessee from the proclamation, Lincoln saw he had no choice but to do so. "The Exception in favor of Tennessee will be worth much to us," Johnson assured Lincoln in early January 1863. Slavery had already been significantly weakened and thousands of enslaved people had been emancipated, but the state's exclusion from the proclamation gave slavery's defenders in Tennessee hope for preserving it.[4]

Despite Tennessee's exclusion, the first half of 1863 witnessed the slow but steady conversion of key Unionists to emancipation and, consequently, the emergence of the factional split between free-state and proslavery Unionists. For the next two years, these two factions vied for control of Tennessee's restoration. Johnson, William G. "Parson" Brownlow, and (eventually) Horace Maynard led the free-state forces, while Emerson Etheridge (a former ally of Lincoln who broke with him over emancipation), former governor William B. Campbell, and Thomas A. R. Nelson were leading conservatives. Although Unionist politics had originally reflected the traditional divisions that dated from the antebellum era, as well as individual loyalties since secession, differences over emancipation eventually became paramount. In this respect, the experiences of Andrew Johnson can be seen as representative. Although Johnson owned several slaves before and even during the war, he detested slavery and especially the planter elite. As the defender of the common (white) man, Johnson hated slavery not for what it did to the enslaved people but rather for the inequalities it produced in white society. He always maintained that ending slavery would liberate many more white people than enslaved black people, and he loathed the idea of racial equality as vehemently as he did slavery. Johnson and his supporters moved to emancipation slowly, and their shift resulted from various factors, but ultimately the central one was the threat from proslavery Unionists to gain control of the state and restore it to the Union with slavery as a legal institution.[5]

Until Lincoln's reelection in November 1864 doomed the Confederacy, Johnson faced a series of attempts by conservative Unionists to achieve their goals. At the same time, he had to deal with calls from free-state Unionists, from Lincoln himself, and from black Tennesseans—who had very different ideas about the process of Reconstruction—to organize a loyal state government that would abolish slavery. Throughout this entire process, Johnson steadfastly maintained that no state reorganization could take place until largely Unionist East Tennessee had been liberated from Confederate control, a policy that his conservative critics maintained was a stalling tactic designed to preserve his hold on power.

Although the split between free-state and conservative Unionists was almost complete by mid-1863, both factions adhered to the illusion that they still might work together. During the spring, Unionists repeatedly urged Johnson to organize a convention that would lead to electing a civilian government and restoring Tennessee to the Union. Johnson was reluctant to endorse this movement, but it was backed by a wide spectrum of Unionists. After much jockeying, a state convention met on July 1 in Nashville, attended by more than two hundred delegates. Despite Johnson's opposition to the convention, it behooved his supporters to participate so as to prevent proslavery Unionists from gaining the upper hand. The convention quickly divided along factional lines, and the conservative Unionists' objectives became clear. They proposed holding elections under the antebellum constitution for a state government and for members of Congress. These elections, moreover, would take place in August—presumably *before* Unionist East Tennessee could be liberated. They thus hoped to overthrow Johnson and capitalize on Tennessee's exemption from the Emancipation Proclamation by restoring the state before abolition became a condition for state restoration.

After acrimonious debate, the convention approved resolutions that appeared to strike a compromise but in fact marked a defeat for the conservatives. The resolutions called on Johnson to organize legislative elections for early August 1863, with the legislature to convene in early October, but they made no provisions for the gubernatorial or congressional elections the conservatives had advocated. Although neither slavery nor emancipation were mentioned, the resolutions affirmed the use of federal power "to guarantee to every State a Republican form of Government"—a phrase that was coming to be associated with abolishing slavery. The resolutions also endorsed Johnson's administration as military governor. Following the Emancipation Proclamation, Johnson and his allies had fended off this initial attempt by conservative Unionists to hijack the state restoration process and restore Tennessee under its antebellum constitution.[6]

Although Johnson did not authorize the proposed legislative elections, conservative Unionists moved forward with their plan to hold a gubernatorial election. They nominated William B. Campbell for governor and secured endorsements from key newspapers in Memphis and Nashville, which gave their plan a patina of credibility. The election took place on August 6, though only in certain parts of West and Central Tennessee and without Johnson's authorization. Campbell received some 2,500 votes in what one scholar has called a "farcical contest," and his supporters declared him the winner. Johnson ignored this election, prompting conservatives to castigate him further.[7]

Meanwhile, Emerson Etheridge pressed the case for Campbell. In late September 1863, he penned a long letter to Lincoln condemning Johnson's administration and his abuse of power as military governor and advocating the recognition of Campbell as the civilian governor of Tennessee. "The election of Gen. Campbell has been, in all things, in conformity with the Constitution and laws of Tennessee," Etheridge claimed, adding that it was "the desire of nearly every Union citizen of Tennessee" to see Campbell "inaugurated or installed" as governor. Loyal Tennesseans "have confidence in his honor, his honesty, and his courage," Etheridge assured the president. Lincoln evidently ignored Etheridge's letter, since no record of a reply exists. This rejection of the Tennessee conservative Unionists may not have been as forceful as the one Lincoln issued to Louisiana conservative Unionists in late June 1863, after they had similarly proposed holding elections for a state government under the antebellum constitution, but there was no denying its implications.[8]

In response to this initiative, Johnson intensified his rhetoric against the rebels, endorsed immediate abolition more strongly, and hinted that state elections would soon be held. Following the Union occupation of Knoxville and Chattanooga in early September 1863, Johnson appeared ready to proceed with organizing a free-state government, a goal Lincoln heartily endorsed. "I see that you have declared in favor of emancipation in Tennessee, for which, may God bless you," Lincoln commended Johnson. "Get emancipation into your new State government—Constitution—and there will be no such word as fail for your case." Johnson had indicated that state elections would be held in October, but the Union disaster at Chickamauga on September 19–20 and the subsequent Confederate siege of Chattanooga halted this plan. Even though Johnson continued to express his commitment to immediate abolition throughout the fall, the military situation in East Tennessee precluded any further action. Not until late 1863 would the area finally come under Union control, and Confederates remained active in the state for another year.[9]

Even as federal forces liberated Chattanooga in early December 1863, following General U. S. Grant's victory at Lookout Mountain, the conservatives struck back. The irrepressible Emerson Etheridge, through a strange confluence of events, was Clerk of the House at the convening of the Thirty-Eighth Congress, which had been elected during the fall of 1862, when Republicans had suffered severe losses and their majority had been greatly reduced. Along with Ohio Democrat Samuel S. "Sunset" Cox, Etheridge was at the center of a bizarre plot in which northern and border-state Democrats and southern conservative Unionists attempted to seize control of an evenly divided Congress. They planned to declare invalid the credentials of a number of northern Republicans while seating several members-elect from the border states and Union-occupied South, including three conservative Unionists from southern Louisiana. The Etheridge plot came to naught, and Lincoln later remarked that Etheridge "ain't worth more than a squirrel load of powder anyway." Still, as Herman Belz noted, northern Democrats and their southern allies had essayed a legislative coup d'état at the very moment that Congress was turning to the now-interrelated questions of Reconstruction and emancipation.[10]

Into the spring of 1864, free-state and conservative Unionists in Tennessee continued to advocate, though on different bases, holding elections and organizing a new government. This pressure had increased following the December 1863 announcement of Lincoln's 10 percent plan, which provided for organizing loyal governments in the states that had seceded—governments that were expected to abolish slavery—once a number of (white, male) persons equivalent to 10 percent of the voters in 1860 had taken an oath of *future* loyalty to the United States and had pledged to abide by all wartime antislavery measures. While white loyalists were calling for a new government, black Tennesseans were demanding both abolition and racial equality. In marches, parades, and other public demonstrations organized largely by soldiers, ministers, businessmen, and other leaders and representing churches, schools, benevolent associations, and other institutions and organizations, the black community celebrated the progress already made toward emancipation while rejecting methods of Reconstruction—including Lincoln's—that left black people without any voice. Johnson recognized the need to act, but he continued to fear the possibility of an unholy alliance between conservative Unionists and ex-Confederates that might seize control of a new government. In turn, conservative Unionists countered that Johnson was stalling so as to hold onto power, conduct a vindictive campaign against his opponents, and most implausibly, implement racial equality and abolish slavery.[11]

In late January 1864, Johnson finally authorized holding local elections in early March as "an initiatory step" toward a state convention that would organize a new government, abolish slavery, and restore Tennessee to the Union. Johnson's local election plan did not quite follow Lincoln's blueprint for Reconstruction. But more important, Johnson's conservative critics condemned the plan for what they called Johnson's "damnesty oath," a far more stringent loyalty oath than Lincoln's and one that they charged—not without justification—was designed to exclude them from the state restoration process. They protested to Lincoln, arguing that individuals who had subscribed to the oath in the 10 percent plan could still be excluded by Johnson's oath. Lincoln supported his military governor, even though the damnesty oath indeed contravened Lincoln's goal of inducing Confederates to abandon the rebellion and resume their former allegiance. Although Johnson's oath, unlike Lincoln's, made no specific mention of upholding wartime measures against slavery, it called for the support of all laws and proclamations made in pursuance of reestablishing the U.S. Constitution, thereby indirectly requiring support for emancipation. Ironically, the stringent loyalty provisions of Johnson's oath allowed proslavery Unionists to object to that oath without having to oppose explicitly its emancipation provisions.[12]

The elections were held on March 5 with mixed results. Voting was light in parts of Central and West Tennessee, but Memphis, Nashville, and other areas reported heavy turnout and hotly contested campaigns. Johnson was encouraged by the results. In a series of speeches, he endorsed a state convention that would abolish slavery and reorganize a state government. "Indications on the part of the people were much better than I anticipated in regard to the emancipation of Slavery," he informed Lincoln in early April. "As Soon as practicable there must be a Convention, which I believe will Settle the Slavery question definitely and finely [sic]." Johnson also explicitly endorsed, evidently for the first time, the amendment to the U.S. Constitution abolishing slavery, which the Senate was just then debating and about to pass. Also by April, local officials who were elected in March were beginning to assume office, and although the military situation in Tennessee was far from secure, a civilian government was taking shape.[13]

Perhaps sensing that public opinion in Tennessee was shifting on the slavery question, some conservative Unionists again attempted to circumvent Johnson by calling a convention of their own. In mid-April, they assembled in Knoxville in hopes of putting forward their own restoration plan. Although free-state Unionists, including Johnson, managed to attend the convention, the conservatives were clearly in the majority. They condemned Lincoln's 10 percent plan and Johnson as military governor. They also made clear their disapproval of Lincoln's—and now Johnson's—emancipation policy and called for Tennessee's continued exemption from the Emancipation Proclamation (although some were evidently amenable to gradual, compensated emancipation). Despite a vitriolic speech by Johnson condemning secession and slavery, which was received enthusiastically, the convention revealed deep divisions on emancipation among East Tennessee Unionists, the very people who Johnson had long insisted were essential to the state's reconstruction.[14]

The convention adjourned after four days of bitter, acrimonious debate. Although another conservative Unionist initiative had failed, the Knoxville convention hardly boded well for a state convention that would have to deal with the contentious issues of abolition and its consequences. The whole thing had been an embarrassment to Johnson and potentially called his entire program into question. Hoping to minimize the damage, free-state Unionists immediately held their own "grand mass meeting" in Knoxville, with Parson Brownlow, Johnson, and others delivering addresses emphasizing that slavery, though largely defunct, remained to be legally abolished. "This thing called Slavery is lying dead; we can't hold on to it any longer," Johnson insisted. "Then why not determine the question at once. Now is the time to exercise this power." Despite considerable progress, by mid-1864 Johnson had no choice but to delay the state convention, which was supposed to have followed soon after the March local elections as Tennessee worked toward reconstruction.[15]

State restoration remained on hold in Tennessee during the summer of 1864, as the nation was consumed with military campaigns and the presidential election. In Tennessee, the election further exacerbated the divide among Unionists, as the rival factions put forward competing plans for conducting it. By August, the nadir of Lincoln's presidency, the conservatives had formally constituted themselves into the Conservative Union Party and proposed William B. Campbell as George B. McClellan's running mate. They hoped that a coalition of northern War Democrats, border-state conservatives, and southern conservative Unionists might defeat Lincoln and overthrow the Johnson regime. Campbell refused to have his name put forward, however, and the plan was further undone by the ascendancy of the Peace Democrats at the party's national convention in Chicago. Undaunted, Tennessee conservatives attempted one final push to defeat Lincoln and an abolitionist war. They cobbled together a slate of presidential electors; unleashed an all-out newspaper attack on Johnson, Lincoln, and abolitionism, which they equated with racial equality; and denied the free-state Unionists' contention that slavery was dead in Tennessee.[16]

Meeting in Nashville in early September 1864, only days after the Democrats had nominated McClellan for president on a peace platform and the federals had taken Atlanta, free-state Unionists announced their own plan for Tennessee's participation in the presidential election. In no mood to show their conservative opponents any quarter, the free-state Unionists proposed a loyalty oath for voting even stricter than Johnson's damnesty oath. They also endorsed Johnson's administration as military governor and Lincoln's reelection and advocated for the abolition of slavery "by all suitable and proper amendments" to both the state and federal constitutions. Through September, Johnson issued a series of proclamations that further dismantled the slave regime: requiring that all black people be dealt with legally as free people of color (essentially suspending the state's slave code) and calling up the state militia and providing for the enrollment of all able-bodied adult males, "white and colored." In addition, Tennessee would participate in the presidential election on the terms proposed by the recent convention.[17]

Wary of being excluded entirely from the presidential election and the state restoration process, conservative Unionists drew up a formal protest that was presented to Lincoln in mid-October. Signed by their ten presidential electors, including Campbell, Etheridge, and John Lellyett (the latter personally submitted it to Lincoln), the petition objected to the free-state Unionist election proposal and charged Johnson with trying to rig the Tennessee election. Incongruously, the petitioners protested Lincoln's supposed interference in the presidential election in Tennessee while seeking his intervention. The intemperately worded appeal could hardly have been expected to gain Lincoln's approval. When Lincoln, both in person and later in writing, firmly rejected their demands, the petitioners, determined to have the last word, published in Democratic newspapers an even more scathing diatribe against Johnson and Lincoln. Johnson, acting under Lincoln's authority, they charged, had unleashed a "reign of terror" in Tennessee, while Lincoln's own course amounted to "a doctrine of despotism in 'irrepressible conflict' with the principles of public liberty." Perhaps hoping to claim a moral victory in defeat, the conservatives grudgingly withdrew their ticket. "There will be no election for President in Tennessee in 1864," they contended. Realizing that further obstructionism only played into Johnson's hands, some conservatives abandoned McClellan, swallowed their pride, and endorsed the Lincoln-Johnson ticket. "The McClelland [sic] party is a mere *faction*, led on by a set of sore-headed Union men, some of them old Democrats, but most of them old Whigs, who have a bad Union record," Brownlow assured Johnson on the eve of the election. "They have played out."[18]

If conservative Unionists were in retreat, black Tennesseans pushed relentlessly forward. Although excluded from formal politics, black leaders in Memphis, Nashville, and other cities continued—and indeed intensified—the campaign for equal rights, calling in particular for black suffrage and the removal of all legal distinctions and barriers based on race. The black community also actively campaigned for the Lincoln-Johnson ticket, equating a Republican victory with racial equality, even though Johnson and other advocates of emancipation steadfastly eschewed that policy. In October, the state sent a delegation to the convention in Syracuse, New York, that founded the National Equal Rights League (NERL). Ransom Harris of Nashville was elected to the national organization's executive board, and in early 1865, a state chapter of the NERL would be formed in that city.[19]

A black torchlight procession in Nashville on the evening of October 24, 1864, provided the setting for one of the most unusual public addresses of Andrew Johnson's political career, his famous "Moses of the Colored Men" speech. The address was demagogic, as was Johnson's wont, and it patronized and condescended toward its overwhelmingly black audience. Yet Johnson explicitly, forcefully, and even eloquently condemned the systematic sexual exploitation of black women under slavery and the irreparable harm slavery had done to black families and black lives. Rarely, if ever, had Johnson, who largely hated slavery for its damaging effects on white society, spoken so sympathetically about what slavery did to the enslaved people themselves. "Colored men of Tennessee," Johnson proclaimed, "your wives and daughters shall no longer be dragged into a concubinage, compared to which polygamy is a virtue, to satisfy the brutal lusts of slaveholders and overseers." "Thank God! Thank God!" exclaimed Johnson's listeners, roaring their approval. This speech and much of his career as military governor stand in stark contrast to Johnson's abysmal record as one of the worst presidents in U.S. history.[20]

The black residents of Nashville conducted an unofficial election in which all but one of nearly 3,500 votes cast went for Lincoln. These votes were not counted; neither did Congress ultimately count Tennessee's electoral votes, on the grounds that no legitimate election had taken place. The 35,000 votes cast statewide—of which Lincoln received some 30,000—amounted to one-fourth of the vote in the 1860 presidential election. Lincoln's reelection sounded the Confederacy's death knell, but the fate of slavery in Tennessee and the organization of a loyal government were yet to be determined.[21]

Johnson's forthcoming elevation to the vice presidency meant that free-state Unionists now had but months to accomplish goals that had evaded them for years. Soon after the election, they called for a state convention to carry out their objectives, but the late fall Confederate military campaign in Central Tennessee, which resulted in disastrous defeats at Franklin and Nashville, delayed the convention until early January. Considerable debate took place over its actual purpose since the original call was not for a constitutional convention per se, but rather for a convention to nominate delegates to a subsequent constitutional convention. Nonetheless, with Johnson playing a key role, the gathering organized itself as a constitutional assembly and approved amendments to the state constitution that abolished slavery immediately and that provided for organizing a new government. The convention also scheduled a plebiscite on the amendments for February and state elections for March; it nominated Brownlow for governor; and it named a "general ticket" of legislative candidates that voters would accept or reject in its entirety.[22]

Significantly, while providing for the abolition of slavery, the convention took no measures regarding black political or legal rights—despite Johnson having recommended eliminating racial distinctions in the state's penal code. "Control and punish the negro, then, by the same laws that you have to punish white criminals," he advised. (Johnson also rejected black suffrage entirely and suggested a system of apprenticeship for the formerly enslaved people.) But the issue of civil rights could not be avoided. As they had on numerous previous occasions, black Tennesseans attempted to be heard. The newly formed Tennessee branch of the NERL presented a petition to the convention that contained the signatures of more than sixty "American citizens of African descent," among whom were many war veterans, that demanded universal male suffrage and equality before the law in addition to abolishing slavery. "This is not a Democratic Government," the petition read, "if a numerous, law-abiding, industrious, and useful class of citizens, born and bred on the soil, are to be treated as aliens and enemies, as an inferior, degraded class, who must have no voice in the Government, which they support, protect and defend, with all their heart, soul, mind, and body, both in peace and war." The convention extended to the petitioners the courtesy of receiving the document and even debated it. A few delegates expressed private support for black suffrage, mostly out of the practical concern that former Confederates would otherwise gain control of the state once the war was over. But with Johnson, Brownlow, and other influential Unionists opposed, the measure stood no chance. The convention approved a constitutional provision that authorized the legislature to enact black suffrage, but this was unlikely to happen in Tennessee or any other southern state.[23]

In the campaign for the amendments and a new state government, conservative Unionists charged that the convention had exceeded its authority in revising the constitution. But with former Confederates barred from voting by the stringent oath and with conservative Unionists boycotting the elections, the amendments were overwhelmingly approved. Slavery was formally abolished in Tennessee. Brownlow was subsequently elected governor, and free-state or "Radical" Unionists secured control of the legislature. Among the new government's first acts upon its inauguration in April was ratification of the Thirteenth Amendment, which the House of Representatives had passed in late January. A week after Tennessee ratified the amendment, Lincoln's assassination made Johnson president.[24]

Although Tennessee had been the one state of the Lower Mississippi Valley entirely excluded from the Emancipation Proclamation, the proclamation precipitated the split among Tennessee Unionists into free-state and proslavery (or conservative) factions. The contest between these factions for control of the state restoration process served as the driving force behind the transformation of military emancipation into the constitutional abolition of slavery. Despite the state's exclusion from the proclamation, thousands of enslaved people were emancipated beginning in early 1862 under various federal antislavery measures. In much the same way that northern War Democrats supported a war for Union (and could even endorse military emancipation) but eschewed an abolitionist war, conservative Unionists in Tennessee (and Louisiana and, to a lesser degree, Arkansas) undertook to restore their state to the Union while preserving slavery. Andrew Johnson, Parson Brownlow, and other leaders of what slowly became after January 1, 1863, the free-state cause detested slavery, and they eventually came to see the inextricable bond between slavery and secession. Consequently, they were determined, despite their firm support for white supremacy, not to allow proslavery Unionists, who always maintained that slavery could be divorced from secessionism, to restore Tennessee as a slave state.

By early 1863, congressional Republicans and Republicans in general had come to the conclusion, in debating Reconstruction, that the seceded states could only be restored to the Union on the basis of abolishing slavery. Throughout 1863 and most of 1864, even after the December 1863 introduction of the federal abolition amendment in Congress, most Americans continued to believe that slavery would be abolished by the states and not the federal government. Ironically, only after Lincoln's reelection in November 1864 did the Thirteenth Amendment come to be seen as the be-all and end-all of abolition, and only then did federal abolition supplant state action. Before late 1864, if the states were thought to be the main loci for abolishing slavery, then the contest over wartime Reconstruction in the states of the Lower Mississippi Valley—which followed inevitably from federal military success in the region during the first half of 1862—transformed the emancipation of enslaved people as a military necessity into the constitutional abolition of slavery.

A coda. In his mid-January 1865 letter to Lincoln, with which this chapter began, Johnson added, after applauding Tennessee's impending abolition of slavery: "I hope that Tennessee will not be included in the bill now before Congress and be made an exception if the bill passes." He was referring to Reconstruction legislation that would have required the states that had seceded to adopt equality before the law and perhaps even black suffrage as conditions for restoration to the Union, in addition to abolishing slavery. Johnson wanted no part of it. "All is now working well and if Tennessee is now let alone will soon resume all functions of a State according to the genius and theory of Government."[25] The Reconstruction bill did not pass. When Memphis exploded in violence not quite a year and a half later, the issues the bill had tried to address—the place of black people in the new social order, the political fate of former Confederates, and the conditions for restoring the rebellious states to the Union—were still unresolved.

NOTES

1. LeRoy P. Graf et al., eds., *The Papers of Andrew Johnson* (Knoxville: University of Tennessee Press, 1967–2013), 7:404 (hereinafter *PAJ*).

2. The focus on the Emancipation Proclamation pervades the scholarship on the destruction of slavery. Works on the Thirteenth Amendment, which are by definition exceptions, include Michael Vorenberg, *Final Freedom: The Civil War, the Abolition of Slavery, and the Thirteenth Amendment* (Cambridge: Cambridge University Press, 2001); and Leonard L. Richards, *Who Freed the Slaves? The Fight over the Thirteenth Amendment* (Chicago: University of Chicago Press, 2015). By contrast, Gary W. Gallagher, *The Union War* (Cambridge, Mass.: Harvard University Press, 2011), emphasizes a war to preserve the Union, while James Oakes, *Freedom National: The Destruction of Slavery in the United States, 1861–1865* (New York: Norton, 2013), posits an abolitionist war from the start.

3. Previous works on wartime Reconstruction and emancipation in Tennessee include John Cimprich, *Slavery's End in Tennessee, 1861–1865* (Tuscaloosa: University of Alabama Press, 1985); Stephen V. Ash, *Middle Tennessee Society Transformed, 1860–1870* (Baton Rouge: Louisiana State University Press, 1988), chaps. 4–6; Louis S. Gerteis, *From Contraband to Freedman: Federal Policy toward Southern Blacks, 1861–1865* (Westport, Conn.: Greenwood, 1973), chaps. 7–10; William C. Harris, *With Charity for All: Lincoln and the Restoration of the Union* (Lexington: University Press of Kentucky, 1997), chap. 10; and Peter Maslowski, *Treason Must Be Made Odious: Military Occupation and Wartime Reconstruction in Nashville, Tennessee, 1862–1865* (Millwood, N.Y.: KTO Press, 1978).

4. *PAJ* 6:85–86, 114; Harris, *With Charity for All*, 46–55; Cimprich, *Slavery's End in Tennessee*, 98–101.

5. On Johnson as military governor, see Hans L. Trefousse, *Andrew Johnson: A Biography* (New York: Easton, 1989), chap. 9; and Paul H. Bergeron, *Andrew Johnson's Civil War and Reconstruction* (Knoxville: University of Tennessee Press, 2011), chap. 1.

6. *PAJ* 6:278–79, 288–89. Convention proceedings appear in the following articles in the *Nashville Daily Union*: "Convention," July 1, 1863, 3; "Union State Convention," July 2, 1863, 2; "The State Convention," July 3, 1863, 2; "The State Convention," July 7, 1863, 2 (quotation); "State Convention," July 8, 1863, 2.

7. Harris, *With Charity for All*, 108–9.

8. Emerson Etheridge to Abraham Lincoln, September 28, 1863, ser. 1, General Correspondence, 1833–1916, Abraham Lincoln Papers, Library of Congress, Washington, D.C.

9. Roy P. Basler, ed., *The Collected Works of Abraham Lincoln* (New Brunswick, N.J.: Rutgers University Press, 1953), 6:440–44 (hereinafter *CWL*).

10. Herman Belz, "The Etheridge Conspiracy of 1863: A Projected Conservative Coup," *Journal of Southern History* 36 (November 1970): 549–67, Lincoln quote at 564.

11. Harris, *With Charity for All*, 212–13; Cimprich, *Slavery's End in Tennessee*, 104–5.

12. *PAJ* 6:xliii, 594–96, 600–601; *CWL* 7:209–10.

13. *PAJ* 6:658–60; Harris, *With Charity for All*, 215.

14. Harris, *With Charity for All*, 215–17.

15. *PAJ* 6:674; Harris, *With Charity for All*, 215–17.

16. Harris, *With Charity for All*, 218–19; Cimprich, *Slavery's End in Tennessee*, 107–8.

17. *PAJ* 7:141–43, 159–61, 203–5; Harris, *With Charity for All*, 219–21.

18. *CWL* 8:58–72; *PAJ* 7:267.

19. Cimprich, *Slavery's End in Tennessee*, 104, 107, 109–13.

20. *PAJ* 7:1, 251–53.

21. Harris, *With Charity for All*, 223; Cimprich, *Slavery's End in Tennessee*, 111–12.

22. *PAJ* 7:xxxiv–xxxvii, 314–15, 369, 371; Harris, *With Charity for All*, 223–24; Bergeron, *Andrew Johnson's Civil War*, 53–55.

23. *PAJ* 7:396; Ira Berlin et al., eds., *Freedom: A Documentary History of Emancipation, 1861–1867*, ser. 2: *The Black Military Experience* (Cambridge: Cambridge University Press, 1982), 811–16; Harris, *With Charity for All*, 224–25; Bergeron, *Andrew Johnson's Civil War*, 55–56.

24. Harris, *With Charity for All*, 226–27; Bergeron, *Andrew Johnson's Civil War*, 57; Cimprich, *Slavery's End in Tennessee*, 115–16.

25. *PAJ* 7:404.

Structural Violence
The Humanitarian Crisis before the Memphis Massacre

JIM DOWNS

Violence took many forms in Memphis in May 1866. It transpired when a group of seven men woke Lucy Smith up in the middle of the night, forced her to make them supper, ransacked the home where she lived, stole money, choked her, and then raped her so badly that one of the men thought "she [was] near dead." Violence also erupted when a black boy, about twelve years old, ran down an alley to see the commotion unfolding on the street; he was discovered by a white police officer, who shot him. The boy miraculously managed to get up and flee down an empty road. No one knows his name or the officer's. Stories such as these can be found in the testimonies that 170 men and women delivered to the congressional delegation charged with investigating the massacre.[1]

Violence also takes less graphic and chilling forms. Violence can be defined as the ways in which social orders and economic structures create oppression. That form of violence is known as "structural violence," a term coined by anthropologist Johan Galtung in 1969.[2] Structural violence is a concept used by anthropologists to explain the ways in which racism, sexism, and other forms of oppression systematically create suffering. While historians often require precise evidence to make particular claims about the past, anthropologists do not require specific documents in order to show how poverty or racism or inequality creates suffering. They point to structures—problematic economic systems or unequal social conditions—as acts of violence that produce suffering.[3]

Before the Memphis Massacre, freedpeople in the city suffered from structural violence. When the Union army occupied Tennessee in the spring and summer of 1862, enslaved people in Memphis and the surrounding area began to escape from slavery. Although they were liberated, they struggled to survive. While many in the Union government believed that the war would lead to emancipation, no one prepared a plan to address how formerly enslaved people would find food, shelter, or even work. Some military officials imagined that the Union army would employ some formerly enslaved people as laborers in Union camps—doing laundry, cooking meals, and performing other forms of manual labor. The subject of military enlistment as soldiers had not yet surfaced, and even after it did, not all men were enlisted, nor were all men employed even as manual laborers.[4] This is to say nothing of women, children, and elderly or disabled people.[5] No policy or plan was in place to deal with their emancipation. This illustrates the meaning of structural violence. While these freedpeople were not victims of direct abuse or torture, the lack of a political structure or economic opportunity and the ambiguity of their social status exemplify how collective structures conspire to produce suffering.

Typically, historians describe enslaved people breaking free from chattel slavery as a victorious narrative, and it absolutely was, but that is not the entire story. The Union army had occupied Memphis in June 1862 as a military tactic to develop a base that would enable it to defeat the Confederacy and consequently cared very little about the predicament of the formerly enslaved people who lived there. While some military officials recruited a fraction of the men to serve in the Union army, the rest of the population of freedpeople, which was estimated as five thousand, took refuge in the city.[6]

Under Union occupation, slavery was legal, but no authority enforced it in Memphis. Word of this quickly spread throughout the Mississippi Delta. Enslaved people from rural plantations broke free from slavery and migrated to Memphis in the hope of gaining their freedom.[7] News of the formerly enslaved people living as "contraband" in Memphis made its way to Chicago, where the *Chicago Times* published a report on their condition in 1862: "Numerous specimens of the darkey [sic] tribe are afloat in the vicinity, the majority of which are runaway slaves. The officers are well waited upon at a small expense, as the darkeys [sic], ignorant of the value of their services, are willing to serve an indefinite time, with the prospect of being their own master by-and-by. Little counter-jumping warriors, who never dreamed of such distinction while plying their trade at home, are waited upon by ebony servitors who quake with fear at the sound of their voices, and stand in perpetual dread of being hung up by the neck or flayed alive for petty misdemeanors."[8]

Freedpeople began creating a makeshift camp near the Union army in Memphis for protection. They did not have a source of food or water. They built shanties out of unused wood, scraps found in city lots, and the Union army's trash—ripped tarps, worn tents, and discarded metals—to protect them from the weather. In order to eat, they had to rely on whatever skills they had to hunt and fish, but they did not have the necessary tools or cooking utensils. As agricultural laborers, they certainly knew how to grow vegetables but that took land, seed, and, most of all, time, which they did not immediately have. Many starved. Their lack of food, shelter, and other necessities was a form of violence. Lacking these basic provisions endangered their health and well-being, making them vulnerable to attacks of disease, bouts of malnutrition, and exposure.

The structural violence that freedpeople endured in Memphis was not uncommon. In many areas throughout the South where enslaved people had liberated themselves from slavery, they lived in close proximity to the Union army. Similar to the situation in Memphis, this proximity offered protection from the Confederate army and a semblance of freedom. But like freedpeople in Memphis, they often lacked the basic necessities to survive. Stationed in New Orleans, Major General Benjamin Butler was the first to refer to the increasing number of newly emancipated people who were arriving at the Crescent City as "contraband," a term that did not clarify their status as either freed or enslaved but did allow them to live within Union jurisdiction. Military officials, the federal government, and northern newspapers soon adopted Butler's term and began to widely use it to describe newly emancipated people. Former bondspeople's alleged freedom was likened to smuggled goods brought into Union camps.

To use the same term—contraband—to refer both to illegal items in Union camps and to people who had escaped from slavery was a form of violence. It was not the same as being beaten or sexually assaulted, but it was a violation. It was an insult that solidified freedpeople's amorphous political status and reflected the nation's attitude toward their emancipation. This demarcation signaled their displacement and the lack of structure to address their status. While there are certainly documents that reveal the suffering that freedpeople endured during this period, the mere evocation of the term "contraband," according to anthropologists' definition of "structural violence," renders any excavation into the archive as theoretically unnecessary. The narrative contours of the term that attempted to describe their status already points to their suffering.

The term "contraband" not only points to structural violence but also exemplifies what literary theorist Gayatri Spivak referred to as "epistemic violence," which means the ways in which acts of language cause harm.[9] Military officials, the federal government, and the press used the term to describe freedpeople in Union camps as illegal. The very language describing formerly enslaved people as contraband suggested that their predicament was accidental; it evoked their struggle as unforeseen; and ultimately it meant that they were out of place. The use of the term "contraband" trapped them in a position of inferiority. Language had struck a blow against them long before the massacre erupted.

To avoid this problematic terminology, we ought to use the term "refugee,"

Not property, but a person. Tens of thousands of refugees fled slavery during the Civil War, ca. 1862–1865. Undated carte de visite from the Gladstone Collection, Prints and Photographs Division, Library of Congress, Washington, D.C.

which more accurately represents the plight of newly freed people and the ways in which the Union army controlled their movements.[10] As the war unfolded, more bondspeople fled to Memphis for refuge. The military was unable to offer employment or support to them, so the military expelled the refugees to the countryside. While the countryside theoretically offered refugees the opportunity to create homes, the freedpeople still had to face Confederate guerrillas, who lurked in the fields and threatened to capture them and return them to plantation slavery. Consequently, the refugees had no choice but to return to Memphis. But they still had no place to live, and the military began to refer to them as "vagrants."[11]

Freedpeople begged military officials for food, water, and shelter. Many of their pleas did not get transcribed verbatim or they were not documented in military reports, but their calls for help eventually made it through the military bureaucracy and to Washington, D.C.[12] As historian Barbara J. Fields eloquently explained, "Freed slaves made a nuisance for the army, and they also made an issue that the army had to deal with. And if the army had to deal with it, the War Department had to deal with it. Congress had to deal with it. That means that every fugitive slave who made a nuisance of himself to the local commander eventually made a figure of himself to the Congress of the United States."[13]

Consequently, the federal government began a systematic effort to survey the structural conditions in refugee camps throughout Tennessee. As the superintendent of "Negro affairs" in Tennessee, General John Eaton wrote to various military officials—chaplains, officers, quartermasters—inquiring into the status of freedpeople's clothing, housing, employment, allotment of food, hospital conditions, and relationship with the army. But military leaders wanted to know something even more disconcerting: they wanted to know if formerly enslaved people were intelligent and if freedpeople understood the meaning of liberty and property.[14]

In response to these questions, an unnamed official in Memphis described freedpeople's clothing as "very poor supplied by Government and donations."[15] The official described the freedpeople living in tents and building log cabins. As for their food, freedpeople were allowed to draw rations from the military on the first of each month. It is unclear what these rations included. During the war, Union officials offered variations of hardtack, which is a cracker, salted pork, and cornmeal.[16] It also is uncertain how these rations were distributed. Were freedpeople only given what they could carry in their hands? How did they store the food and then ration it for themselves over the course of a month? Did they share with their neighbors or did they consume much of it in the first week? Without cooking utensils or even wood to build fires, it is also unclear how they prepared this food.

The report also included a telling section about the health of the freedpeople in the camp in Memphis. The official reported that a hospital was established for the freedpeople, which was not common throughout the South in 1863. That said, hospitals for newly emancipated people, for soldiers, or even for other nineteenth-century Americans pale in comparison to modern hospitals. These hospitals often functioned more like soup kitchens or shelters for sick people who lacked family to take care of them. A wartime hospital was often just a building that the military occupied—a hotel, a house—and many times for soldiers on the field, it was simply a tent or a few tents strung together, separate from their living quarters. While the architecture of wartime hospitals lacked sophistication and technological advancements, they were somewhat effective nevertheless, because they offered a place to quarantine infected people away from those vulnerable to an attack of an infectious disease.[17] For instance, a smallpox epidemic exploded during the war, but the Union and Confederate armies suffered few losses compared to freedpeople, about sixty thousand of whom died during the Civil War and Reconstruction.[18]

While the reference to the hospital in the refugee camp in Memphis only included few details, this sparse evidence indicates that it failed, even according to nineteenth-century standards. According to the report, there was no superintendent in charge of the hospital, and the surgeon in charge did not attend to the sick. In response, the writer of the report had sent physicians from his own district to care for sick people in the camp. The report described the hospital as "wretched in the extreme," which is a telling assertion. In the decades before an understanding of bacteria and microbiology, health officials believed that cleanliness was the best protection against the onslaught of sickness; therefore, hospital staffs strived to keep hospitals clean as a defense against illness. The official described the hospital in the refugee camp as "wretched," which in nineteenth-century parlance meant that it was unsanitary and unorganized. The official also reported that the people in the camps were infected with "pneumonia, fevers, and smallpox." Given the unsanitary condition of the hospital, each of these infectious illnesses could easily spread. When outbreaks erupted during the war, some Union doctors created additional "pest hospitals," which were used to quarantine those infected with smallpox, for example. While such measures did little to cure smallpox patients—some succumbed to the virus, while a few survived—at least it separated them from susceptible freedpeople. Yet, since the freedpeople were crowded in the refugee camps, smallpox rates likely spiked. In the late eighteenth century, physicians had begun to develop a vaccination to prevent the spread of the virus. They would scrape a pustule from an infected cow and then administer it to an uninfected person with the expectation that the person would develop a mild version of the virus and fight it off. During the war, it was often hard to obtain and transport this treatment.[19] In Memphis, the official reported that there was no vaccine available for the freedpeople in the camps, which further exacerbated the medical crisis.

Before the Memphis Massacre, freedpeople battled the outbreak of a smallpox epidemic and the onslaught of pneumonia and fever. Malnourished, living in used tents, and dressed in donated scraps of clothing, they stood defenseless against these biological attacks. Violence does not just refer to the gruesome stories, however accurate, of beatings, shootings, and rapes; it must also be defined as attacks against people's very survival. The conditions of the camps exemplified the structural violence and suffering that refugees endured.

When Eaton further probed the situation of those who lived in the camps, he was shocked to discover how much they suffered. Of the thousands in the camps, only eighty-five were employed. The federal government expected that employed people would, at least, have earned a wage that would have improved their condition, but that was not the case. The report described freedpeople's circumstances in desperate terms: they "worked all day in water, drenched, nearly frozen, and then driven to tents for shelter, to sheds for sleep, without covering, and almost without fire and food, they have come back to die by scores. Wages seldom paid—none in hospitals. The services of a large number have been stolen outright."[20]

Life in the Memphis refugee camps was inherently dangerous in terms of people's health, but the camps were also physically violent places. The writer of the report described the relationship between the army and the freedpeople as violent and acrimonious: "Many soldiers and some officers manifest only bitterness and contempt, resulting, among the abandoned, in the violence and abuse of these helpless people, in addition to the injuries heaped upon them by the vicious & disloyal in the community."[21] This description challenges the romantic narrative of emancipation in which Union soldiers are cast as the heroes who rescued black people from slavery, and it instead discloses how hostile these interactions were and how they often erupted into violence. Further, the reference to the "vicious & disloyal in the community" suggests that some freedpeople possibly enacted violence against members of their own community; this is a subject that historians are only beginning to investigate. Contrary to the harmonious portrait of freedpeople living together in unity, this passage suggests that some of them perpetrated violence and abuse on other freedpeople.[22]

In addition to the threat of violence in the camps, the abject poverty, and the biological attacks, the army assaulted freedpeople based on their perceived intelligence. In response to the question about their intelligence, the author of the report wrote, "Higher than I had expected—keen & bright when they wish to understand;—stupid and idiotic when they do not." When the writer answered the question about their notions of liberty, he responded, "A slander to say their notion of liberty is idleness—that is their laziness."[23]

These comments demonstrate the epistemic violence committed against freedpeople. No matter where they turned, no matter what they did, those in power condemned them. The descriptions of their intelligence and notions of liberty became the crucial building blocks for how the government designed the structural conditions that shaped freedpeople's lives in the camps. These were not abstract questions about nationalism but instead functioned as evidence that dictated how the government responded to the wartime conditions of emancipation. The degradations of their intelligence and notions of liberty were yet another blow against freedpeople's humanity, revealing the multidimensional assaults committed against freedpeople during the war.

Before the Memphis Massacre, before the war even ended, freedpeople were under attack. They were threatened not only by the traditional forces of aggression—Confederate guerrillas and, at times, Union soldiers—but also by the structural conditions of the world that they inhabited. Life on the ground, in the refugee camps, revealed how freedpeople were suffering. This humanitarian crisis existed long before the massacre in May 1866. Each day was a fight to survive in a world that had been built without their freedom in mind.

NOTES

1. "Memphis Riots and Massacres," *U.S. Serial Set*, no. 1274, House Report 101, 39th Cong., 1st sess., 197, 155.

2. Johan Galtung, "Violence, Peace, and Peace Research," *Journal of Peace Research* 6, no. 3 (1969): 167–91.

3. Paul Farmer, "An Anthropology of Structural Violence," *Current Anthropology* 45, no. 3 (2004): 305–25.

4. On the lack of policies for freedpeople during emancipation, see Jim Downs, *Sick from Freedom: African-American Illness and Suffering during the Civil War and Reconstruction* (New York: Oxford University Press, 2012), 42–64.

5. Ibid., 12–45.

6. Ira Berlin et al., eds., *Freedom: A Documentary History of Emancipation, 1861–1867*, ser. 1, vol. 3: *The Wartime Genesis of Free Labor: The Lower South* (Cambridge: Cambridge University Press, 1990), 631.

7. Beverly G. Bond and Janann Sherman, *Memphis: In Black and White* (Charleston, S.C.: Arcadia, 2003), 53.

8. *Chicago Times*, June 8, 1862, as quoted in James B. Jones Jr., "Tennessee Contraband Conundrum, 1862–1865: A Documentary Narrative," *Southern History* (May 16, 2014), http://www.southernhistory.co/2014/05/tennesseecontraband-conundrum-1862-1865.html.

9. Gayatri Chakravorty Spivak, "Can the Subaltern Speak?," in *Marxism and the Interpretation of Culture*, ed. Cary Nelson and Lawrence Grossberg, 271–313 (Urbana: University of Illinois Press, 1988).

10. On the cultural use of the term "contraband," see Kate Masur, "'A Rare Phenomenon of Philological Vegetation': The Word 'Contraband' and the Meanings of Emancipation in the United States," *Journal of American History* 93, no. 4 (2007): 1–65. On the use of the term "refugee" as opposed to "contraband," see Downs, *Sick from Freedom*, 4, 22, 51.

11. Berlin et al., *Wartime Genesis of Free Labor*, 631.

12. I explain the process in which freedpeople alerted the military to their suffering in Downs, *Sick from Freedom*, 13.

13. Quoted in "The Beast," episode 3 of *The Civil War*, directed by Ken Burns (PBS, 1990).

14. Excerpts from Chaplain John Eaton Jr. to Lt. Col. Jno. A. Rawlins, April 29, 1863, O-328 1863, Letters Received, ser. 12, Adjutant General's Office, RG 94, National Archives and Records Administration, Washington, D.C., as published in Berlin et al., *Wartime Genesis of Free Labor*, 684–98.

15. Ibid.

16. On Civil War food, see http://www.civilwar.org/education/pdfs/civil-war-curriculum-food.pdf (accessed January 9, 2017).

17. Downs, *Sick from Freedom*, 65–94.

18. Ibid., 95–119.

19. Ibid.

20. Eaton to Rawlins, April 29, 1863.

21. Ibid.

22. On violence among enslaved people, see Jeff Forret, *Slave against Slave: Plantation Violence in the Old South* (Baton Rouge: Louisiana State University Press, 2015). On sexual assault and rape committed by Union soldiers against freedwomen, see Crystal N. Feimster, "'What If I Am a Woman': Black Women's Campaigns for Sexual Justice and Citizenship," in *The World the Civil War Made*, ed. Gregory P. Downs and Kate Masur (Chapel Hill: University of North Carolina Press, 2015), chap. 10. On black soldiers raping formerly enslaved women, see Thavolia Glymph, "Black Women and Children in the Civil War: Archive Notes," in *Beyond Freedom: Disrupting the History of Emancipation*, ed. David Blight and Jim Downs (Athens: University of Georgia Press, 2017), 126.

23. Eaton to Rawlins, April 29, 1863.

Urban Battlegrounds
Reconstruction in Southern Cities

KATE MASUR

The Memphis Massacre was an event of extraordinary violence and national consequence, but conditions in Memphis were not unlike those in other southern cities during the Civil War and Reconstruction. When people discuss the South in the nineteenth century, they often forget about cities, picturing instead farms, plantations, and rural byways. Perhaps they imagine a world untouched by the density, diversity, and commercialism of modern cities. By contrast, I argue here that cities were crucial battlegrounds during the Civil War and Reconstruction.[1] Cities were laboratories for the egalitarian experiments of emancipation and Reconstruction because of their concentrated and heterogeneous populations, public spaces, transportation infrastructure, and local governments charged with keeping the peace and overseeing economic development. Yet those same features also made cities especially combustible, and at moments of high tension whites were prone to inflict murder and destruction on their black neighbors. In this chapter I focus on a few key features of urban life in this period: African Americans' wartime migration into cities, their claims on public spaces, tensions with police and other white residents, and the longer-term development of institutions and opportunities for African Americans in southern cities.

In the antebellum South as elsewhere, cities emerged as hubs of trade and transportation. They were places where farmers brought agricultural goods to market, selling directly to customers or to agents who transported staple crops to distant places. Rural residents also visited cities to purchase manufactured goods to take home, take care of legal and financial business, and socialize with friends. Thus cities were home to professionals, including bankers, lawyers, accountants, and journalists. Slavery persisted in cities, where enslaved people often worked as domestic laborers and sometimes in industry. Free African Americans, a small minority of the southern black population, also often made their homes in cities, where they were able to find employment in the more varied urban economy and build institutions, such as churches and mutual aid societies, that strengthened the bonds of community and cultural life.

Cities were strategically critical during the Civil War because of their locations and infrastructure. To facilitate the movement of agricultural and other products, southern cities were often located on waterways: the Atlantic Ocean, the Gulf of Mexico, or rivers such as the Mississippi. Located on the peripheries of the South and boasting amenities such as transportation connections to inland places, warehouses and other large buildings, and professional services, cities were appealing targets for military occupation. The U.S. Army often established headquarters in cities, and soldiers remained for lengthy periods in places like Norfolk, New Orleans, Charleston, Memphis, Natchez, Nashville, St. Louis, and Washington, D.C. Occupying armies helped make cities especially desirable destinations for enslaved people who were struggling to escape from bondage.

Southern cities quickly became laboratories for freedom. Enslaved people across the South had followed the political events that led to war and knew that an invasion by U.S. forces could open opportunities to claim their freedom. As the army moved across the countryside and took up residence in cities, enslaved people left the farms and plantations where they had long been forced to labor. Many found work for the army as teamsters, cooks, draymen, and laundresses.[2] The U.S. military provided not only jobs but a modicum of protection for those trying to escape from slavery. Particularly after the Emancipation Proclamation of January 1, 1863, southern cities were also hubs for black men's enlistment as U.S. soldiers. In Natchez, army officers ordered the men of the Sixth Regiment of Mississippi Infantry, most of whom had been recruited out of slavery in the nearby countryside, to tear down the infamous buildings associated with the Forks of the Road, one of the largest slave markets in the South. The order went out in the evening, wrote a news correspondent, and the men worked "with a terrible earnestness" through the night, recounting stories of the "cruelty of traders, of sad partings of husband and wife, of inhuman fathers selling their own children." When dawn came, the slave pens were destroyed, and laborers used the wood to construct barracks for American soldiers.[3]

In many cities, existing black communities galvanized to welcome and try to help migrants from rural areas. With thousands of new people in town, black churches swelled and multiplied. In many instances, even before the war ended, congregants pooled their money to buy churches from whites or construct their own houses of worship. Independent African American churches flourished in southern cities, serving not only as places of religious gathering, but also as hubs of the community, sites of schools, and foundations for mutual aid societies and other organizations. Urban black communities, some-

"The Camp of the Contrabands on the Banks of the Mississippi," *Frank Leslie's Illustrated Weekly*, November 27, 1862, 140. Courtesy of Charles Deering McCormick Library of Special Collections, Northwestern University Libraries.

times led by pastors, moved quickly to create educational institutions as well. Black organizations frequently applied for and received aid from northern missionary societies looking to send teachers south. For a limited time they also benefited from the Freedmen's Bureau, which was particularly helpful in securing buildings in which to hold classes.[4]

Southern cities offered hope for freedom and community self-determination, but conditions were often difficult and even dire. Housing shortages were common, and urban residents faced health crises as smallpox and other diseases spread through crowded neighborhoods. In occupied cities, the U.S. Army had established refugee camps known as "contraband camps." The army that oversaw the camps was overtaxed and often unable to prevent the spread of disease; residents frequently fell ill and died. The squalid and dangerous conditions of the camps are a reminder that the war was a force of destabilization and crisis, even as it helped produce the destruction of slavery. Despite the sometimes harrowing conditions, however, migration to cities continued after the war, as freedpeople sought economic opportunities and a respite from white southerners' violent efforts to keep them on plantations and control virtually all aspects of their lives. As Henry McNeal Turner, an African Methodist Episcopal minister and Georgia politician, told a congressional committee,

"Celebration of the Abolition of Slavery in the District of Columbia by the Colored People" (April 19, 1866), *Harper's Weekly*, May 12, 1866. Prints and Photographs Division, Library of Congress, Washington, D.C.

people "leave the country in many instances because they are outraged, because their lives are threatened; they run to the cities as an asylum."[5]

Having made their way into cities amid the turmoil of war, and in the process having helped destroy slavery, urban African Americans took further action to assert and define freedom. For instance, before the Civil War, municipal laws had required people of African descent living in cities to carry passes, subjected them to special curfews, and banned them from central and ceremonial urban spaces. Black people now rejected such rules, advancing into spaces from which they had previously been banned and demanding their right to participate in civic culture as equals to whites. In Natchez, Mississippi, for instance, African Americans convened in the park on the high bluffs of the Mississippi River. In Charleston, South Carolina, they assembled on the battery that looked out on the harbor and Fort Sumter, and in Washington, D.C., they began attending sessions of Congress and public receptions at the White House. I have called such actions "upstart claims" to denote how African Americans advanced their ideas of freedom, equality, and belonging without receiving permission and before any "right" was acknowledged.[6]

In cities across the South, African Americans began to organize and turn out for large public parades, celebrating holidays like July 4 or the passage of Reconstruction legislation by Congress. Parades were opportunities for African American civic associations to publicly claim their places in the city. Militias, Sunday school organizations, benevolent societies, social clubs, and other groups took to the streets in organized formation, displaying banners and touting their accomplishments. These, too, were upstart claims. African Americans were insisting on their right to equal participation in civic life. They were displaying pride in their own institutions and also demanding respect, both as individuals and as members of a group entitled to integrity and standing in the broader urban community.[7]

In the aftermath of the war, municipal, state, and federal officials vied for power as they struggled to bring order out of chaos. The agents of the U.S. government who remained in southern cities—typically, soldiers or Freedmen's Bureau agents—were there to keep order and to protect the freedom and basic rights of African Americans and white Unionists. In many cases, bureau agents worried about urban crowding and shared local whites' view that freedpeople were best off in the countryside, where they could continue to labor on farms and plantations. Although some freedpeople returned to farms and plantations, many refused because they feared violence and repression by their former owners and hoped the city would allow them to pursue new economic opportunities and maintain the bonds of family and community.[8]

Black U.S. soldiers were a particular source of controversy. Empowered and often armed, black soldiers and veterans embodied the revolutionary impact of the war—the reality that the abolition of slavery might lead to the elevation of black men and women to positions of equality with whites. Realizing that many southern whites saw black soldiers as particularly provocative, army commanders sought to transfer most black enlisted men out of the urban South. Yet, as in Memphis in the spring of 1866, black soldiers remained in many southern cities as they waited for orders or to be discharged. White soldiers stationed in southern cities sometimes treated black soldiers and civilians disdainfully, and at times white and black U.S. soldiers clashed openly.[9]

As the U.S. Army demobilized, Confederate veterans increasingly outnumbered U.S. soldiers and were often better armed. In many cities, ex-Confederates donned their gray uniforms and took to marching in military formation—a gesture designed to menace African Americans and any remaining U.S. soldiers in their midst. Urban police forces were particularly implicated in postwar friction. Charged with enforcing the law and keeping the peace, urban police in the South had long concerned themselves with regulating the movements and livelihoods of free and enslaved people of African descent. Po-

"The Irrepressible Conflict," *Harper's Weekly*, August 4, 1866. Courtesy of Charles Deering McCormick Library of Special Collections, Northwestern University Libraries.

lice were none too happy with wartime developments, including military occupation and the arrival of thousands of people escaping from slavery. In some instances, Confederate veterans had strong connections in city government and on the police force. And in most places, city officials generally viewed black freedom and freedpeople's migration into cities as a "problem" brought on by the U.S. government—a government they viewed as a source of oppression and coercion. The tense combination of assertive freedpeople, hostile white populations, and heavily armed police, soldiers, and veterans made southern cities highly combustible.[10]

Tensions were acute in the spring and summer of 1866—the months surrounding the Memphis Massacre—and in many cases, local police instigated or abetted violence against freedpeople. The coordinated attack on a political convention in New Orleans at the end of July is now, like the Memphis Massacre, well known as a nationally significant event.[11] In addition to Memphis and New Orleans, however, Charleston, Norfolk, Savannah, and Washington, D.C., all experienced violent outbreaks that summer, and such incidents may have occurred in other cities too. In Norfolk in April, for example, a black-led celebration of the Civil Rights Act of 1866, the first federal civil rights law, generated daytime tensions. That night, uniformed ex-Confederates, marching in formation, attacked occupying U.S. Army forces. The army was able to restore order, but tellingly, white newspaper editors spun a narrative of white victimization, insisting that the white community was besieged by lawless black people and that the U.S. government was at fault for bringing about such disruption.[12] Such narratives of black instigation and white victimization would become all too familiar as Reconstruction continued.

In Washington, D.C., that summer, white residents regularly attacked African Americans, sometimes delivering beatings, throwing bricks, or firing shots as the police stood by or, in some cases, joined in. Savannah was on edge too, and in July a white teacher of freedpeople was shot dead in the street amid a brawl that began with a black man refusing to give way to a white one. In Charleston that summer, African American soldiers and civilians clashed repeatedly with the local police.[13] All these conflicts, while not as lethal as the Memphis Massacre, reveal southern cities as fields of battle in the struggle over the revolutionary potential of the Civil War and emancipation. African Americans fought for freedom and dignity with whatever resources they could. Sometimes they received critical support from U.S. soldiers; elsewhere, their large numbers and militancy allowed them to withstand attacks. In the longer term, however, the urban upheavals of the summer of 1866 reveal a white population reluctant to acknowledge black freedom itself. All this turmoil occurred *before* the onset of Radical Reconstruction and before voting rights for African American men.

In the spring and summer of 1867, Congress passed the Reconstruction Acts, which demanded that southern states remake their constitutions and allow black men to vote and hold office. Black men's enfranchisement had specific implications for cities. With their large concentrations of African American people and institutions, cities were excellent places to mobilize new voters. Many African American men who emerged as Republican Party leaders and elected officials had learned about leadership and cultivated constituencies through previous work in black institutions, including mutual aid societies, schools, and churches. Such men helped build Republican organizations, often collaborating with white Unionists or former Whigs who were willing to imagine a biracial political coalition capable of combating the dominance of the Democratic-oriented elite. Working to galvanize people to register and vote, Republicans regularly held meetings in black churches and in public squares, places where they could reach entire communities, not just the men who would ultimately cast the ballots.[14]

Black communities could hope to wield real political power in the localized world of urban politics. Black-majority wards could elect African American

"First Municipal Election in Richmond since the End of the War," *Harper's Weekly*, June 4, 1870. Prints and Photographs Division Library of Congress, Washington, D.C.

men to city councils, and once in office those officials could direct resources toward black neighborhoods or ensure that African Americans received political appointments and employment in public works. Much more attention is typically paid to the African American elected officials who served in the U.S. Congress or in statewide office, but during Reconstruction many black men were also elected to city councils and other municipal posts. By 1871, Natchez voters had elected an African American mayor, Robert Wood. In at least twelve cities, black men were hired as police officers and firefighters. New Orleans was most notable for its Metropolitan Police, which the state government created in 1868 to displace the Confederate-dominated New Orleans municipal force. At the outset, the Metropolitan Police was majority African American, and the board of commissioners that governed it was 50 percent black. Black men's enfranchisement meant major changes in political power and policy priorities in southern cities.[15]

Black men's enfranchisement helped inspire African American urbanites to broaden their demands. In many cities, African Americans pressed for equal access to the era's preeminent form of urban transportation—streetcars. When streetcars first emerged in southern cities, operators typically excluded black passengers entirely or forced them to ride on the platform in front. During the war, black soldiers stationed in Washington, D.C., and New Orleans had demanded equal access to streetcars and won some concessions.[16] Demands for equality on streetcars expanded and enjoyed growing success after the Reconstruction Acts, when African Americans could turn to friendlier city governments and to newly empowered federal forces for support. By 1872, Charleston, Richmond, Louisville, Mobile, and Savannah (in addition to New Orleans and Washington, D.C.) had all seen conflicts over access to streetcars and other public accommodations. In many cities, streetcars remained desegregated until the 1890s.[17]

It was in southern cities, then, that Reconstruction's equal rights revolution advanced the furthest. In New Orleans, African Americans and white allies successfully pressed for the desegregation of white public schools. Southern cities became home to institutions of black higher education, including LeMoyne Normal and Commercial School in Memphis, Fisk University in Nashville, Howard University in Washington, and many more. In Charleston, Richmond, and New Orleans, black longshoremen and stevedores—who were excluded from white labor unions—managed to organize their own unions in the late 1860s. African Americans developed businesses that served the black community and became the basis for a growing black middle class.[18]

Black urban institutions flourished despite white opposition, which sometimes took the form of arson and murder. And many of those institutions were durable enough to survive well beyond the Democratic Party's rise to power and its counterrevolutionary movement against Reconstruction. During the war, cities had become centers of African American mobilization and assertions of freedom, and they remained so far into the period commonly known as Redemption. They became places where people could congregate more freely, where they could pursue a more advanced education than was available in the countryside, and where they could build institutions to help cement the bonds of community. In short, cities could provide a respite from the extraordinarily repressive conditions that so often prevailed in rural areas.

That is not to say that cities were safe. With black men's disfranchisement, urban black businesses, schools, and churches were almost entirely at the mercy of white Democrats, who increasingly monopolized political power. As the Democratic Party regained control, officeholders took deliberate steps to reduce urban African Americans' political influence, sometimes redistricting city councils to disempower largely black wards or putting cities under the direct supervision of state governments. Democrats removed black men from positions of authority and repealed or simply ignored laws that prohibited racial discrimination in public accommodations. Indeed, the racial order of segregation had a distinctly urban flavor; many white southerners believed the density of urban life required the systematic and heavily policed separation of two supposedly antagonistic races.[19]

In this context, black institutions, including homes, businesses, and neighborhoods, were tremendously vulnerable. An economic shift, a quotidian crime, or rumor of a rape could provoke white neighbors to frenzied violence. Many white people continued to believe that black people did not deserve to be free or equal or fully vested members of the urban community. Convinced that they were entitled to power and privilege, whites found ways to justify all manner of cruelty and lawlessness. White urbanites attacked their black neighbors again in Wilmington, North Carolina, in 1898; New Orleans in 1900; Atlanta in 1906; Springfield, Illinois, in 1908; and dozens of cities in the summer of 1919, when the presence of black and white soldiers once again made conditions combustible and black communities vulnerable. The loss of black life and property in these episodes was tremendous. The psychological costs on black communities surely were as well. Few perpetrators were ever brought to justice, and white communities generally chose to "forget" the criminal rampages they committed, turning instead to narratives of black deviance and unassimilability.

To publicly remember the Memphis Massacre and to recognize it for what it was is to invoke the larger history described here. It is to begin to acknowledge, collectively, some of what white Americans have taken from black Americans. When we talk about this history, people often ask, where do we go from here? The history itself—a history of black people's struggles to build lives in freedom, of white people's violence against black people, of white destruction of black property and well-being, and of authorities' complicity in that destruction—provides no sure answer. But telling the whole history, the true story, is surely a critical step.

NOTES

1. For a twenty-first-century effort to place southern cities more squarely in the history of the Civil War and Reconstruction, see Andrew L. Slap and Frank Towers, eds., *Confederate Cities: The Urban South during the Civil War* (Chicago: University of Chicago Press, 2015). African Americanists have long recognized the significance of black urbanization during the period. Crucial earlier accounts include John W. Blassingame, "Before the Ghetto: The Making of the Black Community in Savannah, Ga.," *Journal of Social History* 6 (Summer 1973): 463–88; Blassingame, *Black New Orleans, 1860–1880* (Chicago: University of Chicago Press, 1973); and Howard N. Rabinowitz, *Race Relations*

in the Urban South, 1865–1890 (New York: Oxford University Press, 1978). Readers interested in additional sources might consult Slap and Towers, *Confederate Cities*, for an extensive and relatively recent bibliography.

2. In addition to the overview in Rabinowitz, *Race Relations*, 18–30, see, for example, Kate Masur, *An Example for All the Land: Emancipation and the Struggle over Equality in Washington* (Chapel Hill: University of North Carolina Press, 2010), 13–50; and Tera Hunter, *To 'Joy My Freedom: Southern Black Women's Lives and Labors after the Civil War* (Cambridge, Mass.: Harvard University Press, 1997), 9–20. Chandra Manning, *Troubled Refuge: Struggling for Freedom in the Civil War* (New York: Knopf, 2016), also contains scattered references to urban experiences.

3. "Letter from Natchez," *Milwaukee Daily Sentinel*, February 17, 1864. Thanks to Mimi Miller and the Historic Natchez Foundation for this source.

4. See, for example, Hilary N. Green, "African Americans' Struggle for Education, Citizenship, and Freedom in Mobile, Alabama, 1865–1868," in Slap and Towers, *Confederate Cities*; Leon F. Litwack, *Been in the Storm So Long: The Aftermath of Slavery* (New York: Knopf, 1980), 310–16; Blassingame, "Before the Ghetto," 471–74; Rabinowitz, *Race Relations*, 152–67.

5. Turner quoted in Rabinowitz, *Race Relations*, 22.

6. For "upstart claims," see Masur, *Example for All the Land*, 7–8; Justin Behrend, "Black Political Mobilization and the Spatial Transformation of Natchez," in Slap and Towers, *Confederate Cities*, 195; Wilbur Jenkins, *Seizing the New Day: African Americans in Post–Civil War Charleston* (Bloomington: Indiana University Press, 1998), 134; Mamie Garvin Fields with Karen Fields, *Lemon Swamp and Other Places: A Carolina Memoir* (New York: Free Press, 1983), 55–56; Kate Masur, "Color Was a Bar to the Entrance: African American Activism and the Question of Social Equality in Lincoln's White House," *American Quarterly* 69 (March 2017): 1–22.

7. See, for example, Peter J. Rachleff, *Black Labor in the South: Richmond, Virginia, 1865–1890* (Philadelphia, Pa.: Temple University Press, 1984), 39; Robert Perdue, *The Negro in Savannah, 1865–1900* (New York: Exposition Press, 1973), 41; Michael Fitzgerald, *Urban Emancipation: Popular Politics in Reconstruction Mobile, 1860–1890* (Baton Rouge: Louisiana State University Press, 2002), 52–54; Masur, *Example for All the Land*, 41–49.

8. Litwack, *Been in the Storm So Long*, 316–22; Hunter, *To 'Joy My Freedom*, 23–24; Masur, *Example for All the Land*, 68–69.

9. Rabinowitz, *Race Relations*, 33–34; Ira Berlin et al., eds., *Freedom: A Documentary History of Emancipation, 1861–1867*, ser. 2: *The Black Military Experience* (New York: Cambridge University Press, 1982), 734–36; Fitzgerald, *Urban Emancipation*, 31–32.

10. Masur, *Example for All the Land*, 55–56; Rabinowitz, *Race Relations*, 129–32; Elna C. Green, *This Business of Relief: Confronting Poverty in a Southern City, 1740–1940* (Athens: University of Georgia Press, 2003), 88–90. Regarding police abuses and discrimination in general, see, for example, Rabinowitz, *Race Relations*, 35–36, 41. The U.S. govern-

ment's ability to protect freedpeople was severely hampered by a lack of resources and questions about jurisdiction. See, for example, Gregory P. Downs, *After Appomattox: Military Occupation and the Ends of War* (Cambridge, Mass.: Harvard University Press, 2015).

11. Dennis C. Roussey, *Policing the Southern City: New Orleans, 1805–1889* (Baton Rouge: Louisiana State University Press, 1996), 114–18. African American veterans also formed militia organizations as early as the spring of 1866. See, for example, Masur, *Example for All the Land*, 118, 121–23.

12. John Hammond Moore, "The Norfolk Riot, 16 April 1866," *Virginia Magazine of History and Biography* 90 (April 1982): 155–64.

13. Masur, *Example for All the Land*, 115, 123; Jacqueline Jones, *Saving Savannah: The City and the Civil War* (New York: Knopf, 2008), 262–64; Melinda Meek Hennessy, "Racial Violence during Reconstruction: The 1876 Riots in Charleston and Cainhoy," *South Carolina Historical Magazine* 86 (April 1985): 102–3.

14. See, for example, Elsa Barkley Brown, "Negotiating and Transforming the Public Sphere: African American Political Life in the Transition from Slavery to Freedom," *Public Culture* 7 (Fall 1994): 107–46; Behrend, "Black Political Mobilization," 199; Blassingame, "Before the Ghetto," 474–79; Fitzgerald, *Urban Emancipation*, 98–107; and Masur, *Example for All the Land*, 132–33, 146–47. Howard N. Rabinowitz, ed., *Southern Black Leaders of the Reconstruction Era* (Urbana: University of Illinois Press, 1982), contains several profiles of urban black leaders.

15. Rabinowitz, *Race Relations*, 265–66; Roussey, *Policing the Southern City*, 135–39. See also Behrend, "Black Political Mobilization," 205.

16. Roger A. Fischer, "A Pioneer Protest: The New Orleans Street-Car Controversy of 1867," *Journal of Negro History* 53 (July 1968): 220; Masur, *Example for All the Land*, 100–112.

17. Rachleff, *Black Labor in the South*, 42; William C. Hine, "The 1867 Charleston Streetcar Sit-Ins: A Case of 'Successful Black Protest,'" *South Carolina Historical Magazine* 77 (April 1976): 110–14; Marjorie M. Norris, "An Early Instance of Nonviolence: The Louisville Demonstrations of 1870–1871," *Journal of Southern History* 32 (November 1966): 487–504; Edmund L. Drago, *Black Politicians and Reconstruction in Georgia: A Splendid Failure* (1982; rev. ed., Athens: University of Georgia Press, 1992), 98–100; Blassingame, *Black New Orleans*, 183–96; Fitzgerald, *Urban Emancipation*.

18. Jenkins, *Seizing the New Day*, 65–68; Rachleff, *Black Labor in the South*, 42–44; Hunter, *To 'Joy My Freedom*; Loren Schweninger, *Black Property Owners in the South, 1790–1915* (Urbana: University of Illinois Press, 1990), 166–71, 179–82; Rabinowitz, *Race Relations*, 100–101; Blassingame, "Before the Ghetto," 464–68; and Blassingame, *Black New Orleans*. As Hunter, Rabinowitz, Rachleff, and others have shown, southern cities later became hubs for the Knights of Labor.

19. Masur, *Example for All the Land*, 176–77, 214–56; Hunter, *To 'Joy My Freedom*, 45–50, 98–105; Rabinowitz, *Race Relations*, 104–27, 259–328.

Christianity and Race in the Memphis Massacre of 1866

ELIZABETH L. JEMISON

During the Memphis Massacre of May 1866, all of the city's African American churches were destroyed. The white mob deliberately attacked these structures, burning wooden buildings and even demolishing a stone one. Lincoln Chapel, one of the largest churches, had been dedicated only five months earlier to "the immortal name of that man whose fiat has stricken the shackles from four million slaves."[1] The church building had also housed a school for formerly enslaved people. Standing amid the building's ashes with several of his congregants in "great sorrow and depression," Rev. Ewing O. Tade assured them that "there were ashes enough . . . to build another Lincoln Chapel" and that they could meet in the shade of a large tree nearby in the meantime.[2] Both the destruction of the churches and the immediate commitment to rebuild testified to the importance of black Christianity in freedpeople's fight for equal citizenship in the post-emancipation South.

But the targeted destruction of black churches amid a violent white rampage demands an explanation of the connections among Christianity, race, and politics at that time. What did black churches offer to newly freed people in their efforts to establish themselves as equal citizens? Why would white southerners, most of whom identified as Christians, target black churches and the congregants who attended them? In this chapter I seek to explain why black Christianity in Memphis in 1866 aroused such fear and hostility in white southerners by exploring the relationship among Protestant Christianity, race, and slavery before emancipation, during the Civil War, and in the early post-emancipation South. I argue that bitter conflicts over slavery left persistent divisions between white southern Christians, who maintained their belief that the Bible supports slavery, and black Christians and their northern allies, who viewed emancipation as a modern-day retelling of the miraculous Exodus story. For these competing groups of Protestants, what it meant to be a Christian differed dramatically. Even when congregations in the Mississippi

River valley shared identities as Methodists or Baptists, the stark differences in their understanding of what Christianity meant for the post-emancipation society rendered dialogue almost impossible. White southern Christians stressed the importance of promoting order in society and defended a plain-sense reading of the Bible, while African American Christians saw themselves as participants in a miraculous transformation of injustice, much like the emancipation of the Israelites from Egypt. Amid these deep differences, people from many sides appealed to Christian behavior as a model for their fractured society, making their contradictory ideas of what Christian behavior entailed all the more significant.

Antebellum debates over slavery created and reflected widely different interpretations of what true Christianity entailed, and these divides along lines of race and region persisted after emancipation. Christianity has had a long, complex history in American slaveholding societies, and by the antebellum period, slavery was the single most contentious issue dividing American Christians of all stripes. While some eighteenth-century evangelicals, most notably Methodism's founder, John Wesley, expressed concerns about slavery, nearly all major Christian groups had made peace with American slavery by the early nineteenth century.[3] As slavery became more concentrated in the southern states and as antislavery activism grew, white southern Christians developed theological defenses that claimed that slavery was more biblical and more humane than free labor systems. Many northern Christians disagreed, forcing schisms within major Protestant denominations. Enslaved people often described Christianity in the antebellum South as two contradictory religions: the proslavery Christianity of slaveholders and true Christianity or "real preachin'," as formerly enslaved Lucretia Alexander termed it. Frederick Douglass, a prominent antislavery activist who had been enslaved, explained: "Between the Christianity of this land, and the Christianity of Christ, I recognize the widest possible difference. . . . I love the pure, peaceable, and impartial Christianity of Christ: I therefore hate the corrupt, slaveholding, women-whipping, cradle-plundering, partial and hypocritical Christianity of this land. Indeed, I can see no reason . . . for calling the religion of this land Christianity."[4] Many enslaved people joined Douglass in distinguishing proslavery Christianity and true Christianity, yet white southerners insisted on the opposite: true, biblical Christianity supported slavery while only unorthodox, politically motivated Christianity opposed it. By the eve of the Civil War, slavery had divided American Christians sharply.

The Christianity of enslaved people has been cited as an inspiration for their resistance, even violent revolt, and it has also been dismissed as an opiate dulling enslaved people's discontent. Historian Albert Raboteau's groundbreaking

Slave Religion: The "Invisible Institution" in the Antebellum South charted this history more than forty years ago. He showed that despite slaveholders' efforts to teach a version of Christianity centered on obedience to masters, enslaved people created complex spiritual cultures combining African religious retentions and Christian practices. Christian conversion experiences and ongoing devotional practices defended the humanity and the individual identity of those caught in a system designed to dehumanize them. Raboteau concluded with the observation of black theologian Howard Thurman: "By some amazing but vastly creative spiritual insight, the slave undertook the redemption of a religion that the master had profaned in his midst."[5] On the eve of emancipation, the religion of enslaved people had become a vital cultural force. As spirituals—the theological writings of enslaved people—maintained, the God who brought the Israelites out of slavery in Egypt, destroyed the walls of Jericho, and protected Daniel in the lion's den would upend the social order to free enslaved people from bondage. Enslaved Christians worked for and longed for that divinely directed emancipation.

The belief that true Christianity must be opposed to slavery inspired some bondspeople to revolt against the injustices and inhumanity of slavery, believing that God was on their side. Communities of enslaved people outside of organized white churches, such as the secret "hush harbors" that Raboteau described, were important ways for revolutionary enslaved people to connect with each other. African Methodist networks in South Carolina helped Denmark Vesey plot an alleged revolt that local whites claimed to have discovered before it happened. Nat Turner, a Baptist preacher and leader of the most violent revolt of enslaved people in U.S. history, believed that God had called him to take up arms, and his revolt killed more than two dozen white Virginians. Many slaveholders had long feared that Christianity would inspire rebellion among enslaved people, and especially before the nineteenth century, slaveholders often prohibited Christian missionaries from preaching to the people they owned. While examples like Turner and Vesey were rare, the aversion of slave owners to teaching enslaved people about Christianity showed that many enslaved people understood Christian teachings as an indictment of the evils of slavery and the hypocrisy of Christian slaveholders.[6]

At the same time, white southerners boldly insisted that supporting slavery was a Christian duty that marked them as more pious than their antislavery critics. In the face of stronger antislavery activity in the antebellum period, white southern Christians developed arguments defending slavery: it was more biblical and thus more morally sound than free labor systems. During these years, white southern ministers wrote the majority of the defenses of slavery, whether theological, economic, or legal, showing how important religious leaders were to the intellectual justification of slavery. Proslavery Christianity united white southerners across lines of denomination and class, even though only a minority of white southerners actually enslaved people.[7]

In the mid-1840s, the bitter debates over slavery in the largest Protestant denominations—Methodist and Baptist—split each into two regional bodies, with the Methodist Episcopal Church, South, and the Southern Baptist Convention embracing explicitly proslavery positions. These denominational schisms also severed some of the nation's strongest ties, since Methodists and Baptists had been the largest national nongovernmental organizations before the 1840s. White southern Christians' embrace of proslavery theology set them apart from both black Christians and northern white Christians. The denominational schisms removed the opportunity for debate on this topic. After the mid-1840s, northern and southern Methodists and Baptists had neither an obligation nor an opportunity to debate the issue of slavery with their coreligionists who held opposing views.[8]

Proslavery writers argued that a direct, plain-sense reading of the Bible found nothing inherently sinful about the institution of slavery. Antislavery Christians, white southerners claimed, must be using extrabiblical political and philosophical ideas to charge that slavery was sinful, a strategy that showed insufficient devotion to the Bible. Slavery, such arguments continued, had existed in the worlds in which the Old and New Testaments had been written, and nowhere did Jesus or a biblical author explicitly condemn slavery as a sinful institution. Instead, New Testament authors in four different places explicitly told enslaved people to obey their masters, a clear indication that the institution of slavery was biblically sound. Each of those New Testament passages appeared near instructions for wives to obey their husbands, and proslavery writers argued that slavery belonged within broader biblical frameworks for household order alongside marriage and parent-child relationships.[9] Recognizing that few antislavery activists supported complete equality for women, slavery's apologists argued that slavery was justified in part by its parallels to marriage. Nineteenth-century marriage gave a husband legal rights and powers over his wife, and slavery too relied on benevolent patriarchal oversight of lesser members of a household by the white male head. The potential for the abuse of this patriarchal authority over wives, children, and enslaved people did not invalidate it. Some fathers might have been guilty of physical violence toward their children, some husbands might have abused their wives, and some slaveholders might have been especially cruel to the people they owned. But even when less than benevolent, patriarchy remained God's plan for household organization, according to proslavery writers. To be clear, the material realities of the lives of married white women, white children, and enslaved black people differed vastly in the antebellum South, but in the rhetorical work of slavery's apologists, these groups shared their subordination to the divinely ordained authority of the white male head of household.

This defense of slavery as a part of biblical household order and as the self-evident conclusion of a plain-sense reading of the Bible enabled much of this theology to persist beyond emancipation. Situating slavery within stable, accepted household hierarchies meant that God's orderly benevolent patriarchy undergirded slavery's defense. The start of the Civil War led the next two largest Protestant denominations—Presbyterian and Episcopalian—to schism along regional lines. By then, white southern Christians were convinced that their northern counterparts had abandoned their fidelity to the Bible and embraced Enlightenment-derived ideas of inalienable rights and human equality. As they launched themselves into war, southern white Christians believed that they alone held fast to the plain meaning of the Bible. God, they were certain, would reward their fidelity with a victory for their slaveholding republic.

For people from every background, white or black, enslaved or free, woman or man, the Civil War and emancipation brought tremendous change. One of the central ways that many different groups coped with this change was to look to their Bibles for models of what they were experiencing. When they read biblical accounts of wars, trials, and emancipation, different communities in the South believed they were reading about themselves. This allowed them to situate their chaotic, unprecedented experiences in an ancient sacred history and helped them to find legitimacy and stability in a deeply unstable world. The widely differing ways that these communities read themselves into the biblical narrative shaped how they interpreted the events of the war and how they acted after the Civil War ended.

Unsurprisingly, the start of the Civil War held an opposite theological meaning for enslaved people than it did for white southerners, who were eager to vindicate their slaveholders' republic on the battlefield. The war, enslaved people hoped, would bring freedom, and they ushered in that freedom by emancipating themselves over the course of the war. West Tennessee Methodist exhorter Isaac Lane, who was enslaved, led prayer meetings where enslaved people prayed for freedom. When local whites learned of his prayer meetings, they severely beat him.[10] This violence testified to the strong potential for liberation that white southerners recognized in black Christianity. As many enslaved people fled their owners and struck out for refugee camps, they joined religious meetings in the camps supported by antislavery northern Christian missionaries and teachers. Gathering outdoors under large shade trees and in Union-occupied buildings, the fugitives, who insisted they were free people, formed Christian communities in alliance with white antislavery activists.

Many formerly enslaved people recognized emancipation, despite the privations of the makeshift camps, as an answer to their prayers and the fulfillment of the promise of Exodus. An older woman who had escaped slavery and lived in early 1864 in a cramped tent in Vicksburg, Mississippi, with many of her relatives, explained to a white missionary that the missionary's presence was an answer to her prayers. Rather than seeing herself as the recipient of charity, the freedwoman saw herself as the agent who had brought the missionary to her: "I know 'de' Lord sent you here 'cos' I's prayed dese many days . . . and 'jist' last night I struggled and prayed all 'de' night 'wid' 'de' Lord to send me help and now it's come." Because she had long wrestled with God in prayer, even all night like the patriarch Jacob had done, this formerly enslaved woman was responsible, she explained, for the missionary's decision to come to help her.[11] During a prayer meeting in Natchez, a Mississippi Delta town, a formerly enslaved woman thanked God, saying, "O Lord, thou hast said if we would *believe* we should see the glory of God; for long years we have prayed for this hour to come." In her prayer, this woman echoed the Gospel of John when Jesus raised his friend Lazarus back to life from the grave.[12] Like the biblical witnesses to miracles, formerly enslaved people saw emancipation and the presence of northern Christian missionaries as answers to their prayers and as the present-day fulfillment of biblical promises.

The missionary teachers understood preaching and teaching throughout the Union-occupied Mississippi River valley as sacred work. When the Vicksburg freedwoman said that her prayers had brought a missionary to help her, the missionary responded gratefully that she "felt more than ever that God was with me and directing my steps."[13] From Corinth, Mississippi, in 1863, Rev. George Carruthers described that he felt as "I should have felt had I been with Moses when he was leading the children of Israel out of Egypt" when "a cavalry raid sent out this morning [would] break the chains of the captives and bring him into our lines a *freeman.*" He linked a Union army raid in northern Mississippi with the biblical call for justice.[14] One of his colleagues echoed this sentiment: "I can truly say that amid all the *deep sorrows and privations* of war, it [is] a *great privalige* [sic] to live in this our day, and to be *identified with the Almighty God* in *his* great work. For it is indeed the Lords work & it is marvelous in our eyes."[15] These antislavery missionaries were certain that even without taking up arms, they fought to end slavery and enact the liberation that the Old Testament proclaimed.

Simultaneously, many white southerners insisted that God was on the side of the failing Confederate army, despite its many setbacks and internal disarray. White southern Christians' belief that their proslavery theology alone correctly interpreted the Bible fortified their belief that God supported the Confederacy. Rather than being signs of divine judgment or of imminent Union victory, military defeats and enslaved people's self-emancipation constituted temporary trials to purify and test the faithful white Christian South. White Christians across the South buoyed themselves with a deep faith that God would vindicate their righteous cause. In this reasoning, Confederate weakness would make God's work to support the South more obvious because only miraculous intervention could help the Confederacy. Leading theological writers echoed these sentiments. The *Southern Presbyterian Review*, a respected theological journal, published an article in April 1864 that claimed because the Confederate cause was "unquestionably just and righteous" and "dictated by a righteous and peace-loving spirit," Confederate supporters could "boldly approach God's throne of justice and judgment, and . . . confidently entreat and anticipate His intervention on our behalf." Without irony, it warned of the "slavery" of white Christians submitting to the Union government and supported the "liberty" of "peaceful independence under a confederate republic" of Christian slaveholders.[16]

Such theological claims also appeared in diaries, sermons, and articles from laywomen, laymen, and their ministers and shaped the white South's interpretation of war rumors and news. A young white woman in Natchez, Kate Foster, responded to Union occupation by insisting that the arrival of "a great many Yankees" in 1863 was only a chapter in the South's "war of Independence." As Foster recorded the Union army's control in her diary, she reflected that "we will come out of the furnace doubly purified for the good work & fight that God has given us to do. For to the people of this Confederacy is given the sublime mission of maintaining the supremacy of our Father in Heaven." Amid Confederate defeats, Foster repeated rumors of resounding victories for General Robert E. Lee's army (rather than the reality of Gettysburg's carnage) and averred, "Even now day is breaking" with "hopes of our once more basking in the sunshine of God's smile."[17]

Interpreting rumors to fit the assumption that God supported the Confederacy continued through the close of the Civil War. In late April 1865, a Presbyterian minister in northern Mississippi, Rev. Samuel Agnew, reported that many of his congregants believed the news of President Abraham Lincoln's assassination but not the news of Lee's surrender to General Ulysses S. Grant. "It is wonderful," he recorded after the Sunday service, "the multitude of lies which are circulated to disapate [sic] the depression caused by the fall of Lee and his army." Even as Agnew chided his congregants for their naïveté in the face of Confederate defeat, he was reluctant to acknowledge emancipation. He complained about the independence of the formerly enslaved people whom he hired and then expressed surprise that they chose to stop working for him.[18] For Agnew as well as for laypeople, their belief in the theological defense of slavery and their self-interest as antebellum slaveholders led to resistance to accepting the reality of emancipation.

Freedpeople's civil and political rights remained deeply uncertain even after the Confederates were defeated and the Thirteenth Amendment brought a final end to slavery. The U.S. Supreme Court in *Dred Scott v. Sandford* (1857) had declared that no person of African descent, whether free or enslaved, was a citizen of the United States. What citizenship entailed on the state level was ambiguous, but until the ratification of the Fourteenth Amendment in 1868, national citizenship was unavailable to black people. Without clear access to civil and political rights through citizenship, freedpeople drew on their religious identity as Christians to argue for their inclusion in the social framework of the post-emancipation South. They insisted that they deserved civil and political rights, in part, because they were fellow Christians with white southerners and thus were capable of participating in the civic life of a Christian society. Yet white southern Christians refused to acknowledge black people as fellow Christians, which contributed to the targeted destruction of all of the black churches during the Memphis Massacre.

White southern Christians claimed that emancipation did not invalidate their belief that the Bible supported the institution of slavery. In their antebellum arguments that only proslavery Christians interpreted the Bible faithfully, white southern Christians had staked not only their war effort but also their understanding of the authority of the Bible on the validity of their defenses of slavery. After 1865, all the major southern denominations reiterated their unchanged theological views on slavery, and they claimed that northern denominations' inadequate piety prohibited the national reunion of the Methodist, Baptist, or Presbyterian denominations.[19] Instead, the Confederate defeat and emancipation were divinely sent afflictions meant to purify white Christians. Experiencing these defeats did not imply any wrongdoing on the part of the afflicted who, like the ancient Job, might face terrible suffering without deserving it. White southern Confederates took solace from the many biblical stories where God's people faced military defeat, economic devastation, or exile. From these stories, they concluded that even in times of trial or affliction, God had remained with the Israelites, just as God would remain with the defeated Confederates.

A telling example of how white southerners reconciled proslavery ideas with the reality of emancipation came from an esteemed Methodist minister in the Mississippi Delta. In December 1865, President Andrew Johnson declared a national day of thanksgiving, and Rev. John G. Jones preached a sermon where he called on his listeners to give thanks for their afflictions. Afflictions were lessons "intended to instruct, discipline and confirm us in a religious life." Biblical heroes Abraham, Jacob, and Job had experienced afflictions without wrongdoing. Jones drew on his personal experience of affliction by talking about the death of his young son many years before as a lesson that helped him empathize more deeply with his congregants' losses. Turning to the present, Jones enumerated "the peculiar afflictions of the last five years," of which the final affliction was emancipation, a loss on par with wartime deaths and destruction. He explained: "Emancipation has caused the ruin of the white people and the death[s] of thousands of negroes who have been decoyed away from comfortable homes to perish from poverty and disease [in] the large cities." Describing plantations as enslaved people's "comfortable homes" revealed Jones's ongoing view of slavery after emancipation.[20] Throughout this thanksgiving sermon, Jones used the concept of affliction to show how Confederate defeat did not show divine judgment on the institution of slavery. If emancipation was an affliction, then slavery had been divinely blessed.

Unsurprisingly, freedpeople had little interest in white-controlled southern churches that did not repudiate proslavery theology after emancipation. Around one in ten enslaved people had been members of antebellum white denominations, but after emancipation, these several hundred thousand black Christians quickly left to form their own churches. The departures alarmed white Christians, who did not understand why formerly enslaved people would not want to remain as second-class members in segregated balconies. Black church membership grew dramatically, far outpacing membership rates under slavery and showing how attractive independent churches were. For newly emancipated people, building churches, which could also house schools and community gatherings, was an urgent priority. Freedpeople in rural areas and in towns built rough church buildings almost overnight, sometimes with the aid of the Freedmen's Bureau or northern benevolent organizations and at other times entirely on their own. Given how deeply uncertain freedom was and how emancipation rarely meant equality, churches played an especially important role in black community life. These churches hosted day, night, and Sunday schools for black adults and children, as well as political gatherings and other mass meetings.

Independent black churches helped freedpeople across the South, including in Memphis, try to claim more equal status by arguing that they deserved civil and political rights because they were fellow Christians with white southerners. As a major port city on the Mississippi River, Memphis served as a gathering point for freedpeople from across the Mississippi River valley, including black soldiers mustered at Fort Pickering, the soldiers' families, freedpeople from rural areas, and long-time Memphis residents. The churches that black Memphians and their northern allies built in the first year after the Civil War were community gathering points for the black neighborhoods that grew along the southern bluffs of the Mississippi River. These churches' role in defending black people's rights was evident in the congressional investigation following the massacre, when ministers were asked how they approached issues of civil and political rights in their sermons and other statements to their congregations. Such questions revealed the ways that black churches advanced their members' rights, in the eyes both of congregants and of outside political officials. During the years when citizenship was either unavailable or uncertain, religious claims worked to bolster freedpeople's equality in the postemancipation South.[21]

Using Christian identity to argue for black people's civil and political rights was an especially astute strategy because political leaders, military officials, and clergy alike stated the importance of Christian behavior as a collective standard for mid-nineteenth-century Americans. In his initial response to the Memphis Massacre, General George Stoneman wrote to the city's mayor, John Park, that "the people of Memphis" must "govern themselves as a law-abiding and Christian community" or face further military oversight.[22] Such language showed that Christian identity was an important marker of belonging and of civil participation, and freedpeople's articulation of their Christian identity placed them squarely in the ranks of those who defended this Christian social cohesion. Racial identity was often a fixed, rigid category, but religious identity could change. Evangelical preachers had long stressed that Christian conversion was available to all, whether enslaved or free, black or white, man or woman. The more fully that black residents could insist that Christian identity should signify who belonged in Memphis, the more they could put themselves in that category of belonging. Religious identity gave black Memphians a more malleable category to use instead of the fixed category of race, which excluded them from whiteness and from citizenship.

For all of this, white southerners deeply resented black churches. White Christians, influenced by proslavery theology's emphasis on household order, believed that black people needed the paternalistic oversight of white men in all areas of life, from religion to commerce to politics. It was unimaginable for white southerners that their black neighbors should be their political or religious equals, so whites saw black churches as little more than Republican or Union political tools, not as organic institutions at the center of free black communities. Once black churches were delegitimized as pawns of corrupt, coercive northern political groups, black Christians became clearer targets for their white Christian neighbors' murderous violence, as the Memphis Massacre showed.

The incommensurability of black and white southern Christianities remained long after the congressional inquiry finished its report on the Memphis Massacre. The report chided white southern churches' hypocrisy by pointing out that after the massacre's destruction of black churches, no white congregation opened its doors to a black congregation. Despite the decimation, black congregations rebuilt their churches rapidly after May 1866, and these churches continued to host schools, community gatherings, and political rallies. The Memphis Massacre helped to spur the passage and ratification of the Fourteenth Amendment, which affirms the national citizenship of every person born in the United States and promises equal protection under the law. While black citizens' civil and political rights remained deeply uncertain in the post-emancipation era, black Christianity remained a strong force arguing for the civil and political rights of those who were not only fellow citizens but also fellow Christians with white southerners.

NOTES

1. "Memphis Riots and Massacres," *U.S. Serial Set*, no. 1274, House Report 101, 39th Cong., 1st sess., 12–13.

2. Ibid.

3. Christine Leigh Heyrman, *Southern Cross: The Beginnings of the Bible Belt* (New York: Knopf, 1997); Cynthia Lynn Lyerly, *Methodism and the Southern Mind, 1770–1810* (New York: Oxford University Press, 1997).

4. "Lucretia Alexander," Federal Writers' Project: Slave Narrative Project, vol. 2, Arkansas, pt. 1, Abbott-Byrd, 1936–1938, Library of Congress, Washington, D.C., https://www.loc.gov/item/mesn021 (accessed February 20, 2018); John Wesley, *Thoughts upon Slavery* (Philadelphia, 1778), http://docsouth.unc.edu/church/wesley/wesley.html; Frederick Douglass, *A Narrative of the Life of Frederick Douglass, an American Slave, Written by Himself* (Boston: Anti-Slavery Office, 1845), 119, http://docsouth.unc.edu/neh/douglass/douglass.html.

5. Albert J. Raboteau, *Slave Religion: The "Invisible Institution" in the Antebellum South* (1978; rev. ed., New York: Oxford University Press, 2004), 332–33; Howard Thurman, *Deep River: An Interpretation of Negro Spirituals* (Mills College, Calif.: Eucalyptus Press, 1945), 40.

6. Katharine Gerbner, *Christian Slavery: Conversion and Race in the Protestant Atlantic World* (Philadelphia: University of Pennsylvania Press, 2018).

7. Stephanie McCurry, *Masters of Small Worlds: Yeoman Households, Gender Relations, and the Political Culture of the Antebellum South Carolina Low Country* (New York: Oxford University Press, 1995).

8. Mark Noll, *The Civil War as a Theological Crisis* (Chapel Hill: University of North Carolina Press, 2006).

9. Ephesians 5:22, 6:5; Colossians 3:18, 22; Titus 2:3–5, 9–10; 1 Peter 2:18, 31. (All Bible citations are from the King James Version.) Among many theological defenses of slavery, see "The Relation of the Church to Slavery" and "The Christian Doctrine of Slavery," in *The Collected Writings of James Henley Thornwell, D.D., L.L.D.*, vol. 4: *Ecclesiastical*, ed. John B. Adger and John L. Girardeau (Richmond, Va.: Presbyterian Committee of Publication, 1873); Richard Furman, *Rev. Dr. Richard Furman's Exposition of the Views of the Baptists Relative to the Coloured Population of the United States* (Charleston, S.C.: A. E. Miller, 1823); Frederick Augustus Ross, *Slavery Ordained of God* (Philadelphia, Pa.: Lippincott, 1857).

10. Isaac Lane, *Autobiography of Bishop Isaac Lane, LL.D. with a Short History of the C. M. E. Church in America and of Methodism* (Nashville, Tenn.: Publishing House of the M. E. Church, South, 1916), 51, http://docsouth.unc.edu/fpn/lane/lane.html.

11. L. A. Eberhart to Rev. C. H. Fowler, Vicksburg, February 1, 1864, document 71588, American Missionary Association Archives, Amistad Research Center, Tulane University, New Orleans, La. (hereinafter AMA).

12. Rev. Samuel G. Wright to Rev. Henry Cowles, Natchez, Mississippi, March 15, 1864, document 71614, AMA. The opening line of the woman's prayer references the words spoken to Martha of Bethany before Jesus raised her brother Lazarus from the dead: "Jesus saith unto her, Said I not unto thee, that, if thou wouldest believe, thou shouldest see the glory of God?" (John 11:40).

13. Eberhart to Fowler, February 1, 1864, document 71588.

14. Rev. George N. Carruthers to Simeon S. Jocelyn, Corinth, Mississippi, June 12, 1863, document 71552/71553 (emphasis in original), AMA. Carruthers's language here parallels Psalm 107:44; Psalm 116:16; and especially Isaiah 58:6 (King James Version).

15. A. O. Howell, Natchez, Mississippi, January 19, 1864, document 71594 (emphases in original), AMA. The final sentence of this quote references Psalm 118.

16. Thomas Smyth, "The Character and Conditions of Liberty," *Southern Presbyterian Review* 16, no. 3 (1864): 204–5, 235–36.

17. Catherine (Kate) Olivia Foster Diary, 1863–1872, item Z0869, July 28, 1863, entry, Mississippi Department of Archives and History, Jackson. The phrase "war of Independence" comes from the June 25, 1863, entry.

18. April 22, 1865, entry, folder 10, vol. 8, Samuel A. Agnew Diary, no. 923, Southern Historical Collection, Wilson Library, University of North Carolina, Chapel Hill.

See also entries from May 8, May 16, and May 25, 1865. http://finding-aids.lib.unc.edu/00923.

19. Luke E. Harlow, "The Long Life of Proslavery Religion," in *The World the Civil War Made*, ed. Gregory P. Downs and Kate Masur (Chapel Hill: University of North Carolina Press, 2015), 132–58. The Episcopalians, a far smaller group than the other three denominations, did reunite.

20. Box 2, John G. Jones Papers, Archives of Mississippi Methodism, J. B. Cain Library, Millsaps College, Jackson, Miss.

21. "Memphis Riots and Massacres," 13.

22. Ibid., 4.

Words of Resistance

African American Women's Testimony about Sexual Violence during the Memphis Massacre

HANNAH ROSEN

Early in May 1866, Rebecca Ann Bloom and her husband, Peter, made their way through the streets of downtown Memphis, Tennessee. The Blooms had once been enslaved, but they were now free people. Although the freedom they had obtained during the Civil War had been a tremendous victory, these were also terrifying and trying times for the Blooms and for other African Americans, who were facing almost daily life-or-death struggles over the meaning of their newly won liberty. Just several days before, freedpeople in Memphis had been subjected to murderous attacks by gangs of white men who roamed the Blooms' neighborhood of South Memphis and intruded into freedpeople's homes, robbing, assaulting, and killing residents and setting fire to houses, churches, and schools.[1] The Blooms were headed now to the offices of the Freedmen's Bureau to testify to what had happened when five white men entered their room on the second night of this violence.[2]

Seated before an agent of the Freedmen's Bureau, Peter Bloom explained that the intruders had barged into the couple's room under the pretext of searching for weapons. Yet instead they had stolen fifty dollars in cash, a gold watch, and a packet of razors—the tools of Peter's trade as a barber.[3] Rebecca Ann Bloom testified that the men were upset that there was no candle to light the room, and so they took her husband out to look for one. She then explained that she was raped by the one man who remained behind. In her affidavit, Rebecca Bloom described this man's words and actions: "He wanted to know if I had anything to do with white men. I said no. He held a knife in his hand, and said that he would kill me if I did not let him do as he wanted to. I refused. He said, 'By God, you must,' and then he got into bed with me, and violated my person, by having connexion with me, he still holding the knife."[4]

Bloom was among five freedwomen who recounted being subjected to rape during the three days of violence known as the Memphis Massacre.[5] Not only in Memphis, but throughout the former Confederate states during Recon-

"Shooting down negroes": scenes of the Memphis Massacre. Drawing by Alfred R. Waud, *Harper's Weekly*, May 26, 1866. Prints and Photographs Division, Library of Congress, Washington, D.C.

struction, freedpeople testified before federal officials about sexual attacks by white men. Freedpeople spoke about the violence they had either witnessed or suffered to congressional investigating committees, to federal prosecutors, and, as Bloom did, to agents of the Freedmen's Bureau. In these spaces, freedpeople's determination to report violations of their rights and to seek redress coincided with federal interest in documenting the violence of former Confederates. Together, these phenomena created a unique historical record of black women speaking about rape.[6]

Freedwomen's testimony about rape is painful to read. It is nonetheless crucial that we pay attention to their words. These women met the challenge of recounting their painful experiences in a forum dominated by white men, suggesting that it was important to those who testified that their stories be heard. Cynthia Townsend, for example, told the congressional committee investigating the massacre that a group of white men had raped a freedwoman living near her home. She also explained that she found it difficult to speak about such things: "I do not believe that I could express what I saw." Still, Townsend managed to describe the assault she had witnessed, adding, "I am telling you the truth and I know I have to give an account of it."[7] Other black women who testified about rape similarly found the words they needed and spoke with remarkable forthrightness, and they met white officials' efforts to reshape their testimony or even question their veracity with open resistance.[8]

Examining freedwomen's testimony about rape also helps us understand the full history of the massacre and of the violence of Reconstruction more generally by taking into account the role of gender and sexuality in the life-and-death struggles in which African Americans were engaged after emancipation. Freedwomen's words about rape reveal that central to their expectations for what it was going to mean to be free were bodily integrity and the right to live free of sexual abuse. Their words also illuminate the place of gender in the efforts of many white southerners to reestablish racial difference and a race-based hierarchy after emancipation.[9]

To understand the significance of freedwomen's testimony about sexual violence during the Memphis Massacre, we need to place their words in the context of the everyday political conflicts in Memphis leading up to the violence, particularly contests over the meaning of race that transpired in various arenas of the city's public space. Public life in Memphis had been dramatically transformed by the Civil War and emancipation. In the antebellum years, the city's relatively small black population had been almost entirely enslaved, and their public conduct was strictly regulated and severely circumscribed by city ordinances.[10] In Memphis, as in most antebellum southern cities, laws prohibited enslaved people's travel through the city without a pass, hiring out their own time, living on their own separate from a slave owner, or congregating for social or political activities. Though these laws were never fully enforced, city police were nonetheless empowered to interfere with and constrain the actions of African Americans in the city at all times.[11] Moving about the streets of antebellum Memphis, white and black people observed and experienced racial difference in their everyday lives in part through inequalities in their power to utilize the city's public spaces.

The Civil War disrupted these racial dynamics in Memphis. The occupation of the city by the Union army in June 1862 brought thousands of African American migrants to the city, and this increased the black population almost threefold.[12] The army's designation of Memphis as the recruiting and administrative center for black troops in the Upper Mississippi Valley in 1863 also drew thousands of slaves-turned-soldiers to the city's streets.[13] The significance of this migration for social relations and public activity in Memphis, though, lay not only in its size. In the past, African Americans had been brought to Memphis by force to be sold in slave markets and to labor in white-owned businesses and homes. After the Union occupation, African Americans came to Memphis by choice, seeking, as one formerly enslaved person described it, a "city of refuge," a space in which they would be free.[14]

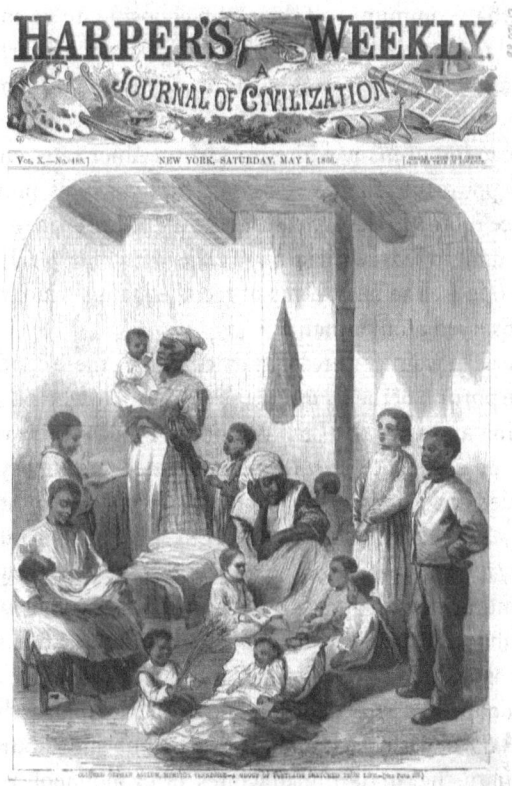

Among those who found refuge in postwar Memphis were orphaned children. Founded during the Civil War by northern missionaries, the Memphis Colored Orphan Asylum sheltered fifty children at the time of the massacre. *Harper's Weekly*, May 5, 1866. Tennessee State Library and Archives, Nashville.

During the Civil War and the years immediately following, refugees from slavery rapidly entered various public spaces in Memphis in anticipation of new rights and freedoms. At the time, their formal political status was uncertain. They were no longer enslaved, yet before black men secured suffrage in 1867, they had no formal political rights. And until a federal Civil Rights Act was passed in April 1866, just a few weeks before the massacre, African Americans were denied even nominal legal recognition as citizens.[15] Nonetheless, freedpeople made use of the limited power available to them to claim many aspects of citizenship. They began their lives in Memphis with expectations for freedom that included the ability to enjoy free movement, social life, and family in an urban community of their own choosing, to be compensated for their labor, and to have these rights protected by law in the form of the Freedmen's Bureau and the police power of the occupying Union army, a power enforced often by black Union soldiers. Freedpeople expected to be citizens of the city. The reaction of many whites to African Americans' entry into public life shows how powerfully their activities disrupted whites' previous norms of racial difference rooted in slavery. Conflicts over public space ensued, as white Memphians sought to redraw racial boundaries, discredit black people's public presence, and oppose the new forms of racial equality evident in what white Memphians observed around them.

African American women were key participants in these conflicts. They constituted a large portion of the formerly enslaved people who migrated to Memphis both during and after the Civil War.[16] And affidavits left with the Freedmen's Bureau indicate that many women migrated specifically in search of a free life. They fled conditions reminiscent of slavery in the countryside, such as physical violence, work with no pay, or forced separation from family.[17] Once in the city, they took advantage of the new opportunity to freely fashion social lives and communities with other African Americans. Women were at the center of many public and visible spaces of black community life, such as picnics and fairs they sponsored to raise money for independent black churches and the grocery-saloons and street corners of South Memphis, where they often gathered and danced with black soldiers into the morning hours.[18]

Black women further undermined whites' prior monopoly on public life by utilizing the power of African American Union soldiers and the federal authority of the Freedmen's Bureau and its court to secure and defend their rights. The bureau's court held jurisdiction in all legal conflicts involving African Americans in Memphis. It was established because the state courts continued to refuse to hear testimony from black witnesses. In this court, freedwomen pressed charges against whites to claim unpaid wages and to protest violent assaults.[19] The impact of legal action at times spilled over from the court into the streets, when whites resisted verdicts and clashed with black soldiers who were making arrests and collecting fines.[20] These clashes were reported and commented on by the city's newspapers.[21] So even when cases did not lead to convictions, freedwomen's actions brought charges of white abuse against blacks prominently into the public eye and thus provided evidence of the new rights and powers of people of African descent.

White Memphians quickly experienced the reality of emancipation and the changed meaning of race through African American women's movement in public spaces and their use of public authority. Some whites responded by attempting to cast black women's new public presence in a disparaging light. For instance, the rhetoric of newspaper editors and the focus of most reporting in the city's conservative press suggest efforts to stigmatize the public activities of freedwomen in the city. Conservative papers often insinuated connections between black women's presence and an alleged increase in crime and disorder, specifically of supposed "lewd women" or prostitutes allegedly threatening white Memphians in the city's streets and alleys.[22] This newspaper reporting drew on a bifurcated concept of womanhood, imposing onto the actual activities of real women—in all their variety and unpredictability—one of two options. As was common in nineteenth-century depictions of urban life in the United States, women were represented as either delicate, chaste, and virtuous "ladies" or vicious, rude "public women" (prostitutes).[23] In post-emancipation Memphis, this binary imagery operated along racial lines. By representing black women as "bad" and often as sexually indiscriminate and "dangerous," these newspaper reports cast black women's presence in the city's public spaces as illegitimate and challenged their claim to the status of equal citizens.

This pattern is evident in the language that conservative journalists used to describe black women. A press report describing a confrontation between a freedwoman named Neely Hunt and a white family, whom she believed was holding her child in the family's home, employed typical terms. When the white mother of the family denied any knowledge of the child, Hunt enlisted the assistance of a squad of black Union soldiers to forcibly search the house. Hunt, who had used state power to assert her rights as a mother, was subsequently characterized by the *Memphis Daily Appeal* as a "negress" who was "enraged," "raving," "threatening," and "us[ing] very abusive and insulting language." In contrast, the women of the white family were described as "ladies of the house" whose supposedly delicate constitutions were unsettled by this confrontation.[24] The *Appeal* thus characterized Hunt not as simply angry about a crime committed against her family, which she no doubt had reason to be, but also as crazed and aggressive.[25] Furthermore, when the press identified black women with terms such as "negress," they avoided describing them as "women," distancing them from images of respectability and associating them with disrepute. News items also often described black women as "wenches," a term meaning "young female" but also implying servitude and sexual wantonness.[26] One report of five black women arrested for disorderly conduct labeled the women "female roughs of African descent" and speculated on the origins of black women's alleged misbehavior: "Freedom seems to have an intoxicating effect on colored females."[27]

Language in the press that associated black women in Memphis with disrepute was reinforced by police action against freedwomen, such as frequent arrests for "lewdness," "vagrancy," and "drunk and disorderly conduct." These arrests, often under false charges and amounting to harassment of black women by police, were then highlighted and exaggerated in newspaper accounts. Phrases such as "six *more* negro prostitutes were yesterday arrested" implied an epidemic of prostitution not indicated by other sources.[28] Another report that "three colored prostitutes were arrested, charged with vagrancy, and hired out to contractors" asserted that those arrested were engaged in the sex trade, but the charge of vagrancy did not necessarily indicate that this was the case.[29]

No doubt, some black women exchanged sex for money when necessary to survive, and others worked more or less full time in prostitution, but many arrests were fraudulent. Amanda Olden, an African American woman living in South Memphis, claimed this was the case when she went to the Freedmen's Bureau to complain about a police officer harassing her in her home just days before the massacre began. Olden recounted that "a city policeman, came to my house, and compelled me to give him twenty-two dollars at the same time falsely charging me with keeping a house of ill-fame." The policeman told Olden that this money would cover her fine for the charged offense. But when she went to court the next morning "ready for an investigation of these false charges, . . . the policeman did not appear, nor had he made any report of this action in [her] case to his proper officer."[30] Similar efforts at extortion under charges of prostitution were reported by freedwomen as having occurred in the midst of the Memphis Massacre.[31]

Ongoing conflicts between freedpeople and white Memphians, as well as the manner in which the city's conservative newspapers depicted these conflicts, appear to have given shape to the violence that black women suffered during the Memphis Massacre. For instance, many of the women who were attacked understood that they were targets of violence because of their relationship to black Union soldiers. Such a connection figured prominently in the stories of four of the five women who testified about having been raped. Harriet Armour was married to an African American Union soldier who was in Fort Pickering during the first days of May. Early in the morning on the second day of the violence, two white men carrying revolvers came to her room. Molly Hayes, a white woman who lived in the adjacent house, overheard these men confronting Armour. Hayes later told the congressional investigating committee: "There were two men who came there and asked her where her husband was. She said he was in the fort. They said, 'Is he a soldier?' She said, 'Yes.' . . . The last word I heard him say was, 'Shut the door.'"[32] Armour testified that after they barred her door shut, both men raped her.[33]

White men participating in the massacre had encountered black Union soldiers on a daily basis in the city's streets as representatives of black male power, of freedpeople's protection in public, and of federal and military authority in

Memphis. By telling women they were being attacked because of their relationship to black Union soldiers, the assailants portrayed their actions as a reassertion of their power over black men. It is important to note, though, that assailants additionally made clear during their attacks that they were also resisting the changed power dynamics between white men and black women themselves. This can be seen in the ways that assailants often initiated their interactions with black women, making oddly casual requests for sex that implied that black women were always available to white men for sex. For instance, sixteen-year-old Lucy Smith testified that the seven men who broke into the home that she shared with Frances Thompson first insisted that they be served supper.[34] Thompson remembered the intruders saying, "they must have some eggs, and ham, and biscuit." She continued, "I made them some biscuit and strong coffee, and they all sat down and ate." When they had finished, the intruders then announced that "they wanted some woman to sleep with." Thompson testified to the congressional committee, "I said that we were not that sort of women, and they must go." Her refusal to have sex proved unacceptable to the intruders. The men physically attacked her.[35] Smith also refused the intruders' demands. She testified, "[When] they tried to take advantage of me . . . I told them that I did not do such things, and would not." In response, one of the men "choked me by the neck . . . [and] said he would make me."[36]

Like the men who attacked Thompson and Smith, the man who assaulted Rebecca Ann Bloom first solicited her for sex—asking if she "had anything to do with white men"—before employing force when her answer was no.[37] "To do with" was a phrase also used by Harriet Armour and Frances Thompson in their testimony to refer to sexual intercourse. By asking Bloom if she had intercourse with white men, this man forced her to engage in a dialogue that positioned her as a woman with whom a strange man might speak about sex, that is, as a woman without virtue. In drawing attention to his whiteness, his words identified her blackness at the same time that he refused to recognize her identity as a wife, even though her husband had just been dragged from the bed in which she still lay. When Bloom refused to participate in his fantasy, he forced her to do so under threat of deadly violence.

These sexual assaults were not spontaneous acts of sexual aggression that occurred when white men were released from "normal" restraints in the pandemonium of a riot. They were, rather, enactments of fantasies of racial domination and superiority that were based on gendered constructions of racial difference and that concluded in rape. The assailants placed black women in the role of the kind of women who could not or would not refuse the sexual advances of a white man. In these fantasies, white men demanded sex, black women acquiesced, and white men experienced their dominance and superiority through black women's performed subservience and lack of virtue. These men attempted to make meaningful to themselves, in a tangible way, the racist discourses on black women's gender and sexuality already circulating in Memphis at the time, particularly in the conservative press. By dishonoring black women, the white assailants joined with the press in contesting the power these women exercised in the public spaces of Memphis. Identifying black women as "lewd" was to imply that they were the kind of women who endangered the community if they were free and unrestrained in public.

Although generally unable to prevent rape in the midst of the massacre, black women were able to resist the meanings that assailants attributed to their violence. Women did this both by verbally refusing requests for sex and subsequently by narrating events from their own perspective when they had the chance to testify. In the days and weeks after federal troops put an end to the massacre, freedwomen told their stories to the Freedmen's Bureau and to the committee sent to Memphis by Congress to investigate. For the women who testified about sexual violence, this committee created a forum of unprecedented state power where they could counter the racist meanings for black womanhood that white men had attempted to articulate through their violence and could claim new rights for themselves.

Freedwomen's testimonies employed a language of violation and harm and thus identified the assailants' actions as rape rather than as illicit or casual sex. Rebecca Ann Bloom maintained before the Freedmen's Bureau that the man who got into bed with her had "violated my person, by having connexion with me."[38] Before the congressional committee, Frances Thompson affirmed that she and Lucy Smith were "violated" by the men who intruded into their home.[39] Smith chose similar words to describe the men's actions: "[they] tried to violate me . . . [and] they hurt me."[40] Another freedwoman who testified about rape, Lucy Tibbs, reported, "I had to give up to them. They said they would kill me if I did not."[41] Stressing that sex was imposed against their will, freedwomen in effect refuted the negative image on which the assailants had insisted, namely that black women had no virtue and so had no reason to resist sex.

Tibbs's comments were made in response to a question from a member of the congressional committee about the assault she described. "Did you make any resistance?" he asked.[42] Harriet Armour also came under this sort of questioning by committee members. When she explained that she had seen no possibility of escape from the white men who attacked her because one of the men had barred her door shut, one congressman asked, "What did he do with the window?" Armour explained that she could not have fled through the window because two slats were nailed across it. "And you made no resistance?" he asked. "No," she answered, repeating that "they had barred the door. I could not get out, and I could not help myself." Yet suspicions and implicit criticism from the committee continued. "Did I understand you that you did not try to prevent them from doing these things to you?" another congressman asked. "Could not the people outside have come to help you?" Armour tried again to explain her strategy to survive the attack: "No, sir; I did not know what to do. I was there alone, was weak and sick, and thought I would rather let them do it than to be hurt or punished.... I should have been afraid to call [for help].... I thought I had just better give up freely; I did not like to do it, but I thought it would be best for me."[43]

Armour had yielded to the men's demands in order to protect herself from other forms of violence and harm. Yet her judgment about what to do in such a situation did not conform to the patriarchal framework within which the elite white men on the committee appear to have imagined rape. When faced with the congressmen's critical response to her testimony, Armour defended her actions and made clear that as much as she had suffered from the violence she experienced, she did not share the assumption that rape would damage her in ways that were worth risking death to prevent. Armour thus struggled to make intelligible to the committee a perspective that grew out of her experiences of Reconstruction-era violence but also possibly out of her experiences while enslaved. All the women who testified about rape had recently lived under a system in which many women faced the grim choice between submitting to coerced sexual intercourse with white men or risking other physical harm to themselves and their loved ones. For them, honor may well have depended more on surviving and protesting this injustice than on privileging and protecting a patriarchal notion of women's sexual virtue.

Despite their efforts, freedwomen's testimony did not lead to the arrests of the white men guilty of assault. On the other hand, the majority of the congressional committee's final report did highlight the rapes of black women as "the crowning acts of atrocity ... committed during these terrible nights."[44] This characterization appeared in the thousands of copies of the report distributed by Congress and reprinted in newspapers across the country.[45] Freedwomen's efforts had, at least temporarily, forcefully challenged conservative public discourse about black women in Memphis. They had successfully represented themselves as honorable women and shown white men to be the ones who were dishonorable and criminal. The women who testified circulated recognition that the rape of black women was a reality as never before. The conservative press, which had earlier been so full of condemnations of black women as disreputable and depraved, was at least temporarily silenced by the overwhelming evidence of the violence enacted by white men.

Ten years later, however, conservatives in Memphis stumbled onto a chance to vindicate the white men of Memphis. In 1876, Frances Thompson was arrested for "being a man and wearing women's clothing."[46] Because Thompson's testimony before the congressional committee had occupied such a prominent place in the committee's final report, her arrest—which might have received only passing mention in the local press under different circumstances—filled the city columns of conservative newspapers for days. Her arrest also served the interests of conservatives in the 1876 presidential election campaign, which would ultimately lead to the Compromise of 1877, the withdrawal of federal troops from the former Confederate states, and the end of official Reconstruction. In this context, the conservative newspapers contended that Thompson's apparent gender nonconformity proved her testimony about rape to have been a lie.[47]

Thompson paid dearly for her supposed crime. After her arrest, she was placed on the city's chain gang, where she was forced to wear men's clothing and suffered constant ridicule from crowds drawn by mocking press reports.[48] While in custody, she protested to a newspaper reporter that the jail house keeper was treating her "very grossly whenever an opportunity presented," taking "evident delight in exhibiting [her] to the curious eye of the public." Thompson alleged further abusive treatment that the paper described only as "other acts which we cannot place in print."[49] So in addition to public humiliation, imprisonment, and hard labor, it is possible that Thompson was subjected to further sexual violence at the hands of those guarding her in jail. As she had done a decade earlier, she protested this violence using the avenue available to her. In 1866, it had been a congressional committee; in 1876, it was a far less effective mechanism: a curious newspaper reporter. Thompson, still defiant, was nonetheless physically weakened by her time in prison. After she completed her term of one hundred days, she moved to a cabin in North Memphis, where she was soon discovered alone and seriously ill by members of the black community. These people moved her to the city hospital, where she died of dysentery on November 1, 1876.[50]

The men who intruded into Frances Thompson's home during the Memphis Massacre may well have known of Thompson's probable transgender identity and may have targeted her for that reason.[51] It is also possible that who Thompson was mattered little to her assailants. Most important to them may have been the gendered scripts of racial domination that they imposed on all of their victims. We may never know for sure.

We do know, though, that the conservative newspapers in Memphis vilified Thompson in ways meant to refute charges of white southerners' brutality against African Americans and to oppose the Republican Party. The press decried Thompson's alleged "utter depravity" and accused her of using her appearance as a woman to facilitate her alleged work as a "procuress" of young women for prostitution.[52] The papers used these charges to condemn their Republican opponents, reminding readers that what they now referred to as "the Frances Thompson Radical Party" had relied on Thompson's words to condemn white men in Memphis.[53] And they also used Thompson's arrest to discredit all the black women who had testified that they had been raped.[54] The *Appeal* claimed: "Whenever you hear Radicals talking of the persecutions of the black race in the South, ask them what they think of Frances Thompson and the outrages committed on her . . . during the celebrated riots. These pretended outrages in the South are all of a piece with this Frances Thompson affair. It is out of such material as this that all their blood-and-thunder stories are manufactured."[55] In the final years of formal Reconstruction, as black political leaders' ability to influence public discourse began to wane and as the spaces in which black women could testify to being raped were closing down, the conservative press in Memphis boldly declared that all black women who testified about rape had lied.

Thompson's experience raises more questions than we can answer. Perhaps most important, though, are the ways that Thompson's history illuminates the politics of memory surrounding the massacre. Freedwomen's testimony about sexual violence during the Memphis Massacre shows how white men's politicization of gender and sexuality shaped a perilous terrain upon which African American women have had to struggle in order to render freedom meaningful for themselves and their communities. Defenders of the perpetrators of the massacre tried in the late 1870s to hide that history from us. But the courage of Rebecca Ann Bloom, Harriet Armour, Lucy Tibbs, Lucy Smith, and Frances Thompson and their willingness to speak despite the risks and challenges they faced allow us nonetheless to remember.

NOTES

This chapter was first presented at "Memories of a Massacre: Memphis in 1866." I am grateful to Beverly Greene Bond and Susan Eva O'Donovan for organizing this important conference and for inviting me to be a part of it. I also thank New York University Press and the University of North Carolina Press for permission to reprint portions of my earlier published work on this history.

1. On the history of this violence, see Stephen V. Ash, *A Massacre in Memphis: The Race Riot That Shook the Nation One Year after the Civil War* (New York: Hill and Wang, 2013). See also Hannah Rosen, *Terror in the Heart of Freedom: Citizenship, Sexual Violence, and the Meaning of Race in the Postemancipation South* (Chapel Hill: University of North Carolina Press, 2009), chaps. 1 and 2; Barrington Walker, "This Is White Man's Day: The Irish,

White Racial Identity, and the 1866 Memphis Riots," *Left History* 5 (Fall 1997): 31–55; Kevin R. Hardwick, "'Your Old Father Abe Lincoln Is Dead and Damned': Black Soldiers and the Memphis Race Riot of 1866," *Journal of Social History* 27 (Fall 1993): 109–28; Altina Waller, "Community, Class, and Race in the Memphis Riot of 1866," *Journal of Social History* 18 (Winter 1984): 233–46; George C. Rable, *But There Was No Peace: The Role of Violence in the Politics of Reconstruction* (Athens: University of Georgia Press, 1984), 33–42; Bobby L. Lovett, "Memphis Riots: White Reaction to Blacks in Memphis, May 1865–July 1866," *Tennessee Historical Quarterly* 37 (Spring 1979): 9–33; Patrick W. Riddleberger, *1866: The Critical Year Revisited* (Carbondale: Southern Illinois University Press, 1979), 177–201; and James Gilbert Ryan, "The Memphis Riots of 1866: Terror in a Black Community during Reconstruction," *Journal of Negro History* 62 (July 1977): 243–57.

2. For their testimony, see affidavits of Rebecca Ann Bloom and Peter Bloom, in "Affidavits Taken before Commission Organized by the Freedmen's Bureau" (hereinafter FBC), in "Memphis Riots and Massacres," *U.S. Serial Set*, no. 1274, House Report 101, 39th Cong., 1st sess., 351, 348.

3. Affidavit of Peter Bloom, ibid., 348.

4. Affidavit of Rebecca Ann Bloom, ibid., 351.

5. See testimony of Frances Thompson, 196–97; Lucy Smith, 197; Harriet Armour, 176–77; and Lucy Tibbs, 160–62, all ibid. For further information on these rapes, see testimony of Cynthia Townsend, 162–63; Henry Porter, 167–68; Molly Hayes, 186; and Elvira Walker, 193–94; and affidavit of Peter Bloom, 348, all ibid. A longer discussion of sexual violence during the massacre appears in Rosen, *Terror in the Heart of Freedom*, chap. 2; and Rosen, "'Not That Sort of Woman': Race, Gender, and Sexual Violence during the Memphis Riot of 1866," in *Sex, Love, Race: Crossing Boundaries in North American History*, ed. Martha Hodes (New York: New York University Press, 1999), 267–93. See also Beverly Greene Bond, "'Till Fair Aurora Rise': African-American Women in Memphis, 1840–1915" (PhD diss., University of Memphis, 1996), 96–103; and Herbert Gutman, *The Black Family in Slavery and Freedom, 1750–1925* (New York: Vintage, 1976), 25–28.

6. See Darlene Clark Hine, "Rape and the Inner Lives of Black Women in the Middle West: Preliminary Thoughts on the Culture of Dissemblance," *Signs* 14, no. 4 (Summer 1989): 912–20; Danielle L. McGuire, *At the Dark End of the Street: Black Women, Rape, and Resistance: A New History of the Civil Rights Movement from Rosa Parks to the Rise of Black Power* (New York: Knopf, 2010); and McGuire, "'It Was Like All of Us Had Been Raped': Sexual Violence, Community Mobilization, and the African American Freedom Struggle," *Journal of American History* 91 (December 2004): 906–31. On black women's testimony about rape during Reconstruction, see Catherine Clinton, "Bloody Terrain: Freedwomen, Sexuality, and Violence during Reconstruction," *Georgia Historical Quarterly* 76 (Summer 1992): 313–32; Clinton, "Reconstructing Freedwomen," in *Divided Houses: Gender and the Civil War*, ed. Catherine Clinton and Nina Silber (New York:

Oxford University Press, 1992), 306–19; Laura F. Edwards, *Gendered Strife and Confusion: The Political Culture of Reconstruction* (Urbana: University of Illinois Press, 1997), 198–217; and Edwards, "Sexual Violence, Gender, Reconstruction, and the Extension of Patriarchy in Granville County, North Carolina," *North Carolina Historical Review* 48 (1991): 237–60. On black women's testimony about sexual violence during the Civil War, see Crystal Feimster, "How Are the Daughters of Eve Punished? Rape during the Civil War," in *Writing Women's History: A Tribute to Anne Frior Scott*, ed. Elizabeth Anne Payne (Jackson: University Press of Mississippi, 2011), 72–74; and Feimster, "'What If I Am a Woman': Black Women's Campaigns for Sexual Justice and Citizenship," in *The World the Civil War Made*, ed. Gregory P. Downs and Kate Masur (Chapel Hill: University of North Carolina Press, 2015), 256–60. See also Susan Barber and Charles F. Ritter, "'Physical Abuse . . . and Rough Handling': Race, Gender, and Sexual Justice in the Occupied South," in *Occupied Women: Gender, Military Occupation, and the American Civil War*, ed. LeeAnn Whites and Alecia P. Long (Baton Rouge: Louisiana State University Press, 2009), 49–64.

7. Testimony of Cynthia Townsend, "Memphis Riots and Massacres," 162–64.

8. Rosen, *Terror in the Heart of Freedom*, 77–80.

9. These arguments are developed more fully in ibid.

10. Gerald M. Capers Jr., *Biography of a River Town: Memphis: Its Heroic Age* (Chapel Hill: University of North Carolina Press, 1939), 107–8, 110, 164; Kathleen C. Berkeley, "'Like a Plague of Locust': Immigration and Social Change in Memphis, Tennessee, 1850–1880" (PhD diss., University of California, Los Angeles, 1980), 47–48; Berkeley, *"Like a Plague of Locust": From an Antebellum Town to a New South City* (New York: Garland, 1991), table 1, 16; and Armstead Robinson, "In the Aftermath of Slavery: Blacks and Reconstruction in Memphis, 1865–1870" (bachelor's thesis, Yale College, May 1969), 26–28.

11. Article 3 of the city charter, "Of the Board of Mayor and Aldermen—Their Powers, etc.," gave the city government the authority to "pass such laws as may be necessary to control and regulate free negroes and slaves." See *Digest of the Charters and Ordinances of the City of Memphis, from 1826 to 1860, Inclusive, Together with the Acts of the Legislature Relating to the City, and Municipal Corporation Generally* (Memphis, Tenn.: Saunder, Overly, and Jones, 1860), 189; see also 85–91, 269, 272–73, 276, 361–67. Also see "Free Negroes and Slaves," in *A Digest of the Ordinances of the City Council of Memphis, from the Year 1826 to 1857: Together with All Acts of the Legislature of Tennessee Which Relate Exclusively to the City of Memphis* (Memphis, Tenn.: Memphis Bulletin Company, 1857), 122–26.

12. Population estimates for post–Civil War Memphis are inconsistent, but all indicate a dramatic growth in the proportion of African Americans in the city. Ash, *Massacre in Memphis*, 3, 33, 66; Robinson, "In the Aftermath of Slavery," 67–68; Berkeley, "Like a Plague of Locust," 120–21; Ernest Walter Hooper, "Memphis, Tennessee: Federal Occupation and Reconstruction, 1862–1870" (PhD diss., University of North Carolina, Chapel Hill, 1957), 132; and "Census of the City of Memphis, Taken by Joe Bledsoe,

under a Resolution of the City Council, Passed April 25, 1865," Memphis and Shelby County Room, History Department, Main Public Library, Memphis, Tenn.

13. Benjamin Quarles, *The Negro in the Civil War* (1953; rpt., New York: Da Capo, 1989), 195; Hooper, "Memphis, Tennessee," 175.

14. Louis Hughes, *Thirty Years a Slave: From Bondage to Freedom: The Institution of Slavery as Seen on the Plantation and in the Home of the Planter* (1897; rpt., New York: Negro Universities Press, 1969), 187.

15. Eric Foner, *Reconstruction: America's Unfinished Revolution* (New York: Harper and Row, 1988), 250–51.

16. In 1863, women made up more than 40 percent of the 535 adults in the contraband camp in Memphis. John Eaton to Prof. Henry Cowles, March 13, 1863, document H8832, microfilm reel 193, American Missionary Association Archives, Alderman Library, University of Virginia, Charlottesville (hereinafter AMA). Jacqueline Jones found that single black women were generally unable to support themselves and their children in agriculture just after the war and thus were more likely than men or married women to migrate to urban areas. Jones, *Labor of Love, Labor of Sorrow: Black Women, Work, and the Family from Slavery to the Present* (New York: Basic, 1985), 74.

17. Records of the Bureau of Refugees, Freedmen and Abandoned Lands, RG105, National Archives and Records Administration, Washington, D.C. (hereinafter BRFAL), entry 3545: statement of Lizzie Howard, July 26, 1865; statement of Elizabeth Jones, July 27, 1865; statement of Mary Ann [no surname recorded], July 31, 1865; statement of Ellen Clifton, August 3, 1865; statement of Eliza Jane House, August 15, 1865; statement of Mary Rodgers, August 15, 1865; and statement of Jane Coleman, August 26, 1865.

18. In "Memphis Riots and Massacres," see testimony of David T. Egbert, 122; A. N. Edmunds, 140; Tony Cherry, 184; Mary Grady, 187–88; and Captain A. W. Allyn, 245; and exhibit 2: report from Captain Arthur W. Allyn, 358. See also Ewing O. Tade to Corresponding Secretary, August 1, 1865, document H8965, microfilm reel 193, AMA; David Tucker, *Black Pastors and Leaders: Memphis, 1819–1972* (Memphis, Tenn.: Memphis State University Press, 1975), 6–8; and Kathleen C. Berkeley, "'Colored Ladies Also Contributed': Black Women's Activities from Benevolence to Social Welfare, 1866–1896," in *The Web of Southern Social Relations: Women, Family, and Education*, ed. Walter J. Fraser Jr., R. Frank Saunders Jr., and Jon L. Wayelyn (Athens: University of Georgia Press, 1985), 182, 193–94.

19. See, e.g., statement of Catherine Martin, July 31, 1865, entry 3545; and Salena Jones v. Gustavis Fisher, August 1, 1865, and Susan Hill v. H. B. C. Miles, December 1, 1865, Docket of the Freedmen's Court, entry 3544, all in BRFAL.

20. See Michael Walsh to Ira Moore, June 11, 1866, and Michael Walsh to David Ingram, June 5, 1866, entry 3541; Lieutenant S. S. Garrett to Lieutenant J. S. Turner, February 23, 1866, and statement of Betty Maywell, December 5, 1865, entry 3545, all in BRFAL. See also "The Negro Again," *Memphis Daily Appeal*, March 3, 1866, 3.

21. Statement of Elizabeth Burns, February 9, 1866, entry 3545, BRFAL; and from the *Memphis Daily Appeal*: "Cruel Treatment," February 15, 1866, 3, and "Cruel Treatment," February 23, 1866, 3.

22. Rosen, *Terror in the Heart of Freedom*, 40–60. See also Clinton, "Reconstructing Freedwomen," 313–14.

23. Mary Ryan, *Women in Public: Between Banners and Ballots, 1825–1880* (Baltimore, Md.: Johns Hopkins University Press, 1990), esp. 73, 76–92.

24. "The Negro Again."

25. Ultimately, Hunt paid dearly for the pursuit of her child. The son of the white woman she confronted was the president of the Tennessee National Bank. Although Hunt did find her child (the record does not indicate where), the bank president filed a complaint against Hunt with the Freedmen's Bureau, claiming that the child had never been in his home. Accepting the bank president's version of events, the provost marshal of freedmen had Hunt arrested and fined ten dollars and costs. Unable to pay, Hunt was at once hired out to labor for a planter for the amount of her fine. (The record does not reveal what happened to Hunt's child while she labored in the country to work off her fine.) This exploitation of Hunt as convict labor was justified by the bureau through the same language by which Hunt had been described in the press. The provost marshal imagined her exile to the countryside to be for the public good. Referring to the planter who bought Hunt's labor, the provost marshal wrote to the bank president, "I trust he may be able to keep her there for the good of this community. I am satisfied that she is a bad woman." Letter to George R. Rutter, Esq., from Provost Marshal of Freedmen, March 3, 1866, entry 3541, BRFAL; and "The Negro Again."

26. See, e.g., "Sharp Wench," *Memphis Daily Appeal*, March 2, 1866, 3.

27. "Female Roughs," *Memphis Daily Appeal*, March 2, 1866, 3.

28. "Freedman's Bureau," *Memphis Daily Appeal*, November 11, 1865, 3.

29. "Freedman's Court," *Memphis Daily Appeal*, November 29, 1865, 3.

30. Statement of Amanda Olden, April 30, 1866, entry 3545, BRFAL.

31. Testimony of Elvira Walker, "Memphis Riots and Massacres," 194.

32. Testimony of Molly Hayes, "Memphis Riots and Massacres," 186.

33. Testimony of Harriet Armour, "Memphis Riots and Massacres," 176–77. See also testimony of Lucy Tibbs, 160–62; testimony of Frances Thompson, 196–97; and testimony of Lucy Smith, 197, all in "Memphis Riots and Massacres."

34. Testimony of Lucy Smith, "Memphis Riots and Massacres," 197.

35. Testimony of Frances Thompson, "Memphis Riots and Massacres," 196–97.

36. Testimony of Lucy Smith, "Memphis Riots and Massacres," 197. Compare historian Stephen Ash, who found in evidence of multiple times Thompson was arrested prior to the massacre for "lewdness," for "disorderly conduct," and once for keeping a "disorderly house," and one time that Smith was arrested a reason to question both Thompson's and Smith's testimony about having been raped. He relied especially on

Thompson's and Smith's arrests on April 30, 1866, the night before the violence began, in his decision that the evidence was inconclusive and thus he did not include Thompson's and Smith's stories in the text of his study. He reasoned that because the record of the Freedmen's Bureau court did not note that Smith's fine for "lewdness" had been paid, she might have been in the city workhouse, working off her fine, rather than at home during the following days and nights. See Ash, *Massacre in Memphis*, 236–38n57. My interpretation of the documentary record leads me to a different conclusion. Rosen, *Terror in the Heart of Freedom*, chap. 2 and 235–40.

37. Affidavit of Rebecca Ann Bloom, FBC, in "Memphis Riots and Massacres," 351.

38. Ibid.

39. Testimony of Frances Thompson, "Memphis Riots and Massacres," 196.

40. Testimony of Lucy Smith, "Memphis Riots and Massacres," 197.

41. Testimony of Lucy Tibbs, "Memphis Riots and Massacres," 161.

42. Ibid.

43. Testimony of Harriet Armour, "Memphis Riots and Massacres," 176.

44. "Report" in "Memphis Riots and Massacres," 5.

45. See, e.g., "Report of the Committee of Investigation on the Memphis Riots," *New York Times*, July 16, 1866, 1; "The Memphis Riots: Report of the Investigating Committee," *Daily Cleveland Herald*, August 1, 1866, 2; "The Memphis Massacre," *Chicago Tribune*, July 28, 1866, 2; and Rable, *But There Was No Peace*, 41.

46. "A Mask Lifted," *Public Ledger*, July 11, 1876, 3; and "Local Paragraphs," *Memphis Daily Appeal*, July 11, 1876, 4. See also Elizabeth Meriwether, *Recollections of Ninety-Two Years, 1824–1916* (Nashville: Tennessee Historical Commission, 1958), 180. Among other inaccuracies, Meriwether incorrectly reported Thompson's arrest as occurring in 1868. I thank Gerald Smith for directing me to this source and to Thompson's arrest for gender nonconformity. For a longer discussion of Thompson's arrest and subsequent history, see Rosen, *Terror in the Heart of Freedom*, 235–40. See also Susan Stryker, "To Appear as We Please," *Aperture Magazine* 229 (Winter 2017): 32–35; Stryker, *What Transpires Now: Transgender History and the Future We Need* (forthcoming); and Ardel Haefele-Thomas, *Introduction to Transgender Studies* (New York: Harrington Park Press, 2019), chap. 8.

47. See, e.g., "Under False Colors," *Memphis Daily Avalanche*, July 12, 1876, 4; and "Thompson," *Memphis Daily Appeal*, July 13, 1876, 4.

48. See "Local Paragraphs," *Memphis Daily Appeal*, November 4, 1876, 4. In the *Memphis Daily Avalanche*, see July 18, 1876, 4; July 19, 1876, 4; July 20, 1876, 4; and July 21, 1876, 4. In the *Public Ledger*, see "Ledger Lines," July 13, 1876, 3; and July 17, 1876, 3.

49. "Frances Thompson," *Memphis Daily Appeal*, July 14, 1876, 4.

50. "Frances Thompson Dead," *Weekly Public Ledger*, November 7, 1876, 3. Her death was also noted outside Memphis: "Telegraphic Notes," *Chicago Tribune*, November 4, 1876, 5; and "Death of a Notorious Negro," *Cincinnati Commercial*, November 4, 1876, 3. See also Register of Deaths, Memphis and Shelby County Health Department, 1876–

1884, 24, Memphis and Shelby County Archives, Memphis, Tenn. (hereinafter MSCA); and Stryker, *What Transpires Now*.

51. Both the doctors who examined Thompson when she was arrested and the coroner's report of her death declared that Thompson was anatomically male. Yet one newspaper report explained that some in Memphis had understood that Thompson's genitalia were ambiguous, that she was intersex or, in their words, "a hermaphrodite." She herself claimed, according to another newspaper, to be "of double sex." She also protested the finding that she was "a man and not a woman in any respect" because she "was regarded always as a woman." All that we can be certain about is that Thompson lived and identified as a woman. See "Francis Thomas [sic]," *Memphis Daily Appeal*, July 12, 1876, 4; Register of Deaths, Memphis and Shelby County Health Department, 1876–1884, 24, MSCA; "A Mask Lifted," *Public Ledger*, July 11, 1876, 3; and "Frances Thompson," *Memphis Daily Appeal*, July 14, 1876, 4.

52. See in *Memphis Daily Appeal*, "Thompson," July 13, 1876, 4; "Frances Thompson," July 14, 1876, 4; and "Local Paragraphs," July 18, 1876, 4. In the *Public Ledger*, see "A Mask Lifted," July 11, 1876, 3, and "That Man-Woman," July 12, 1876, 3. In the *Weekly Public Ledger*, see "Frances Thompson Dead," November 7, 1876, 3.

53. "Frances Thompson," *Memphis Daily Appeal*, July 14, 1876, 4; and "Ledger Lines," *Public Ledger*, July 17, 1876, 3. See also "Ledger Lines," *Public Ledger*, July 14, 1876, 3.

54. E.g., "Thompson," *Memphis Daily Appeal*, July 13, 1876, 4; and "Time Makes All Things Even at Last," *Public Ledger*, July 19, 1876, 2.

55. Untitled editorial, *Memphis Daily Appeal*, July 16, 1876, 2.

On Duty in Memphis
Fort Pickering's African American Soldiers

ANDREW L. SLAP

African American soldiers stationed at Fort Pickering were at the center of the Memphis Massacre. Three of them were walking south down Causey Street, just a few blocks from the fort, on the afternoon of Monday, April 30, 1866. Four white policemen approached from the opposite direction. For the last several months, there had been increasing clashes between African American soldiers and the white police officers who patrolled the streets of Memphis in the aftermath of the Civil War. That afternoon was no exception. The soldiers made way for the policemen on the sidewalk, but the two groups started to exchange heated words. One of the soldiers suddenly dashed into the muddy street and fell, a pursuing policeman tripped over him, and a melee ensued. Curses rang out. The police pulled their guns and brandished their knives. They began to whale on the soldiers; one policeman threw a brick. After exchanging more insults and threats, the white police retreated into the city and the black soldiers returned to Fort Pickering. This all took place the afternoon before the actual massacre erupted.[1]

On May 1, dozens of African Americans clad in army uniforms gathered about a quarter of a mile from Fort Pickering—a few hundred yards from where the clash had occurred the previous day—to celebrate their muster-out. The ex-soldiers became boisterous with drink, annoying nearby shopkeepers and residents. By late afternoon, a city official directed four police officers to disperse the crowd. The uniformed black men refused, and tempers flared once again. The outnumbered police grew anxious and started to withdraw, but the former soldiers followed, shouting threats and brandishing clubs. Suddenly one of the African Americans fired a pistol in the air to scare the police. Thinking they were being shot at, the police turned and drew their revolvers. Two policemen fired into the crowd of African Americans, leading more than twenty ex-soldiers to start firing at the police in earnest. The firefight quickly died down and the only person injured was a policeman who had accidentally shot himself, but the situation was too intense and confusing for anyone at the time to know what was happening. Two of the policemen ran back to the police station, chased by some of the ex-soldiers, who seriously wounded one of the policemen. As the situation started to calm down, the ex-soldiers returned for the night to Fort Pickering, where they were still quartered. They were unaware that a white mob, led by some policemen, was organizing and about to descend on African American neighborhoods surrounding the fort.[2]

Violence engulfed South Memphis on the night of May 1, 1866. For three days, whites led by the police attacked African Americans and their property. The violence was not indiscriminate, as whites purposefully targeted African American ex-soldiers and their families. The former soldiers beseeched the commander of Fort Pickering to give them weapons to defend their families, but he refused. Some of the ex-soldiers stayed in the safety of the fort, but many ventured weaponless into the city to protect their loved ones. One former soldier later testified that a policeman stabbed him and declared that the mob was "going to kill the God damned nigger soldiers who were here fighting against their rights—the black sons of bitches." Several ex-soldiers were among the forty-six African Americans killed during the massacre. Four of the five African American women who testified that they had been raped were connected to African American soldiers and the U.S. Army. Veterans and their families were among the hundreds of African Americans beaten or robbed, and they watched while ninety-one houses were burned, along with four churches and twelve schools. On May 4, the U.S. Army commander finally sent troops into Memphis and declared martial law.[3]

But the experience of African American soldiers and their families in Memphis is more than three horrible days in May 1866. Sidney McCargo, also known as Sidney Mack, was born in Montgomery, Alabama, around 1844. He enlisted in the Third U.S. Colored Heavy Artillery at Memphis, Tennessee, during the summer of 1863 and spent the next three years at Fort Pickering. He was mustered out of service on April 30, 1866, and very well may have been one of the soldiers involved in the massacre. Despite the violence, he stayed in the city, working as a janitor and living on the corner of Webster and DeSoto Streets in South Memphis. He met his wife, Ella Baker, in Memphis. Baker was born enslaved and had lived on a plantation in DeSoto County, Mississippi, about nineteen miles from Memphis. She was in Memphis during the massacre, living with her first husband, York Baker, on Gayoso Street at the center of the violence. The spring of 1866 was bad for the Bakers in many respects. Their first child was born in April 1865 but died in March 1866, just a month before the massacre. After the death of her first husband, Ella Baker and Sidney Mack married in 1882 and lived in Memphis for about a decade before moving to

Chicago. They had no children of their own but were surrounded by friends and family, some of whom joined them in a photo taken shortly before Sidney Mack's death.[4]

There are thousands of these individual stories about the lives of the African American soldiers and their families who experienced the Memphis Massacre. As we explore these experiences, though, it becomes clear that these were not isolated individuals. The African American soldiers stationed at Fort Pickering and their families were part of vibrant and dynamic communities from the antebellum period through the Civil War and into the twentieth century. These communities came together in Memphis to protect and help African Americans dealing with racism, government bureaucracy, and violence.

Desertion may seem an odd place to start a discussion of community, particularly since the Third U.S. Colored Heavy Artillery regiment stationed at Fort Pickering had an incredibly high rate. The desertion rate for all U.S. soldiers during the Civil War was a little more than 10 percent, and it was only 6 percent for African American soldiers. The Third U.S. Colored Heavy Artillery, however, had a desertion rate of more than 18 percent. Significantly, more than 40 percent of the desertions involved multiple soldiers from the same company deserting on the same day, which is statistically unlikely. The majority of the simultaneous desertions did not occur in pairs, but in large groups, making it less likely that the soldiers deserted independently. The largest was when fourteen soldiers deserted from Company D on the same day in February 1866. The rough probability of fourteen soldiers individually deserting on the same day is .001 raised to the fourteenth power. Something interesting was going on in the regiment, and examining the desertions shows strong and long-lasting communities.[5]

Jerry Shelton and David Shelton both deserted Company F on September 23, 1863, and they had many other similarities. Besides sharing a last name, both men were born in Panola County, Mississippi, and enlisted on August 27, 1863, and they took their physicals one after the other. They were probably from the same plantation and knew each other before the war. Likewise, Reuben Right and Thomas Clark were both born in Franklin County, Tennessee, enlisted in Company A on June 5, 1863, and deserted on July 19, 1863, while on guard duty on the breastworks. One of the most remarkable cases was John Alexander and James Alexander, who both deserted Company L on December 28, 1863. The two men had taken their army physicals on December 4 with only one person between them in line. More interesting, both returned from desertion more than a year later on exactly the same day, suggesting that they stayed in contact after deserting.[6]

Antebellum community and family connections are likewise evident with the Dunlaps. Nineteen-year-old Lewis Dunlap may have been nervous standing in line on November 28, 1863, for his physical examination to join the Third U.S. Colored Heavy Artillery. The presence of Campbell, Hillman, Henry, and Powell Dunlap immediately behind him, though, probably reassured him, since census and military records suggest that all of them were enslaved on the same plantation in Henry County, Tennessee. Forty-nine-year-old Hillman Dunlap was rejected for being too old, and Campbell Dunlap was turned away because of a hernia, but Lewis, Henry, and Powell enlisted in Company L. The Dunlaps leaving a plantation and joining the Union army together was not an aberration, since many African Americans carried part of their enslaved communities with them into military service. Privates Henry and Powell apparently did not care for the military, since both deserted on January 10, 1864, and then returned, only to desert again on May 2, 1864. Those who stayed in the regiment developed new bonds of community.[7]

Like Henry Dunlap and Powell Dunlap, Isham Knight did not have an exemplary military career. Private Knight enlisted in Corinth, Mississippi, on June 10, 1863, and within two months was in the hospital with a dislocated shoulder, which would bother him for the rest of his life. Knight spent the next six months sick in his quarters before deserting on February 26, 1864. Despite his brief time in the regiment, Knight had made friendships that lasted for decades. When Knight applied for a pension in 1885, David Lipford testified that he had known him since the mid-1850s and had seen the accident in 1863. Further, Lipford said, "I have known him ever since the war[.] we live about 5 miles apart. I see him from two to three times per month and know the effects of the wound." Sergeant James Pharr had only met Knight in the military but knew the veteran still suffered because he was "acquainted with him and living neighbors ever since the war."[8]

For many of the soldiers who served at Fort Pickering, their postwar neighborhood was South Memphis, and the community support there was vital, considering the daily challenges African Americans faced. In September 1865, three young African American soldiers were returning to the fort around midnight when they encountered a few white policemen. Private William Clark was just eighteen years old and had enlisted less than six months earlier. He testified, "I was conducting myself peaceably, walking slowly away to camp, not pestering anybody at all," and "I never saw anything until I was shot." Clark recounted that after he was shot in the leg, the policemen "knocked me over the head with a pistol" and then "fired at me three times while I was lying on the ground." According to his companion Private Richard Smith, "They beat Clark who had been shot and was still lying there over the head with a pistol. They said, 'The other son of a bitch is gone, but here is his cap; we had better go across the street and look under the drays and see if one of them is not there."⁹

Smith remembered more of what happened that evening than Clark did, perhaps because he was not beaten over the head with a pistol. "I was shot while walking on the street one night while going home from Bob Church's, on DeSoto Street crossing Gayoso. A policeman said, 'Halt, where are you going?' I replied I was going to camp. He immediately passed me and wheeled and fired on me. I came across the street and staid [sic] in a colored man's house 'til Sunday morning." Smith did a good job describing the three white policemen, and he recognized the accused, John Mageveny. However, when the judge asked Smith if the accused policeman was present at the time he was shot, the defendant objected to the question before Smith could answer. For some reason, the commission sustained the objection. The officers on the commission did push the surgeon who testified about what the nature of the wounds indicated about the position of the soldiers and police at the time of the shooting. The surgeon was clear that "in every case the wound was inflicted from behind, except perhaps in the case of Clark, which was more from the side."¹⁰

A couple of months later, Mageveny was patrolling with another white policeman, David Roach, in the late afternoon. Five African American soldiers in uniform were gathered in front of First Sergeant Peter Robinson's house on Gayoso Street in South Memphis. A civilian testified that there was plenty of room to pass, but Mageveny "just walked along and shoved him with his elbow as he passed hard enough to push Sergeant [Jack] Buckner out of his place up against the other men." He then heard Buckner tell Robinson "Sergeant, I cant stand that," but Robinson told him to keep quiet and that they should go see the colonel. This was similar to Robinson's account: "A policeman come along with his hand in his bosom and threw his whole weight against Sergeant Buckner and passed along about five feet, when the Sergeant said, 'Don't you see that policeman push me?' The policeman then stopped and turned around with his face toward us. That was about all that occurred. I took the men in charge and retired from the ground immediately for fear there would be some disturbance."¹¹ This incident is strikingly similar to the one that occurred the evening before the massacre and suggests the constant threats to African Americans in Memphis.

The massacre was the culmination of months of attacks on the African American communities that had developed around Fort Pickering in South Memphis. Policeman David Roach was one of the leaders of the white mob. African American veteran Coleman Default described his experience on the first evening of the massacre: "David Roach, policeman, and several other policemen came to where I was, on South street, and fired [at] the house, shot me twice, beat me on the head with pistols and robbed me of what money I had and my discharge from the army.... After Roach shot me, I begged him not to kill me; he said, 'Yes, God damn you, I will. You and all the balance of you.'" Roach seemingly tried to make good on his threat. Two witnesses testified that the next morning, Roach and a white citizen cornered an African American soldier, who pleaded for his life. One witness said, "Roach pulled out his pistol and shot the man in the leg; then this drayman put his pistol right to the man's head, shot the man, and walked on." That same morning, Cynthia Townsend stated, "I saw a man by the name of Roach, a policeman, shoot a negro man; he was driving a dray. Mr. Roach ran up and shot him right in the side of his head." Throughout the day Roach helped burn down African American homes and churches, and one woman stated he was part of a group that said they wanted to kill her brother because he was a soldier. Roach was never prosecuted and continued working as a policeman in Memphis off and on for a decade, patrolling the same streets where he had murdered people during the massacre.[12]

Despite the massacre and other violence, hundreds of African American veterans and their families stayed in Memphis for decades. Extrapolating backward using the special soldiers census in 1890 and mortality rates, about 1,600 African American veterans lived in Memphis in 1870. Almost three decades later, George Crutchfield, the special examiner for the U.S. Pension Bureau in Memphis, commented on the continuing strength of the African American veteran communities while trying to solve a difficult case. In 1899 he had to determine whether Mary Johnson's deceased husband, Robert Johnson, was either of the two men by the same name who had served in African American regiments in the city during the Civil War. After examining the official records and deposing fourteen witnesses, he reported, "I am convinced the claimant[']s husband is not identical with either of said soldiers." For Crutchfield, "the most convincing fact to indicate that claimant's husband did not serve in either of said companies is that there are hundreds of [members of] those two regiments in Memphis Tenn and it is hardly conceivable that he would live here from discharge to 1887 without being known to many of them and without talking of them to his wife and having them at his house."[13]

Veterans from the regiment who lived outside Memphis often testified to regularly coming into the city, suggesting that for some former soldiers Memphis was the center of a veteran cluster. Alex Jones of Company I recounted, "I lived most of my time in DeSoto Co Miss after the war until 1884 when I moved to Memphis but I was in and out of Memphis every three or four months during that period." Similarly, Tony Jordan of Company K reported in 1899, "I lived in Fayette Co Tenn from muster out to 1882 when I moved back to Memphis. The first two years after muster out I made frequent trips to Memphis Tenn and then it was that I saw Robert Johnson," who had been a private in Company H.[14] Coming into the city regularly, buying groceries, meeting a former comrade—these simple acts point to the interconnections between Memphis and the surrounding countryside for black veterans.

Henry Hart's experience shows the importance and strength of African American veteran communities. Hart was born and raised in Henderson County, where he still lived on a plantation during the first years of the war. The twenty-five-year-old Hart enlisted at Corinth in the summer of 1863, was sent to Memphis, and was enrolled in Company H. He soon met Henrietta McKenney, who worked in the hospital where he recovered from smallpox. By February 1864, they were married and eventually had at least five children. Henry Hart tried his hand at several different occupations, keeping a grocery store in 1867 and working as a laborer in 1870 and as a candy maker in 1880. Sometime in the 1870s he also learned to read and write. Henry and Henrietta Hart had a fractious relationship and separated in 1885. But Hart maintained good relations with comrades from his regiment who lived in the city. Four of these men testified for Hart when he applied for a pension increase in 1899. Soon after that, he moved to 13 Jefferson Avenue, just blocks away from two of his comrades. Robert Piles from Company I, who lived less than 350 feet from him, recounted how Hart had helped take care of him while Piles was in the hospital for smallpox during the winter of 1863–1864, and "he was [as] well acquainted with Henry Hart after the war, as he could be with any man."[15]

The area in Memphis where most of the veterans from the regiment lived was about eight blocks south of Jefferson Avenue. The combination of the veterans census and the Company H pension files provides exact addresses for thirty veterans or widows of veterans living in Memphis in the 1890s, a small sample of the hundreds of African American veterans and widows living in Memphis in the late nineteenth century. Almost half of the veterans and widows were living within a few blocks of the intersection of Pontotoc Street and Hadden Avenue. Perhaps not coincidentally, Hadden Avenue Colored Church was in the center of this cluster of African American veterans and widows. Henry Bankel of Company K lived at 44 Hadden Avenue, next door to two regimental widows. A few blocks east on DeSoto Street, Joseph Ferguson lived next door to Emily Morton, the widow of John Morton from Company H. Robert Rawson of Company A, who testified on behalf of William Sikes, lived one block north of Ferguson and Emily Morton. Robert Jones of Company H and Alex Jones of Company I lived together at the rear of 281 Calhoun Street, four blocks south of Hadden Avenue Colored Church, while George Washington of Company C and Stephen Bowman of Company I lived within a few hundred feet of the Joneses.[16]

Another small cluster of veterans and widows lived about ten blocks southwest of Hadden Avenue Colored Church. Mary Anne Weston, the widow of Richard Weston of Company H, lived in this area even after her husband died of yellow fever during the epidemic of 1878. By early 1890 she was living much farther north in the city, on the same block as Robert Piles, who was Henry Hart's friend. Later that year, she moved back to her old neighborhood to a house on Pennsylvania Avenue next door to Henry Beaumont of Company I, a few blocks north of John Abernathy of Company K and two blocks east of Simon Lewis of Company H.[17] The odds of thirty people coincidentally living so closely together in a city of almost sixty-five thousand is small.

David Warrington probably had a photograph taken soon after enlisting in the Union army at Mount Sterling, Illinois, along with his brother James Warrington in late October 1864. The brothers had much in common. Both had been born in Missouri and were twenty-eight-year-old farmers. Even for the mid-nineteenth century, they were on the short side, standing, respectively, five foot five and five foot four. A neighbor later recalled, "Dave Warrington was black and not very tall, a heavy-set man." They agreed to serve as substitutes for two men who had been drafted but did not want to serve in the army. After a little time in Springfield, Illinois, the brothers were sent south to Memphis, where they joined different companies of the Third U.S. Colored Heavy Artillery. The only thing of note in David Warrington's service record was that some clerk incorrectly listed him as David Washington, a seemingly innocuous mistake that the illiterate soldier may never have noticed. The Warrington brothers were mustered out of the army in late October 1865 when their term of service expired. They both settled down in Monroe County, Illinois, a rural area just south of St. Louis, Missouri. The area was described by one person as a "wilderness" where "a few men owned that good land and had negroes and poor whites in shacks down there to work at taking off the heavy timber."[18]

It was not all hard work for the brothers. David Warrington soon met Charlotte "Lottie" Grimes, a young woman who may have been the sister of Frank Grimes, a soldier who had served with the Warringtons in Memphis. After a few years of courtship, David Warrington and the eighteen-year-old Lottie Grimes married on July 25, 1872. Lottie Warrington gave birth to a daughter, Sylvia, ten months later. Around 1878 the couple had a second daughter, Diana, who according to her sister "was always a little weak thing." By all accounts the family was happy. A neighbor recalled, "I well remember Dave going long distances home at night when he and I were feeding [the] threshing machine and saying he had a little baby at home and had to go and I know he was referring to this Diana." Another neighbor gave a similar account—"he was foolish about Charlotte and the two children and would walk home four or five miles from his work just to be with his said wife and said children when he did not have to."¹⁹

Tragedy struck the young family in 1882 when Lottie Warrington died of pneumonia at age twenty-eight. David's sister Mary Warrington moved in to help with the young girls, though he remained devoted to his daughters. A neighbor recalled, "I used to see Dave out on the lake bank fishing and these two children, Sylvia and Dianna [sic] with him, and their mother Charlotte was dead and gone and then he took them along to get them out of the way of his sister Mary." Seven months after his wife's death, however, David Warrington became ill with pulmonary tuberculosis and died in the spring of 1883. James Warrington helped bury his brother.[20]

Frank Grimes took his two young nieces to live with him in St. Louis. Diana Warrington was young enough that she later said that she had no memories of her parents: "the first I can remember I was living here in St. Louis in the house of my Uncle Frank Grimes." In 1893 Frank Grimes applied to get a minor's pension (based on David Warrington's Civil War service) for Diana Warrington, who was still eligible, unlike her older sister. Unfortunately, the small mistake of a clerk almost three decades earlier now had huge consequences, for the pension application listed the soldier's name as David Warrington while the service records only showed a David Washington. Despite periodic correspondence from relatives trying to clear up the confusion, Diana Warrington did not get the pension, although she probably needed the financial support. Similar to her sister's testimony, a government official commented that Diana Warrington "has been very shallow mentally from birth and she is a weak pattern physically." Eventually, in 1923, Diana Warrington wrote the pension office inquiring about the application filed by her uncle thirty years earlier.[21]

Special examiners in the pension office investigated the claim, interviewing people from Illinois to California. One of the key pieces of evidence was a photo of David Warrington wearing his Union uniform. A cousin explained, "I gave to Sylvia Mitchell, David Warrington's daughter, a tintype picture of a man which my mother always taught me is the likeness of her brother David Warrington and the picture resembles him." The special examiners took the photograph with them on their interviews to try to corroborate that David Warrington and David Washington were the same person. Upon being shown the photograph, a former neighbor declared, "I can easily tell you whose likeness that picture is; it is the picture of a man named Dave Warrington I used to know in Monroe County, Ill. I did not have to have you or anyone else tell me whose picture that is." Finally, Diana Warrington received the pension, and the pension office backdated it to 1894, when she should have first received it.[22]

David Warrington had taken care of his little girl with a photograph from

This undated tintype of David Warrington was found in his pension file, placed there by examiners who had used it to verify his wartime service. David Warrington, Civil War Pension File, Certificate 950723, RG 15, National Archives and Records Administration, Washington, D.C. This copy was taken by *Military Images* and is reprinted with permission.

almost sixty years earlier. The sad part is that this photograph was the only image Diana Warrington had of her father, but she did not get to keep it. She had told a special examiner, "he must have been a soldier as I have here a tintype of a man in soldier clothes which my sister says is the likeness of our father. I will lend this picture but wish it returned to me." But the unreturned picture remained buried in the pension files for almost a century.[23]

The memory of the Memphis Massacre likewise remained suppressed for generations. However, in the twenty-first century a community of residents, activists, academics, and institutions, including the University of Memphis, the Memphis branch of the National Association for the Advancement of Colored People, and the Orange Mound Cultural Center came together and have begun to bring those three days of racial violence in Memphis during 1866 back to public consciousness with a symposium, historical markers, and this volume. The research on the Memphis Massacre shows that there is not just a history of racial violence in the city. The vibrant and dynamic African American communities in Memphis, which are reclaiming the history of the massacre, are built on the foundation of powerful African American communities in the city that stretch back centuries.

NOTES

I thank *Military Images* for allowing me to use some material from a previous article in this chapter.

1. "Memphis Riots and Massacres," *U.S. Serial Set*, no. 1274, House Report 101, 39th Cong., 1st sess., 64, 67–68.

2. Stephen V. Ash, *A Massacre in Memphis: The Race Riot That Shook the Nation One Year after the Civil War* (New York: Hill and Wang, 2013), 95–100.

3. "Memphis Riots and Massacres," 171, 36; Kevin R. Hardwick, "'Your Old Father Abe Lincoln Is Dead and Damned': Black Soldiers and the Memphis Race Riot of 1866," *Journal of Social History* 27 (Fall 1993): 128n45.

4. Sidney McCargo, Civil War Pension File, RG 15, National Archives and Records Administration, Washington, D.C. (all pension files hereinafter cited as CWPF).

5. Of the 752 total desertions from the regiment, 234 involved multiple soldiers from the same company deserting on the same day. The regiment existed for a little more than a thousand days, so the probability that a soldier would desert on any given day is approximately one-tenth of 1 percent. The probability of two soldiers independently deserting on the same day is .001 to the second power, or .000001. Simultaneous desertions of more than two soldiers from the same company were 58 percent of all group desertions. Adjutant General's Office, RG 94, entries 112–15: Civil War Regimental Book: 3rd United States Colored Heavy Artillery: Regimental Letter and Order Books, National Archives and Records Administration, Washington, D.C.

6. Benjamin S. Hood, Surgeon's Book, Abraham Lincoln Library, Springfield, Ill.

7. 1860 U.S. Federal Census; Hood, Surgeon's Book; 3rd United States Colored Heavy Artillery: Regimental Letter and Order Books.

8. 3rd United States Colored Heavy Artillery: Regimental Letter and Order Books; Isham Knight, CWPF.

9. MM3338, entry 4, Military Commission Case Files, RG 153, National Archives and Records Administration, Washington, D.C.

10. Ibid.

11. Ibid.

12. "Memphis Riots and Massacres," 162, 337–38.

13. George A. Crutchfield to Green B. Raum, November 4, 1899, in Robert Johnson,

CWPF; *Report on Population of the United States at the Eleventh Census: 1890* (Washington, D.C.: Government Printing Office, 1897) (hereinafter *1890 Veterans Census Schedules*).

14. Robert Johnson, CWPF.
15. Henry Hart, CWPF; 1870 U.S. Census; 1880 U.S. Census.
16. *1890 Veterans Census Schedules*; Robert Johnson CWPF; Simon Lewis, CWPF. The locations of the addresses were found on the 1888 Sanborn map of Memphis.
17. Mary Anne Weston, CWPF; *1890 Veterans Census Schedules*.
18. David Warrington, CWPF.
19. Ibid.
20. Ibid.
21. Ibid.
22. Ibid.
23. Ibid.

Black Organizing Traditions after Slavery

JULIE SAVILLE

Linking the ugly, brutal events of the 1866 massacre in Memphis to the unfolding of emancipation brings clearly into view the contradictions that defined enslaved people's experiences of emancipation. Dangers—at times, lethal—saturated freedom's promises but did not extinguish its appeal. Far from lifting the burdens of enslavement, emancipation could trigger new vulnerabilities, as the events in Memphis in May 1866 suggest. For better or worse, emancipation was not deliverance transcendent of time and place. Rather, its freedoms had to be won on already riven ground. Activist-scholar Angela Davis's examination of the modern prison system and the post-emancipation origins of the death penalty in the United States offers a reminder that some legacies of emancipation's turbulence imbue our own times: "If slavery was declared dead, it was simultaneously reincarnated through new institutions, new practices, new ideologies . . . structures and ideologies of enslavement that were translated into the terms of freedom."[1] Terrorist violence stalked emancipated men and women with impunity. Electoral politics became a blood sport. Legal fictions of contracts disguised the racial subordination of sharecropping. The massacre in Memphis, then, is of a piece with the troubled aftermath of slavery's abolition.

Painful injury and joyous possibility cannot be meaningfully separated in formerly enslaved people's experiences of emancipation, nor should they be. A new emphasis on suffering or trauma as elemental components of emancipation has brought to light previously underappreciated and even previously unknown aspects of the experiences of enslaved women, children, and men in the aftermath of the Civil War and Reconstruction.[2] Injury and violent assault underlay the conditions under which formerly enslaved people sustained efforts to fashion free lives. With threats and with deeds, harm tracked their pursuit of bodily integrity, economic agency, political recognition, and social dignity.

One example from countless possible illustrations must suffice. This event is as unforgettable as it is impossible to fully understand. In June 1865, Frank Frazier quit his owner's plantation when his master refused to issue the weekend pass that he customarily used to visit his wife. As Frazier made his way over the nearly 150-mile route from Clinch County, Georgia, to Liberty County on the Georgia coast, he encountered a group of three black women traveling with their children back to Liberty County, from where they had been removed at some point during the Civil War. Upon reaching the Altamaha River, together they tried to avoid the "rebels with guns" who guarded a river bridge by climbing down a trestle to the water's edge and then crossing on floating logs. Spying their movements, the guards set dogs loose on the travelers to force them to return to shore. Frank Frazier later explained the group's desperate circumstances to the chaplain of a South Carolina black regiment:

> The dogs were pressing us hard. The bank was about fifteen feet high. I went down to the water as quick as I could. I climb[ed] down on the posts of the trestle work to the water. One woman threw down her child to me [and] I caught it. This was her babe. She then threw down to me her little daughter about five years old [but] I could not catch it and the current swept it away and it was drowned. One of the other women threw down her little girl about 7 years of age. I could not catch it, [and] it was swept away and drowned.

The unnamed women and another fugitive black man who had joined the group then climbed down, and, Frazier reported, "The dogs could not get over and we went on."[3]

What combination of desperation, determination, and dread passed through the escapees' minds? From where came the courage that led one mother to toss her child to Frazier just after his attempt to catch another mother's child had failed? Such acts are unfathomable; the thoughts of the mothers whose children drowned as they were trying to get free remain beyond recovery. The women and men who traveled on to Liberty County knew that emancipation was not only a survivors' story. They did not yet know the uncertainties that awaited them behind federal lines, however, even two months after Robert E. Lee's surrender.

Against the backdrop of varied precariousness, formerly enslaved people devised efforts to wrench their lives free from slavery's wreck. They encountered social and legal forms of post-emancipation resubordination that can be placed on a continuum with the types of exploitation and vulnerability experienced by people emancipated in other parts of the early modern Atlantic world. The military leadership that had abolished slavery and declared political independence in Haiti in 1804 distributed prime sugar plantation lands among army generals and instituted a militarized regime of forced labor on sugar estates and in the construction of new state monuments. In 1802, in Guadeloupe, another of France's Caribbean colonies, Napoleonic forces overturned the emancipation of tens of thousands of men and women whose freedom had been proclaimed only eight years earlier, reviving and rebuilding slaveholding regimes that would last almost another fifty years. Both events amplified the rumors of re-enslavement that long enveloped proclamations of emancipation in Caribbean regions. In 1865, just as the reconstruction of societies without slavery was getting under way in the United States, British colonial troops brutally suppressed insurgencies and protests mounted by formerly enslaved rural laborers and small landowners in Jamaica, where slavery had been abolished some thirty years earlier, and a planter-dominated Jamaican assembly relinquished representative local government rather than engage with the concerns that emancipated workers and their allies brought to a contentious political sphere.[4] Declarations of slavery's abolition failed to end compulsory labor, ensure political recognition, or in some instances, even last. As historian Walter Rodney observed, after slavery's abolition in the "post-emancipation era," the outcomes of social conflict determined "the extent to which an alteration of legal status was transformed into substantial social change."[5]

By the time the massacre erupted in Memphis, wartime executive and military declarations and federal occupation had shortened the life of Confederate slavery. Many locales, including Maryland, the District of Columbia, Louisiana, Missouri, and Tennessee itself, had declared slavery abolished, and in December 1865 the Thirteenth Amendment had been adopted. The timing of the massacre underscores the insight of Rodney's observation that declarations of abolition were not sufficient in themselves to end slavery. The massacre, along with many other protracted, unpredictable upheavals that followed in emancipation's wake, should dispel any tendency to view emancipation as a state act that is complete at its enunciation. Emancipation in Memphis, as elsewhere in the Americas, provided openings in which formerly enslaved men and women acted to address both the lingering influences of the slaveholding order and the new problems that stemmed from the terms of state-sponsored emancipation itself. Their actions became the core of social movements—a mass of movements throughout the southern states—that sought to complete or redress what state declarations had enacted or legitimated but had never fulfilled.[6] These movements developed from formerly enslaved people's experiences that changes in juridical status, constitutional amendments, state legislation, and even suffrage itself were insufficient to realize freedom. Therefore, formerly enslaved people and their allies needed to seize the openings that state acts of emancipation and abolition had proclaimed.

Viewed from the grassroots, the social struggles of Reconstruction do not follow the same chronology used to mark milestones in institutional politics. They did not begin with congressional enactment of the Reconstruction Acts in 1867 or end with the overturning of the last post–Civil War southern Republican state governments in 1877. Like the events of May 1866 in Memphis, these struggles implicated relations of power in which the very meaning of politics itself was contested as part of the dismantling of one of the central structuring institutions of nineteenth-century American life. The concept of an "organizing tradition," developed by scholars exploring the aims, strategies, and roles of local freedom fighters in the civil rights movement, can also be used by historians of Reconstruction to explore the ways in which emancipated men and women mobilized for justice after slavery. The organizing-tradition frame is especially useful for calling attention to historically specific conceptions of freedom, forms of social justice activism, and the strengths and limits of various modes of repression in the economic, political, and cultural spheres of postwar African American life.

Grassroots movements after slavery drew on some traditions that did not begin with emancipation. Historians now generally accept that by the time of the Civil War, enslaved people in the United States had been, as Steven Hahn phrased it, "looking out from slavery" for quite some time.[7] Well before the outbreak of the Civil War, the idea of some external events—the action of a distant monarch, the success of slave armies in another part of the world, reports that the United States was fighting against a government that had abolished slavery in Mexico, and indeed the first national presidential campaign of the Republican Party in 1856, dubbed by historian Douglas Egerton "the slaves' election"—had set small numbers of enslaved people, most often men, in motion to create a life without slavery.[8] Their efforts sometimes moved against the tide, however. The eight escapees from slavery who presented themselves at Fort Pickens, a Union garrison in Florida, in March 1861, "entertaining the idea," as the fort's commander reported, that federal troops "were here to protect them & grant them their freedom," were instead transported to Pensacola to be returned to their owner.[9] Nevertheless, in selecting a federal fort as a destination, these escapees from slavery identified a space that would figure often in later runaways' negotiations to secure their reception behind Union lines.

Within slave territory itself, less public spaces—a cabin wall on which abolitionist illustrations were mounted, plantation celebrations, funerals, sparsely traveled woods—became localized neighborhood sites in which momentary interactions that ran counter to slavery's hegemonic power might be experienced.¹⁰ While still enslaved, the previously mentioned adults who traveled toward Liberty County had developed standards of human relationships that highly valued skills to incorporate and coordinate the actions of strangers. Formerly enslaved people brought to emancipation myriad lessons drawn from the unending skirmishes of having lived in bondage. Many enslaved people would have understood why in upstate New York Sojourner Truth had described her own enslavement as combat. "Now the war began," she recalled.¹¹ As veterans of the struggles that preceded those of the Civil War, whether toiling in house, field, or city, emancipated people looked out toward new horizons. The remarkable mobilizations mounted by formerly enslaved women and men in the immediate aftermath of the Civil War responded to unprecedented opportunities and emergent threats. Federal armies of occupation promised liberation; roving armed bands of destitute, hungry men peeled off from demobilizing Confederate armies. Their interactions with both groups prompted emancipated women and men to maintain vigilance and coordinate self-defense. Their lives in slavery had left a legacy not only of deficits but also of skills, formal and informal, that they were ready to harness to advance their interests as free people.¹²

Emancipation revealed not only what had been done to enslaved people but what they did with what was done to them. From coastal South Carolina, a group of formerly enslaved men succinctly described how their community was preparing in the fall of 1865 for a life in freedom: "We have, for the last four yars," they informed President Andrew Johnson, "been studing with justis and the best of our ability what step wee should take to become a people."¹³ Their letter illustrates an important aspect of the organizing tradition as a mode of action that encompasses the most basic aspects of community building. Seizing emancipation as an occasion to restructure their social world—"to become a people"—this group of freedpeople reminds us that organizing traditions look not only to identify and seek redress for external constraints on community development. They also focus internally on the very nature of the group relationship in order to enhance the capacity for social action.

The letter, written at the height of the implementation of the president's policy to restore the lands on which the federal government had settled formerly enslaved people during the Civil War, reveals the most widespread conviction shared by emancipated women and men: the expectation that land would accompany emancipation. The claims for land were most insistent in freed communities from Tidewater Virginia to the coastal mainland and islands of South Carolina, Georgia, and northern Florida, where the federal government had located some sixty thousand people on lands abandoned during the Civil War.¹⁴ More fundamentally, land was central to formerly enslaved people's conception, as overwhelmingly rural, laboring people, of how life was lived and organized. Many enslaved people had customarily enjoyed access to plantations and farmlands on which they grew crops, hunted, fished, and even pastured animals that they and their owners regarded as the enslaved people's property. Familiar with such practices under slavery, they did not expect emancipation to offer any less.

This viewpoint was widely disseminated in the print media of the day, often with assistance from sympathetic northern teachers, missionaries, and religious leaders who lent their skills and presses to the cause. In December 1866, Baptist minister Bayley Wyatt, who had been born enslaved, delivered a speech to a mass meeting of freedpeople, military, and civilian officials on a Tidewater Virginia "government farm" that protested the eviction of the formerly enslaved people from their wartime settlement. The speech was later published in a Quaker journal. Wyatt drew on economic, philosophical, and religious principles to frame his broad protest against government restorations of land to former slave owners and the evictions of formerly enslaved wartime settlers. He anchored freedpeople's rights to land in political economy, Christian morality, restitution for slavery's violations of core human relationships, the simple mutuality of friendship, and the failures of the North and South alike to acknowledge their indebtedness to the wealth that the labor of enslaved women and men had produced:

> I may state to all our friends, and to all our enemies, that we has a right to the land where we are located. For why? . . . Our wives, our children, our husbands, has been sold over and over again to purchase the lands we now locates upon; for that reason we have a divine right to the land. . . . And den didn't we clear the land[,] raise the crops of corn, ob cotton, ob tobacco, ob rice, ob sugar, ob everything. And den didn't dem large cities in the North grow up on de cotton & de sugars and de rice dat we Made? . . . I say dey has grown rich and my people is poor.[15]

However deeply held, the belief that land would accompany emancipation was transient. At times, it revived in hopeful rumors sparked by ex-masters' loud allegations of the government's intent. It greedily absorbed occasional announcements from Union soldiers that a master's lands would be distributed among the people who had labored on the plantation. At times, mythologies of hope misconstrued reports of pending congressional legislation or the meeting of state conventions to write new constitutions in the Union-occupied Confederate states. The schemes of itinerant peddlers in Georgia brought it back to life when they advertised wooden stakes that could be used to claim confiscated tracts. To illustrate freedpeople's perceived gullibility and political unfitness, ex-slaveholders long joked that formerly enslaved people expected "forty acres and a mule." A plantation owner in the neighborhood of Adams Run, South Carolina, recycled the planters' jest when he expressed disgust at the spectacle of the first elections based on universal male suffrage in his neighborhood. Freedmen came to cast their ballots at the polls near Adams Run, he reported, "bringing [with them] halters for mules which they expected to carry home."[16] As a phrase, "forty acres and a mule" appealed to the hopeful and their ridiculers alike, probably helping to ensure the phrase's longevity. Ex-masters read it as cultural incapacity; conservatives heard a plea for government favors for special interests; small farmers and landless, laboring whites saw apparitions of thieves who would threaten their precarious livelihoods in alliance with large landowners; and Radicals heard the muted echoes of eighteenth-century republicanism's tenet that representative institutions require a material economic basis. Within a few years, however, freed women and men came around to the grudging acknowledgment that their emancipation would be landless. Although belief in the likelihood of land redistribution faded, formerly enslaved people's wide belief that landownership was the foundation of the good life animated their most basic efforts at community self-organization.

Because their masters had owned their very persons, formerly enslaved people's programs of social reconstruction addressed intimate areas of household and personal life along with new claims to public life. Reuniting family and other kin separated by sale or wartime relocation was clearly freedpeople's first priority in town and countryside alike. For some families, the searches continued well past the early days of Reconstruction, and notices seeking information about missing family members continued to appear in the African American press until the early twentieth century. The reconstitution of family groups and the establishment of household relationships—no less than the founding of independent churches and schools, mutual benefit societies, and social clubs—drew the energies of social organizing into the institutional infrastructure of an emerging black community. Family members defended their kin against threats of abuse, and relatives accompanied each other to a nearby military post or an office of the Freedmen's Bureau to lodge complaints. Schools and churches opened their doors to mass meetings. Even before the Reconstruction Acts ordered elections in which black men would be eligible to vote, a latent social movement slumbered in this black institutional infrastructure, and new sites of informal political power emerged in the immediate aftermath of emancipation.

This postwar flowering of community organizations is best viewed locally, but freedpeople's efforts to reshape their working lives to meet their own household needs and their pursuit of economic agency show that some patterns of activism were common to plantation workers, farm laborers, and household workers in town and countryside alike. Freedwomen and freedmen reduced the time they spent cleaning, laundering, or farming for others and turned to cleaning, laundering, and farming for their own households. Their postwar reallocations of their working time typically provoked charges of laziness from plantation owners and other employers. Some former slave owners returned to whipping or other forms of physical coercion in attempts to reestablish the workday that they had become accustomed to during slavery. The intentions of extended family groups to farm independently on an employer's land and to structure the timing and pace of work themselves turned topsy-turvy the obligations that farmworkers, both enslaved and juridically free, owed to landowners under antebellum laws of master and servant. When freedpeople left work without permission—whether to attend a political rally with family and friends or to blend work and amusement by taking a break to fish, hunt in the woods, or gather honey—their actions drained meaning from nineteenth-century laws that continued to vest employers with full authority over the work routines, the home lives, and the political expressions of the enslaved people they owned and the juridically free people they hired.[17] Emancipated rural working women and men encountered the rigid legal obligations of enslaved workers and wage-earning workers alike. Two freedmen operating farms in Kentucky in 1866 received an anonymous message that spelled out the challenge for black independent farming settlements. "Believeing this to be a white mans Country," the anonymous writers pledged, "we are bitterly opposed to negroes setting up to farming for themselves therefore we have concluded to brake it up."[18]

It is difficult to overestimate the contribution of work-centered identities to the visions, associations, and aims of the early public lives of emancipated people. In plantation districts of the former Confederate states occupied by federal troops, demonstrations, work stoppages, and laborers committees' public protests displayed the enthusiastic embrace of the public sphere as an available and open arena. Social relationships forged in labor—in both its symbolic and political aspects—proved an important source of formerly enslaved people's remarkable engagement with politics after emancipation. In contrast to the view of their onetime owners, formerly enslaved people understood work as a human obligation, not as an exclusive duty restricted to a subordinated social rank. This belief was a secular source of confidence in their own capacities. Although the social hierarchies of slavery depicted them as dependent, formerly enslaved men and women saw the domain of work as an arena of collective strength. For example, a formerly enslaved man from

Tennessee gave short shrift to the suggestion of a white chaplain who had served in a black army regiment that onetime masters feared that freedpeople would not work without the whip or could not survive without paternalist protection. "We'se made the white people," he said, and further indicated that "it would be a great pity if they could not support themselves, without the white folks to take care of, too."[19]

When Congress wrested control of the process of Reconstruction from President Johnson in March 1867, it brought the authority of the nation within reach of burgeoning local movements seeking to give social and economic content to emancipation. The political expressions of formerly enslaved people's culturally distinctive public sphere included variously named "marching companies" or "drill squads," which mushroomed in the countryside as a new form of associational life, and the participating freedmen and, in some instances, freedwomen pioneered a model of collective public assertion that came to serve as the backbone of emancipated workers' radical clubs, parades, and holiday celebrations. The companies appeared in tandem with Union occupation, and more than one writer credited black Union veterans with their organization. Elements of this new form of sociability and spectacle entertained rural audiences, and some plantation work groups assembled to military cadences that lent variety and fun to work routines. Small in size and generally formed by men who lived on the same plantation or in the neighborhood, early marching companies sometimes doubled as home guards that organized matters of plantation welfare, village self-government, sanitation, patrol, and self-defense. The quasi-military organizations enlivened plantation routines by incorporating staged performances steeped in the symbolism of the military victory that had brought emancipation.

In this context, acting like a soldier could never be only an innocent gesture. Describing his childhood in Reconstruction-era Florida, T. Thomas Fortune reflected on many occasions when leisure pastimes or sports were intermingled with violent attack. "Can you imagine a party of grown-up white persons deliberately shooting into a crowd of Sunday school teachers and children?" he asked, before recalling how he and his schoolmates decided to confront the white boys who stoned them when they passed the white "academy" on their way to school:

> The colored children approached the academy in mass formation whereas in the past they had been going by it in pairs or small groups. Timothy was in the front of his group, [and] when they reached hailing distance of the academy [a] half dozen white boys rushed out and hurled their missiles, acting as if they expected to stampede their opponents. Instead

of scampering away, however, the colored children not only stood their ground and hurled their missiles, but maintained a solemn silence. The white children then, seeing there was no backing down and scampering, as they expected, came rushing out of the four sides of the academy, and charged the colored children, who stood their ground stubbornly. During some fifteen minutes it was a real tug of war between them, with little ground given by either side. In the close fighting the colored children got the advantage, gradually, and began to shove the white children back, and as they pressed the advantage, the white children broke away and ran for the academy. The colored fighters did not follow them but made it hot for the laggards until they also took to their heels.[20]

The practical uses that Fortune and his friends glimpsed in the marching companies were not lost on adults. Marching companies provided self-defense by accompanying voters to the polls after black male suffrage was introduced under the terms of the Reconstruction Acts. In southern Louisiana and the plantation districts of South Carolina, some of these companies were briefly incorporated and armed as state militias. Although they were official units of the states' Republican administrations, the marching companies splintered in the face of better-armed attacks from Democratic rifle clubs and controversy among black Republican voters over the militia's role in breaking up work stoppages and protecting strikebreakers in the rice region after 1874. While they lasted, however, the marching companies were part of a grassroots mobilization of neighborhood associations that pioneered a kind of social movement not previously known in the United States. Not again until the 1960s would so varied a range of social organizations rally to affect political life. Members of marching companies, defense associations, union leagues, loyal leagues, family labor unions, churches, and benefit societies along with students and teachers became the backbone of the organizing Republican Party in the former Confederate states. Together they transformed the meaning of politics, pressing social mobilization beyond the boundaries of deference to a patriarch, a landlord, or political elites. Soon, political engagement became too important a matter to leave only to enfranchised men. The critical roles of freedwomen as political agents and political targets, the frequent presence of children at local political meetings, and the infusion of political partisanship into the concerns of mutual aid associations and labor organizing made political contention a community affair.

The life of Eliza Pinkston, who was born enslaved, did not encompass the plantation belt's extended family groups and public displays of collective organizing. Instead, she lived her life moving between the cotton country of

African American men, dressed to indicate their professions, wait to cast their first ballots as free men. Drawing by Alfred R. Waud, *Harper's Weekly*, November 16, 1867. Prints and Photographs Division, Library of Congress, Washington, D.C.

Canton, Mississippi, where she was born around 1857, and the small farming neighborhoods of Ouachita, Louisiana. Nonetheless, the cultural penetration of the social changes that radicalized Reconstruction also rendered her daily life a field of contending political forces. When she died in Canton in 1883 at age twenty-six, Eliza Pinkston had returned from stints of living and working in Alabama and elsewhere in Mississippi to her place of birth. One of a small number of freedwomen who spoke before the congressional committee that visited New Orleans to investigate the contested election of 1876, Pinkston's testimony sheds light on some social, cultural, and political meanings of household relationships during Reconstruction.[21]

When Congress passed the Reconstruction Acts, Eliza was barely ten years old and still lived in the household of her employer-guardian, a white tenant farmer named Charles Tidwell. As a young enslaved child, her services in Tidwell's household encompassed house and farming chores—and sexual encounters with Tidwell's son, David, "who was the first one that I had ever taken up with in my life"; as "little children," the relationship between Eliza and David had included sex, along with "dew-berry hunting, fishing &c."[22] With no identifiable kin outside the Tidwell household, Eliza's departure from her guardian's employment bore little discernible connection to the Thirteenth Amendment. Instead she first left her childhood residence around the time of the Reconstruction Acts, when the elder Tidwell sent his son away to school because, Eliza reported, David "got so that he did not want to twist or turn without me, and I was getting big enough to know right from wrong."[23] Eliza began her own version of emancipation as a search for recognition as an honorable woman, first by marrying Alabama schoolteacher Adam Finch when she was only thirteen years old. Their union was interrupted when Charles Tidwell wielded his authority as the head of the household in which Eliza had lived and worked by having her husband jailed and then barred from Eliza's company until she was fourteen years old. The couple nevertheless found ways to circumvent the court order; their first child was born around the time of Eliza's fourteenth birthday in 1871.

Subsequently, life and labor took Eliza to northern Louisiana. Now widowed, she resumed farmwork, along with cohabitation and a sexual relationship with David Tidwell, explaining, "I never was sot up as a mistress. . . . I worked; but when nighttime come I done duty too."[24] Farm labor, sexual services, and domesticity seem inextricably entangled in Eliza's experiences as she strove to fulfill her household obligations. Gaining no satisfactory public recognition for faithfully performing her duties in David Tidwell's household, Eliza left him after their twin boys failed to survive infancy, and she married the black sharecropper Henry Pinkston. "My color didn't look on me with honor . . . and for that reason I hid myself as proper as I could after I had them twins. [But] after I married my color I went everywhere, and I had a name. [Previously,] I could not be called 'Mrs. Tidwell'; it was always 'Eliza Finch.' Said I, 'It didn't sound pretty, and didn't look upright and honest, and I am right.'"[25]

The newly married couple, Henry and Eliza Pinkston, together with Eliza's firstborn child, worked a tract of land that the elder Tidwell rented around 1874. The brittle overlapping household relations of labor, guardianship, sexual partnership, and cohabitation that ensued required Eliza's careful tending even before Henry showed enthusiasm for the Republican Party, which had first won county elections in 1868. Some Democrats who were determined to suppress Republican votes in the 1876 elections were connected to the pre-emancipation household networks in which Eliza had grown up, for she recognized most of the men who raided the Pinkstons' cabin in November 1876 from her days living with the Tidwells. Henry's desecration and murder on the eve of the election at the hands of twenty young white nightriders described by a Democratic House minority report as "among the first young men of the parish, moving in the best circles of society," precipitated the investigation in which Eliza Pinkston's lengthy, richly descriptive testimony was recorded.[26] In addition to the castration and shooting of her husband and the murder of their newborn child, Pinkston reported, she had been stabbed, gang-raped by two of the attackers, sliced on her thigh, struck in the head with an ax, cut on the tendon of her left heel, and shot above her right breast. Her bid for social recognition as an honorable wife to Henry Pinkston had been destroyed, together with Ouachita Parish's Republican government and Louisiana's Republican administration.

The personal consequences for Eliza Pinkston of the Republican defeat remain indeterminate. The Democratic press, in an effort to depict the recording and publicity of Pinkston's ordeal as partisan Republican demagoguery, crafted an account in which Democratic attacks on the Pinkston household counted for little, and journalists noted that two years later Eliza Pinkston had resumed a happy domestic life. "Eliza shortly disappeared from the public view," the Macon *Weekly Telegraph* reported in 1878, miraculously recovered from her wounds and removed to Madison, Mississippi, where she had married Raymond Prichard, "a respectable colored man."[27] Five years later, the *New York Times* reprinted a press notice from Jackson, Mississippi, that sketched Pinkston's subsequent tragic decline. She reportedly had died in Canton, Mississippi, "where she was serving a term in jail for larceny and was buried as a pauper."[28]

In death, as in life, Eliza Pinkston's self-realization straddled competing political claims. Neither Pinkston nor the Democratic members of the congressional investigatory committee understood that her testimony addressed matters central to voter suppression. And Pinkston insisted that neither she nor her husband, Henry, "was a politishman."[29] Yet from a distance it is hard to ignore the explosive political contests of the Reconstruction era that collided in her private life. Her desire to achieve respectability as an honorably married woman first gained public expression during the turmoil of Louisiana's Reconstruction-era politics. A Ku Klux Klan–like gang of Democratic sympathizers and friends of David Tidwell, Eliza's white childhood companion and occasional sexual partner who had fathered her deceased twins, launched a nighttime attack. The raiders destroyed her respectable household only days after they had prevented the couple from traveling as a family to a neighborhood Republican meeting.

Similar to Eliza Pinkston's attempts to use labor, travel, and marriage in order to create an honorable household status, collective forms of mobilization pressed against every thread in the fabric of community life, testing the strengths and the limits of the localized neighborhood organizations that responded to the organizing drives of political parties in the wake of the Reconstruction Acts. Both the collective and personal expressions of mobilization wielded by formerly enslaved women and men precipitated a new form of direct, deadly attack on freedpeople's households that had no precedent under slavery.

Whether rooted in personal relations of the household or in collective forms, mobilizations deeply rooted in the business of ordinary life have a kind of double existence. By their very nature, they are simultaneously less and more than they appear. Disappearing from public view by blending into ostensibly nonpolitical roles when under siege, they can sprout without warning precisely when their defeat seems to be most evident. Such resilience makes the impact of repression on social mobilization contingent rather than inherent. Union leagues, a pervasive feature of black rural life in 1868, were virtually unknown a decade later. But through what historian Rebecca Scott, drawing on the political theory of economist A. O. Hirschman, has described as a "transfer of social energy," less deadly arenas of organization, such as schools, churches, orphanages, and a host of various associations, filled a seeming void.[30] Would the impact of the changed political climate on the internal governance of these post-repression community institutions sustain the dynamism of an ascending workers mobilization, or would the community associations themselves become vehicles of repression monitoring personal respectability in cultural form?[31] To pose the question is to concede the potentially political meanings of the ostensibly nonpolitical institutional infrastructure of community organizations.

I recently discovered that Collins Chapel on Washington Street, one of the eight black churches in Memphis that was burned in May 1866, was affiliated with the post–World War II institution of Collins Chapel Hospital. The resilience of those who rebuilt Collins Chapel after the Memphis Massacre formed part of a transfer of energy that provided a safe space for a family that quit Tuscaloosa, Alabama, almost a century later when the adults decided that life in Tuscaloosa had become too risky. In Collins Chapel and other Memphis city hospitals, the male head of the family found a space in which to renew hopes, make plans, and continue his professional skills. As a child in that family, I have only lately understood my indebtedness to those people who returned after May 3, 1866, to rebuild their chapel. The good fruits of the congregation's resilience also suggest a possible moral to the story about mobilization after slavery: if through some combination of grace, wit, and good luck you pass through to the other side of a catastrophe, pause, take a deep breath, give thanks, sift through the ashes, look forward, and then pass it on.

NOTES

1. Angela Y. Davis, *The Meaning of Freedom and Other Difficult Dialogues* (San Francisco, Calif.: City Lights, 2012), 140.

2. Thavolia Glymph, "Black Women and Children in the Civil War: Archive Notes," in *Beyond Freedom: Disrupting the History of Emancipation*, ed. David W. Blight and Jim Downs (Athens: University of Georgia Press, 2017), 121–34; Carole Emberton, *Beyond Redemption: Race, Violence, and the American South after the Civil War* (Chicago: University of Chicago Press, 2013); Kidada Williams, *They Left Great Marks on Me: African American Testimonies of Racial Violence from Emancipation to World War I* (New York: New York University Press, 2012); Nell Irvin Painter, "Soul Murder and Slavery: Toward a Fully Loaded Cost Accounting," in Painter, *Southern History across the Color Line* (Chapel Hill: University of North Carolina Press, 2002), 15–39; Saidiya V. Hartman, *Scenes of Subjection: Terror, Slavery, and Self-Making in Nineteenth-Century America* (New York: Oxford University Press, 1997).

3. Steven Hahn et al., eds., *Freedom: A Documentary History of Emancipation, 1861–1867*, ser. 3, vol. 1: *Land and Labor, 1865* (Chapel Hill: University of North Carolina Press, 2008), 91–93.

4. Johnhenry Gonzalez, "The War on Sugar: Forced Labor, Commodity Production, and the Origins of the Haitian Peasantry, 1791–1843" (PhD diss., University of Chicago, 2012); Laurent Dubois, *A Colony of Citizens: Revolution and Slave Emancipation in the French Caribbean, 1787–1804* (Chapel Hill: University of North Carolina Press, 2004); Thomas C. Holt, *The Problem of Freedom: Race, Labor, and Politics in Jamaica and Britain* (Baltimore, Md.: Johns Hopkins University Press, 1992).

5. Walter Rodney, "Guyana: The Making of the Labor Force," *Race and Class* 22, no 4 (1981): 331–52, 331 (quotation).

6. Francoise N. Hamlin, "Collision and Collusion: Local Activism, Local Agency, and Flexible Alliances," in *The Civil Rights Movement in Mississippi*, ed. Ted Ownby (Jackson: University Press of Mississippi, 2013), 35–58.

7. Steven Hahn, *A Nation under Our Feet: Black Political Struggles in the Rural South from Slavery to the Great Migration* (Cambridge, Mass.: Belknap, 2005), 1–12.

8. Steven Hahn, *The Political Worlds of Slavery and Freedom* (Cambridge, Mass.: Harvard University Press, 2009); Cassandra Pybus, *Epic Journeys of Freedom: Runaway Slaves of the American Revolution and Their Global Quest for Liberty* (Boston: Beacon, 2006); Julius

S. Scott, "The Common Wind: Currents of Afro-American Communication in the Era of the Haitian Revolution" (PhD diss., Duke University, 1986); Susan E. O'Donovan, "Writing Slavery into Freedom's Story," in *Beyond Freedom: Disrupting the History of Emancipation*, ed. David W. Blight and Jim Downs (Athens: University of Georgia Press, 2017), 26–38; Douglas R. Egerton, "The Slaves' Election: Frémont, Freedom, and the Slave Conspiracies of 1856," *Civil War History* 61 (March 2015): 35–63; Armstead L. Robinson, "In the Shadow of Old John Brown: Insurrection Anxiety and Confederate Mobilization, 1861–1863," *Journal of Negro History* 65, no. 4 (1980): 275–97.

9. Ira Berlin et al., eds., *The Destruction of Slavery* (Cambridge: Cambridge University Press, 1986), 9.

10. Stephanie M. H. Camp, *Closer to Freedom: Enslaved Women and Everyday Resistance in the Plantation South* (Chapel Hill: University of North Carolina Press, 2004); Anthony E. Kaye, *Joining Places: Slave Neighborhoods in the Old South* (Chapel Hill: University of North Carolina Press, 2007).

11. Nell Irvin Painter, *Sojourner Truth: A Life, a Symbol* (New York: Norton, 1996), 13.

12. Doug McAdam, *Political Process and the Development of Black Insurgency, 1930–1970*, 2nd ed. (Chicago: University of Chicago Press, 1999), ix–x.

13. Mary Ames, *New England Woman's Diary in Dixie in 1865* (Springfield, Mass.: Plimpton, 1906), 99–100 (spelling per original).

14. Rene Hayden et al., eds., *Freedom: A Documentary History of Emancipation, 1861–1867*, ser. 3, vol. 2: *Land and Labor, 1866–1867* (Chapel Hill: University of North Carolina Press, 2013),211–25; Edward Magdol, *A Right to the Land: Essays on the Freedmen's Community* (Westport, Conn.: Greenwood, 1977); Willie Lee Rose, *Rehearsal for Reconstruction: The Port Royal Experiment* (1964; rpt., Oxford: Oxford University Press, 1978).

15. Speech of Bayley Wyatt, *Pennsylvania Freedmen's Bulletin*, March 1867, 15–16 (spelling per original); Hayden et al., *Land and Labor, 1866–1867*, 336–41.

16. Eric Foner, *Reconstruction: America's Unfinished Revolution, 1863–1877* (New York: Harper and Row, 1988), 302–78; Myrta Lockett Avery, *Dixie after the War* (New York: Doubleday, Page, 1906), 346; Adrienne Monteith Petty, *Standing Their Ground: Small Farmers in North Carolina since the Civil War* (New York: Oxford University Press, 2013), 14.

17. Marek D. Steedman, *Jim Crow Citizenship: Liberalism and the Southern Defense of Racial Hierarchy* (New York: Routledge, 2011), esp. 51–77.

18. Hayden et al., *Land and Labor, 1866–1867*, 55 (spelling per original).

19. Hahn et al., *Land and Labor, 1865*, 126.

20. Timothy Thomas Fortune, *After War Times: An African American Childhood in Reconstruction-Era Florida*, ed. D. Weinfeld (Tuscaloosa: University of Alabama Press, 2014), 15, 16–17.

21. Marek D. Steedman, "Gender and the Politics of the Household in Reconstruction Louisiana, 1865–1878," in *Gender and Slave Emancipation in the Atlantic World*, ed.

Pamela Scully and Diana Paton (Durham, N.C.: Duke University Press, 2005), 310–27; Steedman, *Jim Crow Citizenship*, 51–77.

22. 44th Cong., 2nd sess., *Senate Report 701: Report of the Sub-Committee on Privileges and Elections: Louisiana in 1876* (Washington, D.C.: Government Printing Office, 1877), 2:932.

23. Ibid.

24. Ibid.

25. Ibid., 2:937.

26. Steedman, *Jim Crow Citizenship*, 69.

27. "John Sherman Put to Shame, Eliza Pinkston Acknowledges Having Lied," *Weekly Telegraph* (Macon, Ga.), September 7, 1878.

28. "Death of Eliza Pinkston," *New York Times*, April 26, 1883.

29. 44th Cong., 2nd sess., *Senate Report 701*, 2:915, 917 (spelling per original).

30. Rebecca Scott, *Degrees of Freedom: Louisiana and Cuba after Slavery* (Cambridge, Mass.: Harvard University Press, 2005), 72, 294–95; A. O. Hirschman, *Getting Ahead Collectively: Grassroots Experiences in Latin America* (New York: Pergamon, 1984).

31. Elsa Barkley Brown, "Negotiating and Transforming the Public Sphere: African American Political Life in the Transition from Slavery to Freedom," *Public Culture* 7 (Fall 1994): 104–46; Tera W. Hunter, *To 'Joy My Freedom: Southern Black Women's Lives and Labors after the Civil War* (Cambridge, Mass.: Harvard University Press, 1997).

Black Constitutionalism and the Making of the Fourteenth Amendment

TIMOTHY S. HUEBNER

During the Civil War era, black activists created a new discourse of rights that challenged the U.S. Supreme Court's decision in *Dred Scott v. Sandford* (1857) and laid the groundwork for the postwar passage of the Fourteenth Amendment to the U.S. Constitution. Idealist in their orientation, these black constitutionalists combined the fact that the Constitution referred to enslaved people as "persons" rather than property, the principle of political equality in the Declaration of Independence, and the notion of God-given natural rights into a powerful critique of slavery and white supremacy. In contrast to Garrisonian abolitionists who condemned the Constitution as proslavery, black constitutionalists viewed the document as "the foundation of American liberties."[1] Unlike white abolitionists, who generally narrowly attacked southern slavery, black constitutionalists took aim at the entire legal apparatus of white supremacy in both the North and the South. Through newspapers, pamphlets, and speeches, through organizing in local churches and national conventions, black activists consistently advocated this distinctive brand of American constitutionalism.

Black constitutionalism was an expression of both belonging and aspiration.[2] It revealed the American identity of African Americans, a people whose roots in the country—whether they were free or enslaved—often went back generations and who had a hard time imagining themselves outside the republic. At the same time, black constitutionalism aspired to a better, more inclusive nation in which liberty would triumph over slavery and transcend distinctions of race or color. It included both a reading of the past and an agenda for the future. "We are Americans. We were born in no foreign clime," explained the delegates of the 1840 Convention of the Colored Citizens of New York. "We have not been brought up under the influence of other strange, aristocratic, and uncongenial political relations. In this respect, we profess to be American and republican."[3] More than a rhetorical tradition or "a counter-narrative of slavery and freedom,"[4] black constitutionalism represented the deepest hopes and beliefs of the black community—the desire to claim all that they thought they deserved as Americans, clinging to the promise of human dignity inherent in their Christian beliefs and implied in Thomas Jefferson's Declaration of Independence.[5] To be sure, black constitutionalism was not the only strain in the black protest tradition. Some African Americans advocated emigration, particularly after the passage of the Fugitive Slave Act of 1850, and during the 1850s occasional calls emerged for violent resistance to slavery and racial oppression. But black constitutionalism represented the dominant and most persistent way of thinking in the black community, for it encompassed both principles and processes, which were simultaneously sincere and strategic.[6]

No one personified antebellum black constitutionalism better than Frederick Douglass. Douglass's most famous oration, "What to the Slave Is the Fourth of July?" was a trenchant analysis of enslaved people's relationship to the United States and emphasized the nation's failure to live up to its principles. Delivered in Rochester, New York, in 1852, the speech praised the founders as brave, heroic men who had been willing to sacrifice their lives for the sake of liberty.[7] But Douglass lamented that the ideals that the country enunciated did not apply to those of his race, a fact that made a celebration of the nation's birth little more than a charade. "What, to the American slave, is your 4th of July? I answer: a day that reveals to him, more than all other days in the year, the gross injustice and cruelty to which he is the constant victim. To him, your celebration is a sham; your boasted liberty, an unholy license; . . . your shouts of liberty and equality, hollow mockery." While Douglass criticized Americans for failing to live up to their own principles, in the process he exalted and venerated both the Declaration of Independence and the Constitution, describing the latter as "a glorious liberty document." Offering a critique of the Garrisonian position to which he had earlier subscribed, Douglass characterized the Constitution in favorable terms. "Read its preamble, consider its purposes. Is slavery among them? Is it at the gateway? Or is it in the temple? It is neither."[8] Douglass, in short, argued that both the Declaration of Independence and the Constitution served as foundational texts for black advancement.

Five years after Douglass's speech, Chief Justice Roger B. Taney denied black citizenship in *Dred Scott v. Sandford*. The case involved an enslaved Missourian, Scott, who alleged that his travels and residence in free territory with his deceased master made him a free man. Taney devoted close to half of his opinion to the issue of Dred Scott's citizenship, for only if he was a citizen of Missouri was Scott eligible to bring the case into federal court. Taney ruled that neither enslaved people nor free blacks could claim citizenship under the Constitution. "The legislation and histories of the times, and the language used in the Declaration of Independence," Taney wrote, "show, that neither the class of persons who had been imported as slaves, nor their descendants, whether they had become free or not, were then acknowledged as a part of the people, nor intended to be included in the general words used in that memorable instrument." Taney claimed that blacks "had no rights which the white man was bound to respect."[9] Because the framers had deemed blacks inferior to whites, African Americans—whether enslaved or free—had no legitimate claims to citizenship. Neither could a state confer citizenship on a black person within the meaning of the U.S. Constitution. Taney offered a racial notion of citizenship that presupposed white supremacy and disregarded any legal distinction arising from emancipation. Although the precise legal status of free African Americans under the opinion remained unclear, the decision had an immediate effect on them. In response to the Supreme Court decision, the federal government abruptly halted African Americans' preemption right (the right to settle on new territorial lands), as well as their ability to obtain passports.[10]

Taney's repudiation of black citizenship reflected the dominant view on the Court and in the country. Although most of the other justices wrote shorter opinions that avoided the citizenship question, Justice Peter V. Daniel, a Virginian, struck a similar tone to that of Taney. "The African negro race never have been acknowledged as belonging to the family of nations," Daniel argued. Two antislavery northerners on the Court wrote dissenting opinions in which they attacked this view of citizenship. Justice Benjamin Curtis's dissent in particular made the point that before the adoption of the Constitution, five states had granted blacks the right of suffrage, evidence that Curtis used to contradict Taney's claim that black people were not counted as members of the political community at the time of the founding.[11] Still, the majority of state courts in the North and the South during the era had ruled that African Americans could not be citizens. Even if his "they have no rights" rhetoric went beyond the legal language of those decisions, Chief Justice Taney's attempt to settle the matter of black citizenship probably reflected the general state of white legal opinion—and white public opinion—on the subject.[12]

Douglass rejected Taney's interpretation of the Constitution. Barely two months after the decision, Douglass mocked the idea that Taney had offered the final word on slavery. "The fact is," Douglass argued, "the more the question has been settled, the more it has needed settling." Then, summarizing Taney's opinion, Douglass offered this response: "You will readily ask me how I am affected by this devilish decision—this judicial incarnation of wolfishness! My answer is, and no thanks to the slaveholding wing of the Supreme Court, my hopes were never brighter than now." Describing the decision as "a scandalous tissue of lies," Douglass asserted that abolitionists and African Americans should remain steadfast in their commitment to reform: "This very attempt to blot out forever the hopes of an enslaved people may be one necessary link in the chain of events preparatory to the downfall and complete overthrow of the whole slave system."[13] Remarkably, Douglass grounded his hope in the U.S. system of government. "I know of no soil better adapted to the growth of reform than American soil.... The Constitution, as well as the Declaration of Independence, and the sentiments of the founders of the Republic give us a platform broad enough, and strong enough, to support the most comprehensive plans for the freedom and elevation of all the people of this country, without regard to color, class, or clime." Linking Taney's proslavery view of the Constitution with that of the abolitionist William Lloyd Garrison, Douglass dismissed their interpretation of the nation's founding document with regard to slavery, as well as Garrison's dis-Unionist solution to the problem. The text of the Constitution was not the same as the construction of it given by the Court, Douglass argued, and because the Constitution itself offered no specific "warrant for slavery," he rejected the proslavery interpretation as "a most scandalous and devilish perversion of the Constitution, and a brazen misreading of the facts of history."[14]

If Douglass focused mostly on undermining Taney's proslavery views, others challenged Taney's ruling on black citizenship. In a Fourth of July address, Charles Lenox Remond, a black abolitionist from Massachusetts, offered a sharp critique. "Shame on Judge Taney! Shame on the United States Supreme Court! . . . My God and Creator has given me rights which you are as much bound to respect as those of the whitest man among you, if I make the exhibitions of a man," he stated. "And black men did make the exhibition of manhood at Bunker Hill, and Lexington, and Concord, as I can well testify." To Remond, who had been born to a prominent free black family in Salem, Massachusetts, it was not up to the justices to decide whether blacks possessed citizenship or rights. Instead, black people's humanity, as well as their service and sacrifice in the American Revolution, conferred on them rights and dignity that demanded white Americans' recognition and respect. Noting Taney's "ingratitude," Remond went so far as to lament the price that blacks had paid in participating in the revolution, if such a decision was to be their recompense. "Better that any such man had folded his hands and crossed his knees, during the American Revolution, if this is the reward we are to derive from such hypocrites, such cowards, such pander[er]s to American slavery, as Judge Taney and his co-operators."[15]

Blacks' interpretation of U.S. history played a critical role in making the case for citizenship. A year after *Dred Scott*, black Massachusetts abolitionists William Nell and Lewis Hayden organized in March 1858 a public celebration to honor the memory of Crispus Attucks, one of the first martyrs of the American Revolution. Held at Boston's historic Faneuil Hall, the event included a host of abolitionist speakers, black and white, who drew a seamless connection between black sacrifice and black citizenship. For years, Nell had been researching and writing about Attucks, an enslaved Massachusetts man who had lost his life in the Boston Massacre, and Nell contended that blacks had played an important role in the nation's founding.[16] Some months after the Attucks celebration, in August 1858 the Convention of the Colored Citizens of Massachusetts took a strong stance in opposition to the ruling based largely on this reading of the American past. William Wells Brown, the convention's president, proclaimed that "we have rights, not granted by the American government, but by the Creator" and urged the assembled delegates to "recommend to the State to assume a defiant attitude towards the Dred Scott decision."[17] Lauding Justice Curtis's dissent, delegates agreed with his conclusion that blacks had been citizens in some states at the time of the founding and that article 4 of the Constitution thus affirmed that they possessed "the privileges and immunities of citizens in the several states." Proclaiming their devotion to their "native land" and describing "the claims of colored people" as "the claims of Americans," delegates highlighted the role of Attucks, while also noting black Americans' military sacrifice during the War of 1812. Finally, delegates pledged to oppose the enforcement of *Dred Scott* with all their might, regardless of the cost, and in rejecting the notion of emigration cast their lot with the country of their birth. On this point, Remond spoke for the convention: "We must resolve to remain here, in defiance of Judge Taney."[18]

Blacks' emphasis on citizenship stood in stark contrast to mainstream criticism of the decision. Across the North, Republican newspapers focused mostly on how the *Dred Scott* decision protected the interests of the "slave power" and undermined the possibility of sectional compromise.[19] In August 1858, just weeks after the Massachusetts convention, Abraham Lincoln and Stephen Douglas began their famous debates for the U.S. Senate. They, too, argued *Dred Scott* as a slavery decision rather than as a citizenship decision—as a matter of slaveholders' rights rather than as a matter of black people's rights. On black citizenship, the two were generally of the same mind. Douglas summarized his position in the first debate, which he frequently repeated. "I believe this government was made on the white basis," he announced. "I believe it was made by white men, for the benefit of white men and their posterity for ever, and I am in favour of confining citizenship to white men, men of European birth and descent, instead of conferring it upon negroes, Indians and other inferior races." Although Lincoln avoided such rhetoric, he nevertheless admitted that he had "never complained especially of the *Dred Scott* decision because it held that a negro could not be a citizen."[20] Lincoln did repeatedly attack Taney's claim that Congress could not interfere with slaveholding in the territories, arguing that the founders had no intention to enshrine slaveholding as a constitutional right.[21] But he remained silent on Taney's conclusions about black citizenship.

African American critics went well beyond Lincoln's narrow critique of *Dred Scott*. Taney's claim that blacks "had no rights which the white man was bound to respect" became a rallying point for the growing group of northern black activists who sought not only to end slavery but also to advance the cause of black citizenship and rights.[22] In September 1858, the Suffrage Convention of the Colored Citizens of New York, for example, excoriated the Court. "The Dred Scott decision is a foul and infamous lie—which neither black men or white men are bound to respect," the delegates exclaimed. They expressed particular outrage at Taney's interpretation of the Constitution and the Declaration of Independence: "In order to satisfy the wolfish appetite of the oligarchy, Judge Taney and his concurring confederates were obliged to assume that the once-revered signers of the Declaration of Independence, and the framers of the Constitution, were a band of hypocritical scoundrels and selfish tyrants." Asserting that Taney's opinion violated American principles and precedents, including the Northwest Ordinance of 1787 (which had banned slavery north of the Ohio River), the delegates claimed the common humanity of blacks and whites, affirming a radically inclusive vision of equality. "We therefore, called upon all who subscribe to the theory of human rights set forth in the Declaration of American Independence, to trample, in self-defense, the dicta of Judge Taney beneath their feet, as of no binding authority."[23] The Convention of the Colored Men of Ohio, held in Cincinnati in November 1858, just a few weeks after Douglas's defeat of Lincoln, repudiated the decision in similar terms. "We trample the Fugitive Slave Law and the dicta of the Dred Scott decision beneath our feet, as huge outrages, not only upon the Declaration of Independence and Constitution of the United States, but upon humanity itself." Delegates not only called for the abolition of slavery, but also for the repeal of "all laws that make complexional discriminations." Rejecting emigration, they resolved to remain and "achieve our rights at home."[24]

The following year black leaders continued to criticize the *Dred Scott* decision and to affirm their status as citizens. In August 1859, the president of the New England Colored Citizens Convention, George T. Downing of Rhode Island, made a passionate address in which he argued that African Americans had an "inseparable, providential identity" with the United States that included a deep connection to the principles on which it had been founded, "which were the uplifting of man—universal brotherhood." Although he took note of "Fugitive Slave Laws, Dred Scott decisions, American Colonization Societies," he argued that while such things "annoy," they "cannot permanently affect us." Unwilling to accept the notion of the United States as a white man's country, the assembly crafted a resolution that rejected the decision as "marked by a brutality of spirit, . . . a wanton perversion of the Constitution of the United States with regard to the rights of American citizens [and] an audacious denial of all the principles of justice and humanity." Delegates not only rejected emigration as an alternative, they also decided to form a committee that would, in consultation with black leaders throughout the North, petition Congress to "remove the disabilities under which we now labor, on account of the unrighteous Dred Scott decision."[25]

Overall, black activists remained hopeful and united in their opposition to *Dred Scott*. Never questioning the legitimacy of the U.S. Supreme Court or its power of judicial review, they always argued against the decision on principle, disagreeing with how the Court had interpreted the Constitution and forcefully offering their own interpretation of the country's founding. Linking their humanity, American identity, and historic military service to citizenship, they championed their belief that rights came from God, from the Declaration of Independence, and from the U.S. Constitution. Determined to defy Taney and continue the struggle, they remained confident that history and justice were on their side.[26] Strikingly, free blacks never attempted to distinguish their own legal status from that of enslaved people. Instead, northern free black activists consistently made unequivocal claims to citizenship for all black people. Free Ohio delegates, for example, denounced slavery in no uncertain terms: "Millions of our brethren are publicly sold, like beasts in the shambles, that they are robbed of their earnings, denied the control of their children, forbidden to protect the chastity of their wives and daughters, [and] debarred [from] an education and the free exercise of their religion." Delegates went on to affirm that "the great principles of Liberty and Equality which are the boast of our nation, were intended to apply to us and our unfortunate brethren, the slaves."[27] Taney had grouped all African Americans together, and rather than emphasizing their own legal advantages over enslaved people and free blacks in the South, free blacks in the North accepted the legal challenge posed by Taney's opinion. All blacks—enslaved and free—deserved citizenship.

The presidential election of 1860 and the outbreak of the Civil War abruptly shifted the theater of black activism from the North to the South. When Lincoln, who had pledged opposition to an extension of slavery in the territories, won election to the presidency and southern states seceded from the Union, some enslaved African Americans sensed an opportunity. Barely a week after

Lincoln's inauguration, enslaved people fled to Fort Sumter in Charleston Harbor and to Fort Pickens in Pensacola, Florida. Although federal military officers at both sites sent the escapees back to their owners, the outbreak of war in April 1861 changed the Lincoln administration's policy, thus opening the door for continued action on the part of enslaved people. In May, while in command of Union forces at Fort Monroe, General Benjamin Butler confronted a Virginia planter requesting that three escapees who had fled to the fort be returned to him under the Fugitive Slave Act. Noting that Virginia claimed it was no longer part of the United States, Butler offered to return the enslaved people only if the planter swore an oath of loyalty to the Union. When the Virginian refused, Butler claimed the enslaved people as "contraband of war." In the ensuing weeks, escaping people began streaming into U.S. forts and camps, and by the summer the administration expressed support for this "contraband" policy.[28]

War presented the opportunity for both enslaved and free black men to take up arms in defense of the Union in order to stake a claim to citizenship. Only weeks after Fort Sumter, Douglass began urging the arming of black men. "Let the slaves and free colored people be called into service, and formed into a liberating army, to march into the South and raise the banner of Emancipation among the slaves," Douglass thundered in his monthly newspaper. At the end of May 1861, a meeting of African American activists in Boston boldly described the conflict as "a contest between liberty and despotism" and offered, quoting the Declaration of Independence, to "defend the Government as the equals of its white defenders—to do so with 'our lives, our fortunes, and our sacred honor' for the sake of freedom."[29] Douglass viewed military service as the surest path to citizenship: "Once let the black man get upon his person the brass letters U.S.; let him get an eagle on his button, and a musket on his shoulder and bullets in his pocket, and there is no power on earth which can deny that he has earned the right of citizenship in the United States."[30] John Rock, a free-born black man from New Jersey, agreed with Douglass. "Seventy-five thousand freemen capable of bearing arms, and three-quarters of a million of slaves wild with the enthusiasm caused by the dawn of the glorious opportunity of being able to strike a genuine blow for freedom, will be a power that 'white men will be bound to respect,'" he argued in a January 1862 speech in Boston, mockingly paraphrasing Taney's opinion. Still, Rock argued, military service and sacrifice needed to be explicitly linked to citizenship and rights. "Let the people of the United States do their duty, and treat us as the people of all other nations treat us—as men; if they will do this, our last drop of blood is ready to be sacrificed in defence of the liberty of this country. But if you continue to deny us our rights, and spurn our offers except as menials, colored men will be worse than fools to take up arms at all."[31]

Over time, white Republicans came to see the war as a means of ending slavery, and they enacted policies they believed would hurt the Confederacy, help the Union, and liberate enslaved people.[32] In 1862, Congress and President Lincoln abolished slavery in Washington, D.C., and banned slavery in all existing federal territories and any that might be acquired in the future. Not only did the law liberate the handful of enslaved blacks who resided in Nebraska, New Mexico, and Utah, but the legislation also directly challenged *Dred Scott*, which had denied to Congress the power to prohibit slavery in the territories. Most significantly in terms of citizenship, in November 1862 Attorney General Edward Bates responded to an official query from the secretary of the treasury about "whether colored men can be citizens of the United States." In a carefully reasoned legal opinion, Bates claimed that all people born in the United States possessed U.S. citizenship. Sidestepping the issue of enslaved people born in the United States, Bates concentrated on free blacks and concluded that no person born in the United States could be denied citizenship solely on the basis of their race or color. Bates dismissed the portion of the *Dred Scott* decision that pertained to citizenship as irrelevant, arguing that the ruling applied only to Scott's specific plea and possessed "no authority as a judicial decision."[33]

Black men coming out of slavery wanted the same guarantee of citizenship and rights that the attorney general's opinion offered to free black men. Lincoln's Emancipation Proclamation of January 1, 1863, not only claimed to liberate all the enslaved people in the Confederacy, it also affirmed the recruitment and raising of black Union regiments.[34] But black leaders still wanted to know if citizenship and rights were forthcoming. At a contentious public meeting about enlistment in New York in April 1863, Douglass admonished a crowd of potential recruits for their lack of enthusiasm. According to one observer, a man named Robert Johnson suddenly rose and defended the skeptical attendees, noting that the lack of "a proper respect for their own manhood" lay behind their unwillingness to enlist. "If the Government wanted their services, let it guarantee to them all the rights of citizens and soldiers," Johnson argued, to great applause.[35] In the spring of 1863 in New Bern, North Carolina, white abolitionist Edward Kinsley found that only if he submitted to a list of black men's demands would local African Americans, under the leadership of Abraham Galloway, respond to his efforts to recruit and enlist soldiers for the Union army. A fugitive from slavery who had traveled to the North and to Haiti, Galloway wanted equal pay for black soldiers, provisions for their families, schooling for their children, and the promise that captured soldiers would be treated as prisoners of war, rather than re-enslaved or executed.[36]

Unable to enlist, African American women emerging from slavery made their own claims to freedom and citizenship. Through their interactions with federal military authorities, African American women took unprecedented actions to demonstrate their demand for equality. In wartime Missouri, a state where the Emancipation Proclamation did not even apply, black women claimed freedom and more. They petitioned provost marshals for "free papers," lodged complaints against their former owners in military courts, and "joined the army" by following their husbands to the Union lines to work as cooks, laundresses, and nurses. They sought legal recognition of their marriages, and when their husbands died in battle, they claimed pensions as the widows of war veterans. These assertions of black agency, which often flummoxed Union military officers, showed that African Americans took the lead in ensuring that emancipation and equal rights emerged from the war.[37]

By 1864, an emerging black leadership class in the South joined a more seasoned cadre of black leaders in the North. On April 29, Galloway led a delegation of African Americans to meet with President Lincoln at the Executive Mansion.[38] Remarkably, after thanking Lincoln for issuing the Emancipation Proclamation, Galloway and his colleagues recited the words of the Declaration of Independence to the president—that "all men are created equal"—and pressed their case for black rights, including suffrage. In the days and months that followed, Galloway and other black leaders took their campaign for freedom and equality to the northern public, and in October 1864, 144 black delegates from seventeen states (including some from the South) and the District of Columbia assembled at a convention in Syracuse, New York. Claiming their share of the U.S. heritage of constitutional liberty, they drafted the "Declaration of Wrongs and Rights," a formal statement modeled on the Declaration of Independence, which listed the historical grievances of African Americans while also lauding black military service. Dismissing emigration, the delegates made their claim to citizenship. "Here were we born," they wrote, casting their lot with the country that had mistreated those of their race for nearly two and a half centuries. "For this country our fathers and our brothers have fought, and here we hope to remain in the full enjoyment of enfranchised manhood and its dignities." Asserting themselves as "citizens of the Republic," the delegates defined the rights they sought as "a portion of what we deem to be our rights as men, as patriots, as citizens, and as children of the common Father."[39] In January 1865, Congress passed the Thirteenth Amendment, which provided that "neither slavery nor involuntary servitude" shall exist, and by the end of the year the amendment won ratification.

For African Americans, of course, emancipation was just the start. Citizenship and equal rights—rather than mere freedom from bondage—had always been the goal. While official state conventions met during the summer of 1865 to establish new governments in the southern states in accordance with President Andrew Johnson's lenient program of Reconstruction, African Americans held their own conventions in order to press the case for their rights. In assemblies throughout the ex-Confederate states during 1865, black people repeatedly invoked the spirit of the country's founders and sounded familiar themes: their loyalty to the Union, their service and sacrifice as soldiers, and their shared constitutional inheritance as Americans. Rev. James D. Lynch of Nashville perhaps best captured the spirit of these gatherings when he announced to delegates of his state's freedmen's convention: "We have met here to impress upon the white men of Tennessee, of the United States, and of the world that we are part and parcel of the American Republic." Sergeant Henry J. Maxwell, who had served in the Third U.S. Colored Heavy Artillery in Memphis before traveling to the convention in Nashville, made explicit what African Americans were seeking: "We want the rights guaranteed by the Infinite Architect. For these rights we labor: for them we will die. We have gained one—the Uniform is its badge. We want two more boxes besides the cartridge box—the ballot and the jury box. We shall gain them. Let us work faithfully unto that end."[40]

In September 1865, black leaders came together for the first annual meeting of the National Equal Rights League. Gathering in Cleveland, delegates criticized President Johnson's Reconstruction policies for seemingly leaving the freedpeople in the hands of their former masters. By that time, many southern states had passed laws restricting the behaviors and economic opportunities of formerly enslaved people, laws that derisively became known in the North as Black Codes. Delegates to the National Equal Rights League called for the nation "to guarantee to us the full enjoyment of our liberties, protection to our persons throughout the land, complete enfranchisement... until all are equal as American citizens before the law." Calling on the U.S. Congress to take swift action, the delegates advocated a constitutional amendment that would prohibit any legislation "against any civilized portion of the inhabitants, native born or naturalized, on account of race or color."[41]

Black constitutional activism, bolstered by the bloody Civil War, helped shift the national debate over rights. In April 1866, Congress enacted the first civil rights bill in the history of the United States. The Civil Rights Act of 1866 established citizenship for all people born in the United States and for the first time articulated a list of rights to which all citizens could lay claim. The legislation stated that all citizens possessed the "right to make and enforce contracts, to sue, be parties, and give evidence, to inherit, purchase, lease, sell, hold, and convey real and personal property, and to full and equal benefit of all laws and proceedings for the security of person and property, as is enjoyed by white citizens." The bill also provided that the federal courts would have jurisdiction in cases involving any offenses under the act. Clearly, this act did not include all that African Americans wanted. The rights to vote, hold office, and serve on juries, for example, were not included in the rights of citizenship under the statute.[42] Still, the law did establish the citizenship of all people born in the United States, including all African Americans. Congress overrode a presidential veto and enacted the bill into law with the requisite two-thirds majority in both houses.

Southern violence prompted further congressional action on behalf of formerly enslaved people. During the war, Memphis had drawn thousands of formerly enslaved blacks, who had fled nearby plantations for the safety of the Union-occupied city. The fact that black troops remained at a local garrison especially offended local whites, and a confrontation between black troops and white police officers in early May prompted a three-day white rampage against the black community. At least forty-six African Americans lost their lives, and another seventy to eighty sustained wounds and other injuries. Outraged congressional leaders dispatched a three-man committee to investigate. By the summer of 1866, congressional Republicans saw a new amendment to the Constitution as the best long-term solution to the problems in the South. Johnson's speedy reestablishment of civilian governments in the South had yielded horrific violence, which served to rally Republicans to push for further federal oversight of southern affairs. Republicans favored a constitutional amendment that would reform the South and protect black civil rights, changes that would not be easily repealed by future Democratic majorities in Congress. The Senate had first agreed on the language for a proposed amendment in April, and southern atrocities—Congressman Thaddeus Stevens referred to "the screams and groans of the dying victims at Memphis"—played into the hands of the measure's proponents in the House.[43] In June, the amendment passed in the House of Representatives. The first section of the amendment wrote into the Constitution the principle that all born on American soil are "citizens of the United States and of the state wherein they reside" and guaranteed, as the National Equal Rights League had advocated, "equal protection of the laws." In 1868, after two years of political conflict between President Johnson and congressional Republicans, the requisite number of states had ratified the Fourteenth Amendment.[44]

Constitutional historians and legal scholars have written a great deal about the origins of the Fourteenth Amendment, particularly how the ideas behind it emerged from the antislavery movement.[45] Focused on understanding the original intentions of white lawmakers, they have devoted careful attention to the amendment's legal and doctrinal origins. However, they have all but neglected the sustained role that African Americans played in defining citizenship, resisting *Dred Scott*, and creating a new discourse of human rights in the United States. From the early decades of the republic, black activists had argued that slavery violated the Constitution, that the Declaration of Independence established political equality, and that God granted rights to all human beings. Their efforts surely made a difference.

NOTES

1. *Dred Scott v. Sandford*, 60 U.S. 393 (1857); "Minutes of the State Convention, of the Colored Citizens of Ohio, Convened at Columbus, January 15th, 16th, 17th, and 18th, 1851," as published in *Proceedings of the Black State Conventions, 1840–1865*, ed. Philip S. Foner and George E. Walker (Philadelphia, Pa.: Temple University Press, 1979), 1:262.

2. The term "black constitutionalism" comes from Christopher Waldrep, *African Americans Confront Lynching: Strategies of Resistance from the Civil War to the Civil Rights Era* (Lanham, Md.: Rowman and Littlefield, 2009), 13–38. See also Timothy S. Huebner, *Liberty and Union: The Civil War Era and American Constitutionalism* (Lawrence: University Press of Kansas, 2016); Donald G. Nieman, "The Language of Liberation: African Americans and Equalitarian Constitutionalism," in *The Constitution, Law, and American Life: Critical Aspects of the Nineteenth Century Experience*, ed. Donald G. Nieman (Athens: University of Georgia Press, 1992), 67–90; Benjamin Quarles, "Antebellum Free Blacks and the 'Spirit of '76,'" *Journal of Negro History* 61 (1976): 229–242. Black constitutionalism conforms to Patrick Rael's contention: "Black elites crafted challenges to racial inequality that appealed to cherished American values rather than stepped outside the bounds of the American ideological landscape." Rael, *Black Identity and Black Protest in the Antebellum North* (Chapel Hill: University of North Carolina Press, 2002), 5.

3. "Address of the New York State Convention of Colored Citizens, to the People of the State," as published in Foner and Walker, *Proceedings*, 1:21. I join Stephen Kantrowitz in taking issue with Manisha Sinha's assertion that "black abolitionists drew inspiration from the Haitian rather than the American Revolution." See Sinha, "To 'Cast Just Obliquy' on Oppressors: Black Radicalism in the Age of Revolution," *William and Mary Quarterly*, 3rd ser., 64 (2007): 149–60, 159 (quotation); Kantrowitz, *More than Freedom: Fighting for Black Citizenship in a White Republic, 1829–1889* (New York: Penguin, 2012), 473n68.

4. Manisha Sinha, *The Slave's Cause: A History of Abolition* (New Haven, Conn.: Yale University Press, 2016), 150–51.

5. Jacqueline Bacon, "'Do You Understand Your Own Language?' Revolutionary 'Topoi' in the Rhetoric of African-American Abolitionists," *Rhetoric Society Quarterly* 28 (1998): 55–75. Bacon describes the rhetoric of African American abolitionists as either "adaptory" or "advisory," with adaptory rhetoric being based on common cultural ex-

pectations and advisory being more critical in tone. Black constitutionalism encompassed both.

6. The major countertraditions to black constitutionalism were represented by Henry Highland Garnett and Martin Delany. See Garnett, "Address to the Slaves of the United States of America," and Delany, "Political Destiny of the Colored Race on the American Continent," as published in *Pamphlets of Protest: An Anthology of Early African-American Protest Literature, 1790–1860,* ed. Richard S. Newman, Patrick Rael, and Phillip Papsansky, 160–64, 226–39; Howard H. Bell, "Expressions of Negro Militancy in the North, 1840–1860," *Journal of Negro History* 45 (1960): 11–20.

7. Frederick Douglass, "What to the Slave Is the Fourth of July? An Address Delivered in Rochester, New York, on 5 July 1852," in *Frederick Douglass Papers,* ser. 1: *Speeches, Debates, and Interviews,* vol. 2: *1847–1854,* ed. John Blassingame (New Haven, Conn.: Yale University Press, 1982), 363.

8. Douglass, "What to the Slave," 371, 385. On Douglass's view of the Constitution, see James A. Colaiaco, *Frederick Douglass and the Fourth of July* (New York: St. Martin's, 2006), 73–108; Paul Finkelman, "Frederick Douglass's Constitution: From Garrisonian Abolitionist to Lincoln Republican," *Missouri Law Review* 81 (2016): 1–73.

9. 60 U.S. 393, 407.

10. Herman Belz speculated that Taney intended that they were either "subject nationals" or "quasi-citizens." Belz, *A New Birth of Freedom: The Republican Party and Freedmen's Rights* (New York: Fordham University Press, 1976), 20–21. On preemption and passports, see Leon F. Litwack, "Federal Government and the Free Negro, 1790–1860," *Journal of Negro History* 43 (1958): 269, 272.

11. 60 U.S. 393, 475, 550. On Curtis's dissent, see Stuart Streichler, *Justice Curtis in the Civil War Era: At the Crossroads of American Constitutionalism* (Charlottesville: University of Virginia Press, 2005), 119–50.

12. Mark Graber, *Dred Scott and the Problem of Constitutional Evil* (New York: Cambridge University Press, 2006), 28–30.

13. *Two Speeches, by Frederick Douglass: One on West India Emancipation, Delivered at Canandaigua, Aug. 4, and the Other on the Dred Scott Decision, Delivered in New York, on the Occasion of the Anniversary of the American Abolition Society, May, 1857* (Rochester, N.Y., 1857), 30, 31, 32.

14. Ibid., 35, 43, 45.

15. "Speech of Charles L. Remond," *Liberator,* July 10, 1857, 110, http://fair-use.org/the-liberator/1857/07/10/the-liberator-27-28.pdf.

16. Mitch Kachun, "From Forgotten Founder to Indispensable Icon: Crispus Attucks, Black Citizenship, and Collective Memory, 1770–1865," *Journal of the Early Republic* 29 (2009): 249–86; Kantrowitz, *More than Freedom,* 219–22.

17. "Convention of the Colored Citizens of Massachusetts, August 1, 1858," as published in Foner and Walker, *Proceedings,* 2:97.

18. Ibid., 99, 101. At least one scholar, Todd F. McDorman, made a sharp distinction between Remond's rhetoric about the decision and that of Douglass, labeling Remond's an "insular" response and Douglass's a "redemptive" one. Despite Remond's harder edge, in their common emphasis on citizenship, rights, and American identity in critiquing *Dred Scott*, Remond and Douglass seem more alike than different. See McDorman, "Challenging Constitutional Authority: African American Responses to *Scott v. Sandford*," *Quarterly Journal of Speech* 83 (1997): 192–209.

19. For a sampling of newspaper opinion, see Paul Finkelman, *Dred Scott v. Sandford: A Brief History with Documents* (Boston: Bedford/St. Martin's, 1997), 127–67. For a discussion of the larger political consequences of the decision, see Don E. Fehrenbacher, *The Dred Scott Case: Its Significance in American Law and Politics* (New York: Oxford University Press, 1978), 449–550.

20. "First Debate with Stephen Douglas at Ottawa, Illinois," August 21, 1858, and "Seventh and Last Debate with Stephen A. Douglas at Alton, Illinois," October 15, 1858, in *The Collected Works of Abraham Lincoln*, ed. Roy Basler (New Brunswick, N.J.: Rutgers University Press, 1953), 3:10, 299–300 (hereinafter *CWL*).

21. *CWL* 3:299–300. See also Lincoln, "First Inaugural Address—Final Text," March 4, 1861, *CWL* 4:269–70, where Lincoln portrayed the existence of slavery in the South and the enforcement of the Fugitive Slave Act as settled questions, while describing the issue of the spread of slavery into the territories as the only issue dividing the country.

22. Taney's infamous words may have been some of the most significant in the history of the U.S. Supreme Court. See Timothy S. Huebner, "'The Unjust Judge': Roger Taney, the Slave Power, and the Meaning of Emancipation," *Journal of Supreme Court History* 40 (2015): 249–62.

23. "Suffrage Convention of the Colored Citizens of New York, Troy, September 14, 1858," as published in Foner and Walker, *Proceedings*, 1:99–100.

24. "Proceedings of a Convention of the Colored Men of Ohio, Held in the City of Cincinnati, on the 23d, 24th, 25th, and 26th Days of November, 1858," as published in Foner and Walker, *Proceedings*, 1:336, 335.

25. "New England Colored Citizens Convention, August 1, 1859," as published in Foner and Walker, *Proceedings*, 2:211–12, 214, 219.

26. James Oliver Horton and Lois E. Horton, *In Hope of Liberty: Culture, Community, and Protest among Northern Free Blacks, 1700–1860* (New York: Oxford University Press, 1997), 263. For a contrasting view, see Vincent Harding, *There Is a River: The Black Struggle for Freedom in America* (New York: Harcourt, 1981), 195–218.

27. "Proceedings of a Convention of the Colored Men of Ohio," 1:333.

28. On July 4, 1861, Secretary of the Treasury Salmon P. Chase sent a report to Congress recommending in general terms the seizure and sale of "the property of those engaged in insurrection." Over the next several weeks, the Senate Judiciary Committee crafted legislation that gave statutory structure and authority to Butler's initial order.

Congressional Globe, 37th Cong., 1st sess., app. 5 (1861); Allen Guelzo, *Lincoln's Emancipation Proclamation: The End of Slavery in America* (New York: Simon and Schuster, 2006), 31–46; Laura F. Edwards, *A Legal History of the Civil War and Reconstruction* (New York: Cambridge University Press, 2015), 64–89.

29. Frederick Douglass, "How to End the War," *Douglass' Monthly*, May 1861, as published in *Frederick Douglass: Selected Speeches and Writings*, ed. Philip S. Foner (1950; rpt., Chicago: Chicago Review Press, 1999), 448; "Resolutions of a Negro Mass Meeting," *Liberator*, May 31, 1861, as published in *A Documentary History of the Negro People in the United States*, ed. Herbert Aptheker (New York: Citadel, 1951), 1:464–65.

30. Frederic May Holland, *Frederick Douglass: Colored Orator* (New York, 1891), 301.

31. John S. Rock, "What If the Slaves Are Emancipated?," as published in *Lift Every Voice: African American Oratory, 1787–1900*, ed. Philip S. Foner and Robert James Branham (Tuscaloosa: University of Alabama Press, 1998), 367.

32. James Oakes, *Freedom National: The Destruction of Slavery in the United States, 1861–1865* (New York: Norton, 2013).

33. Edward Bates, *Opinion of Attorney General Bates on Citizenship* (Washington, D.C., 1862), 3.

34. "Emancipation Proclamation," January 1, 1863, *CWL* 6:30. See also Guelzo, *Lincoln's Emancipation Proclamation*.

35. James M. McPherson, *The Negro's Civil War: How American Negroes Felt and Acted during the War for the Union* (New York: Pantheon, 1965), 177. See also Brian Taylor, "A Politics of Service: Black Northerners' Debates over Enlistment in the American Civil War," *Civil War History* 58 (2012): 451–80.

36. David S. Cecelski, *The Fire of Freedom: Abraham Galloway and the Slaves' Civil War* (Chapel Hill: University of North Carolina Press, 2012), xiii–xvi.

37. Sharon Romeo, *Gender and the Jubilee: Black Freedom and the Reconstruction of Citizenship in Civil War Missouri* (Athens: University of Georgia Press, 2016).

38. Cecelski, *Fire of Freedom*, 115–16.

39. "Proceedings of the National Convention of Colored Men, Held in the City of Syracuse, N.Y., October 4, 5, 6, 7, 1864; with the Bill of Wrongs and Rights, and the Address to the American People," as published in *Minutes of the Proceedings of the National Negro Conventions, 1830–1864*, ed. Howard Holman Bell (New York: Arno, 1969), 42–43. Although cited on the title page as the "Bill of Wrongs and Rights," the document itself is titled "Declaration of Wrongs and Rights."

40. As quoted in Steven Hahn, *A Nation under Our Feet: Black Political Struggles in the Rural South from Slavery to the Great Migration* (Cambridge, Mass.: Belknap, 2005), 120. See also Judy Bussell LaForge, "State Colored Conventions of Tennessee, 1865–1866," *Tennessee Historical Quarterly* 65 (2006): 236–37.

41. "Proceedings of the First Annual Meeting of the National Equal Rights League, Held in Cleveland, Ohio, September 19, 20, and 21, 1865," as published in *Proceedings*

of the Black National and State Conventions, 1865–1900, ed. Philip S. Foner and George E. Walker (Philadelphia, Pa.: Temple University Press, 1986), 1:65.

42. Michael Les Benedict, "'Membership of a Nation, and Nothing More': The Civil Rights Act of 1866 and the Narrowing of Citizenship in the Civil War Era," in *The Greatest and Grandest Act: The Civil Rights Act of 1866 from Reconstruction to Today*, ed. Christian G. Samito (Carbondale: Southern Illinois University Press, 2018), 9–36.

43. Stephen V. Ash, *A Massacre in Memphis: The Race Riot That Shook the Nation One Year after the Civil War* (New York: Hill and Wang, 2013); Thaddeus Stevens, "Speech on the Fourteenth Amendment," May 10, 1866, in *Selected Papers of Thaddeus Stevens*, vol. 2: *April 1865–August 1868*, ed. Beverly Wilson Palmer and Holly Byers Ochoa (Pittsburgh, Pa.: University of Pittsburgh Press, 1998), 138.

44. White Republicans acceded to this redefinition of citizenship largely because they witnessed black people's service and sacrifice in the war. Belz, *New Birth of Freedom*, 17–34. See also Carole Emberton, "'Only Murder Makes Men': Reconsidering the Black Military Experience," *Journal of the Civil War Era* 2 (2012): 369–93.

45. See, e.g., Jacobus tenBroek, *Equal under Law* (London: Collier, 1965); William Wiecek, *The Sources of Antislavery Constitutionalism in America, 1760–1848* (Ithaca, N.Y.: Cornell University Press, 1977), 249–75; Belz, *New Birth of Freedom*; Herman Belz, *Emancipation and Equal Rights: Politics and Constitutionalism in the Civil War Era* (New York: Norton, 1978), 108–40; James Kettner, *The Development of American Citizenship, 1608–1870* (Chapel Hill: University of North Carolina Press, 1978), 287–351; Paul Finkelman, "Prelude to the Fourteenth Amendment: Black Legal Rights in the Antebellum North," *Rutgers Law Journal* 17 (1986): 415–82; William E. Nelson, *The Fourteenth Amendment: From Political Principle to Judicial Doctrine* (Cambridge, Mass.: Harvard University Press, 1988); Earl M. Maltz, "Fourteenth Amendment Concepts in the Antebellum Era," *American Journal of Legal History* 32 (1988): 305–46; Louisa M. A. Heiny, "Radical Abolitionist Influence on Federalism and the Fourteenth Amendment," *American Journal of Legal History* 49 (2007): 180–96; Gerard N. Magliocca, *American Founding Son: John Bingham and the Invention of the Fourteenth Amendment* (New York: New York University Press, 2013).

"The Violent Bear It Away"

White Responses to Black Political Mobilization during Reconstruction

CAROLE EMBERTON

The title of this chapter comes from Matthew 11:12 in the New Testament. It is also the title of a southern gothic novel by Flannery O'Connor that explores the inescapable mix of religious fundamentalism and violence that O'Connor saw as endemic to southern society—indeed, its defining characteristic.[1] However, I would like to challenge the conventional assumption that the violence we so often associate with the South is unique to that region. Certainly, the image of the violent South has animated popular thinking about the region and its relationship to the rest of the country for centuries. From Thomas Jefferson's list of distinctive character traits, which he attributed in large part to the South's hotter climate, to the continuing red state–blue state division that dominates much of our current political analysis, the South has functioned as the nation's foil in terms of race, religion, and class.[2] Or, as Shreve McCannon, Quentin Compson's Canadian roommate at Harvard, asked after he heard the bloody, incestuous story of the rise and fall of the archetypal slave owner Thomas Sutpen in William Faulkner's *Absalom, Absalom!*, "Jesus, the South is fine, isn't it? It's better than the theater, isn't it? It's better than Ben Hur, isn't it."[3]

Rather than run off into the night proclaiming that I do not hate the South (as Compson did), here I discuss how the trope of the violent South obscures the ways that Reconstruction-era violence reflected deeply held American ideas and values about manhood and citizenship. Instead of setting the South apart from the broader sweep of American nationalism that emerged after the Civil War, the violent words and actions of white southerners placed them firmly within it. Furthermore, Reconstruction-era violence, in which the Memphis Massacre was but an opening act, did more than simply stamp out much of the grassroots black political organizing in the Deep South or break up freedpeople's efforts to obtain land and economic independence. It did all this, of course, but violent spectacles like the one in Memphis in 1866 and later in Camilla, Georgia (1868); Colfax, Louisiana (1873); Eufaula, Alabama (1874);

Coushatta, Louisiana (1874); Vicksburg, Mississippi (1875); and Hamburg, South Carolina (1876) watered the seeds of white supremacy not only in the South but also throughout the entire nation. In order to fully understand the violent white responses to black political mobilization in the Reconstruction South, we must begin at the end—that is, at the end of Reconstruction, which coincided with the nation's centennial celebration in 1875–1876.

To mark the start of the centennial celebration season, the Washington Light Infantry, a militia unit from Charleston, South Carolina, was invited to participate in the Bunker Hill memorial ceremony in Boston. Organized in 1807, the unit had been involved in most of the major military actions of the nineteenth century. During the Civil War, its primary function had been the defense of Charleston, but some regiments saw action in Virginia, most notably at the Battle of Petersburg. The Washington Light Infantry was reorganized in the mid-1870s as part of the South Carolina rifle club movement, which resulted in the proliferation of paramilitary units dedicated to the "protection" of white men's rights. It also helped Wade Hampton take the governorship in 1876 as part of his Red Shirt organization, whose motto was "peaceably if we can, forcibly if we must."[4]

Not knowing the role that the Washington Light Infantry would play the next year in his administration's violent unraveling, South Carolina governor Daniel Chamberlain, a Massachusetts native, heartily endorsed the unit and its mission of brotherly goodwill. He was not alone. As the company left Charleston Harbor, U.S. troops stationed there bade the infantrymen farewell with a thirty-seven-gun salute. Northern newspapers charted their trip day-by-day, noting the dignitaries that greeted them at each stop. In New York, the city's establishment feted them at the famed Delmonico's restaurant. Upon the soldiers' arrival in Boston, the papers claimed this was "the first appearance on Northern streets of a military unit which had fought for the Confederacy," and cheering crowds turned out to meet them. Local leaders made speeches praising the renewal of bonds based in the two states' shared military history during the American Revolution. "We are strangers and aliens no longer," declared one member of the unit when its members visited Harvard University, "but brothers and fellow-citizens of one common country." General Fitzhugh Lee, a nephew of Robert E. Lee, attended the celebration with the other invited southern regiment, the Norfolk Light Artillery Blues. He summed up the feelings of all involved when he said, "When I reflect that I am an American citizen, and that I too am a descendant of those men who fought at Bunker Hill, and that I too have a right to be here and celebrate their splendid victory, I take courage."[5]

It was a dazzling display of the "mystic chords of memory" that Abraham

Lincoln had so fruitlessly called forth in April 1861. And then a peculiar thing occurred. The commander of the Washington Light Infantry presented the Massachusetts governor with a palmetto cane engraved with the coats of arms of both states. A palmetto cane was the weapon used by South Carolina congressman Preston Brooks to beat Massachusetts senator Charles Sumner to within an inch of his life on the floor of the Senate in 1856. Surely, no one at the event could have missed the irony. According to one attendee, "If the presentation recalled the treatment of Charles Sumner by Preston Brooks, no mention was made of the earlier use of a South Carolina cane."[6] There were other omissions as well. Nowhere in the accounts of the celebration appeared the famed Massachusetts Fifty-Fourth, whose gallantry in South Carolina had so recently been the pride of the Bay State.

What are we to make of the gift of the palmetto cane? Was it meant to be an apology of sorts for the actions of the long-deceased Brooks? Or did the governor and other northern delegates interpret it as an unwelcome reminder of previous hostilities? The lack of commentary makes it difficult to answer these questions with certainty, but it appears that the Massachusetts leaders accepted the gift as a pacifying act of friendship. As such, this moment stands as a prime example of the culture of white reconciliation that emerged toward the end of Reconstruction, a reconciliation premised on a shared tradition of martial manhood that glorified white male violence and erased black military contributions like those so recently made by the U.S. Colored Troops.

It had been less than twenty years since Brooks attacked Sumner, but in that short time, the nation's collective memory had been stretched and reshaped to such a degree that those who had not so long ago decried Brooks's actions as cowardly now embraced the militant southern legacy that he represented. That legacy was rooted in a paramilitary culture that had maintained slavery and, more recently, destroyed black grassroots political activism.

Paramilitarism has a long history in the South. John Hope Franklin traced its origins to antebellum slave plantations.[7] While local militias and slave patrols regulated enslaved people's movements throughout the backcountry, some of the nation's first police forces in southern cities like Charleston and New Orleans patrolled the line between slavery and freedom. Slavery required a considerable amount of surveillance and discipline, so much so that perhaps Michel Foucault should have begun his treatise on the origins of modern disciplinary culture with antebellum slavery rather than with the nineteenth-century prison.[8] In any case, the southern need for armed social and political regulation became in some ways even more crucial after slavery was legally abolished. With what had been the eternal dividing line in southern society—slavery—now gone, policing the boundaries of freedom and citizenship became even more crucial to the ability of southern whites to control the exercise of political and civil rights. The eagerness with which freedpeople seized freedom and the opportunities it afforded them to vote, run for public office, go to school, and work for themselves underlined that reality. So, in one sense, the extent of Reconstruction-era violence signaled the success of Radical Reconstruction.

The costumed nightriders known as the Ku Klux Klan attempted to enforce black subservience in the late 1860s and early 1870s, until a series of federal prosecutions largely broke up the organization. But soon, armed white men who eschewed the now-illegal hoods continued the Klan's terrorist campaign against southern blacks and their white Republican allies. The White Leagues openly embraced violence and were unafraid of being associated with it. While southern elites and Democratic leaders had tended to publicly denounce the Klan as ruffians, undisciplined rabble, and misguided youth, that was not the case with the White Leagues. When their campaign of terror began in 1873 in Louisiana, the valorization of white violence was central to their identity and appeal. Southern newspapers praised how the leagues demonstrated "the aggressive instinct of the white people" to the extent that the brutal suppression of black political independence became naturalized. White Liners in Mississippi declared that their violence against black people was "not only lawful, but eminently proper and essentially necessary for the protection of public and private rights." White Leagues built in a constitutional argument for their violence, which had been absent from the Klan's self-justifications. In New Orleans, the Crescent City White League (CCWL), which was composed of former Confederate officers and the sons of some of the city's wealthiest families, effected a coup d'etat of the state government in September 1874, after the Republican-controlled and racially integrated Metropolitan Police seized a shipment of arms that the CCWL had secretly purchased. Using the Second Amendment as a justification for their armed takeover of the state, the CCWL members referred to themselves as "minutemen" poised to reclaim the rights that their revolutionary forefathers had won a century before.[9]

Hardliners in the Deep South understood violence as the key to political and social change. Through the language and imagery of war, they presented the political contests of the mid-1870s as battles, including the presidential election in 1876. The metaphor of war served to justify the violent Redemption of the South and the reestablishment of what was known as "home rule," but it also situated white paramilitaries squarely in the U.S. revolutionary tradition. The White Leagues were conscious of the need to appeal to outsiders and convince northerners of the validity of their violent struggle. It was the only way to avoid federal interference in situations such as when in 1874, President Ulysses

S. Grant used federal troops to reinstall the elected officials that the CCWL had run out a few days after the league's rebellion. "Is there no language strong enough to awake the people of the North to a sense of the danger which threatens to forever bury their liberties?" wondered a white man from Tangipahoa Parish. That man recognized that southerners were acting on a national stage, not just a local one. In order for the Democratic Party to ultimately succeed, a majority of white northern voters would have to come to feel that the cause of white supremacy was theirs too.[10]

The incidents of violence the White Leagues orchestrated across the Deep South served a number of purposes. First and foremost, they stamped out black political organizations. This was the violence's most straightforward, utilitarian function. But southern violence also possessed a performative function that was less straightforward. On the one hand, participating in these very public actions—forcing elected officials to resign their offices at gunpoint or leading an all-out military engagement with a city police force—allowed white men to perform their revolutionary heritage and appeal to broader American sensibilities about the necessity of fighting to demonstrate one's worthiness as a citizen. That such actions were performed openly, undisguised, in broad daylight demonstrated their legitimacy. On the other hand, the extreme nature of much of the violence against black people—the maimings, murders, postmortem mutilations, and other humiliations—exhibited a level of white rage that far exceeded what was strictly necessary to keep black people from voting. For instance, the massacre of at least fifty-nine freedmen in Colfax, Louisiana, on Easter Sunday 1873 exemplifies what Holocaust survivor Primo Levi called "violenzia inutile," or useless violence. As Levi pointed out in his rumination about the torture of Jewish prisoners in Nazi camps, useless violence is not really useless. It becomes "an end in itself, the sole purpose of inflicting pain." Stripping prisoners naked, refusing them facilities for bathing or relieving themselves, tattooing them with numbers that replaced their names, forcing the sick and nearly dead on thousand-mile journeys in fetid railway cars only to shoot them upon arrival—these gratuitous acts of cruelty dehumanized the victims and gave some perpetrators a sadistic sense of pleasure. More important, Levi argued, the humiliation and degradation forced Jewish prisoners to perform their own inferiority, allowing Germans to feel justified in their persecution. "Before dying," Levi wrote, "the victim must be degraded, so that the murderer will be less burdened by guilt."[11]

There were moments when white southerners exhibited this type of "usless" violence. At Colfax, whites cut the throats of dead bodies in a final silencing of black opposition and dissent. The corpses were "badly shot to pieces" and received "numerous wounds to the head." The faces of some victims had been

Mounted night riders hunting black men in Gibson County, West Tennessee. Drawing by W. Webb Metz, *Frank Leslie's Illustrated Newspaper*, September 19, 1874. Prints and Photographs Division, Library of Congress, Washington, D.C.

virtually erased by head trauma, a calling card of genocidal violence in places like Rwanda in the twentieth century. The U.S. attorney who unsuccessfully prosecuted the perpetrators believed that the aim of the attack had been to wipe out the black population of Grant Parish. He found that the level of violence exhibited "a wantonness of killing uncalled for by anything except that motive."[12]

For Louisiana whites, the Colfax Massacre formed the basis of an emerging violent subjectivity that shaped their understanding of themselves as white people. These gruesome, murderous actions were not dismissed as the work of "ruffians" from other states or even as regrettable lapses in control of otherwise good men. Rather, they represented important messages about the nature of politics and the problem of black freedom. Emboldened by the acquittal of the perpetrators the following year, the White Leagues openly praised the massacre as a "wholesome lesson" to black people who dared to defy white authority. Despite the extreme brutality exhibited at Colfax, the White League newspapers declared it was the work of "cool, determined, and just men, who knew just how far to go." Louisiana, and indeed the rest of the South, needed more men like them, who were "bold and resolute" and not "afraid of a little bloodletting."[13]

While atrocities like Colfax communicated "lessons" to southern blacks about the cost of defiance, they also communicated an important message to whites who were reluctant to join the movement. White unity in the South is often taken for granted, and historians sometimes overlook the political divisions that fractured whites, mainly along class lines. A number of "Fusion" or cooperationist tickets had successfully, albeit temporarily, united moderate Democrats and Republicans in Mississippi and Louisiana. Fusionists campaigned for black votes and in some places endorsed black candidates, much to the chagrin of conservative Democrats and race-baiting hardliners. Fusionists also tended to support industrial interests, like railroads, which threatened to further alienate the former planters, whose interests were in agriculture.

From the beginning, there had been white men opposed to the formation of the White Man's Party in Louisiana, pushing instead for a People's Party that welcomed black support. These Fusionists became the sworn enemies of the White Leagues, who viewed them as far more dangerous than the "deluded negroes," whose ignorance was expected. Even a white man who wanted to avoid politics altogether was "a traitor to his race and to his country, and false to his wife and children, and deserves to be ruled forever by negroes." According to the White Leagues, white men must actively support their cause or risk the leagues' wrath. "Words of sympathy will not do," warned the *People's Vindicator*. "When a war of the races is imminent . . . [whites] should be found on one side with the Caucasian race." The White Leagues declared war on whites as well as blacks, encouraging members to ostracize those who refused to join. The *Franklin Enterprise* in Louisiana advocated keeping a "book of remembrance" of those who refused to join the league so that their progeny would be "forever cast out from all association with the Caucasian race."[14] John R. Lynch, a black congressman from Natchez, Mississippi, recalled how local blacks tried in vain to keep their white allies from deserting them. They were informed that "no white man [who supported black people] can live in the South in the future . . . unless he is willing and prepared to live a life of social isolation and political oblivion."[15]

Threats of ostracization, however vitriolic, paled in comparison to the threats of physical harm or death that hung over whites who failed to hoist the banner of white supremacy high enough. "The white men who ally themselves with negroes in this conflict need not expect any better fate than they—fact is, they will be first to suffer," warned the *Forest Register* in Mississippi. Similarly, the *Yazoo Democrat* called for a "stout rope and short shrift" for any white man who opposed the "Mississippi Plan" of violent Redemption. When a northern observer traveling through the state in 1875 asked one White Liner how he expected to steer all the white people "with all their diverging views" into the movement, the White Liner simply replied, "We'll make it too damn hot for them to stay out."[16]

In the aftermath of Colfax, one witness surmised that "one half of the white population took to the woods" in fear of their lives from marauding whites. "The effect of the Colfax murder and the subsequent murders near Coushatta," he explained, "with the use made of them by keeping them constantly in the minds of the people" was not only a landslide Democratic victory at the polls in the fall (in some parishes, not a single Republican vote was cast), but also the coalescence of white supremacy.[17] Although it had to be forced into existence with brutality, white unity nonetheless emerged from those violent assaults on freedpeople and their white allies. In other words, violence brought white supremacy into being, not the other way around. The Colfax Massacre inaugurated the White League movement in Louisiana, which then spread to Mississippi and South Carolina. Colfax mobilized white southerners by giving tangibility to their cause—not a lost cause but a very winnable one.

To return to the Bunker Hill ceremony, the Washington Light Infantry's gift of the palmetto cane therefore symbolized more than the growing amnesia surrounding slavery, emancipation, and the Civil War. It also represented the shared history of violence that united white Americans. Instead of dividing them, this history brought white men together as soldiers in the common cause of "good government," which by 1875 had become the code phrase for white supremacy. Just minutes before the presentation of the palmetto cane, the former national leader of the Grand Army of the Republic had proclaimed, "All true men are with the South in demanding for her peace, order, and honest and good government, and encouraging her [in] the work of rebuilding all that has been made desolate."[18] Other speakers at the event decried the "mire of corruption and degradation" that had beset South Carolina in the wake of emancipation and black men's enfranchisement. The memory of the American Revolution thus paved the way for sectional reunification by allowing former enemies to see themselves as the torchbearers of revolutionary violence against corrupting elements that sought to destroy the nation's exceptional mission. White paramilitaries throughout the South in the mid-1870s invoked the memory of 1776 in their violent struggles against Republicans. "We complain of grievances a thousand times more monstrous than Boston port bills or paltry taxes upon tea and stamped paper," proclaimed the *People's Vindicator*. In South Carolina, Wade Hampton's Red Shirts marched under banners that read "1776–1876" and "What We Did in 1776 We Will Do Again in 1876."[19]

To gauge the success of white southerners' attempts to make their cause a national one, consider the northern reaction to General Philip Sheridan's efforts to quell the ongoing unrest in Louisiana. When the White League once again took over the state capitol in January 1875, Grant sent Sheridan to the city to restore order. After his arrival, Sheridan dispatched a telegram to the secretary of war, asking that he be allowed to treat the White Leagues as "banditti"—a term that stripped the members of their presumed legitimacy and cast them not as patriotic revolutionaries but as common criminals.[20] The telegram was leaked and published. The reaction in Louisiana was predictable enough. Sheridan was burned in effigy, the windows of his hotel were shot out, and he was hissed and booed in public. But the reaction of northerners was more surprising. "We have never published such a document before," wrote a shocked *New York Times*, "and we must say that nothing like it has ever been seen before under a country with a constitutional government." The *Times* then went on to compare Sheridan to Oliver Cromwell. "It almost induces one to believe that the world has gone back two or three hundred years in the theory and practice of government."[21]

Many northern Republicans publicly disavowed Sheridan's statements in an attempt to distance themselves from the brouhaha and its worsening political implications. Both the Pennsylvania and Ohio legislatures denounced the telegram and Grant's refusal to condemn it and immediately withdraw Sheridan from Louisiana.[22] "We are sorry to find the *Evening Post* [a Democratic paper] identifying the Republican Party with this reckless dispatch," the *Times* corrected. "The Republican Party consists of thousands of persons who have not yet had even an opportunity of expressing any opinion on Gen. Sheridan's blood-and-iron message, and who cannot in any way be held responsible for it." The "wild production of one fevered brain" should not sully the party's reputation for law and order. The Republican Party resented "any violation of the law, either on the part of Gen. Sheridan or of any intemperate or treasonable class at the South."[23]

Even while they acknowledged the "rascality" of Louisiana Democrats, the editors of the *Chicago Tribune* admitted that the Democrats' rhetorical ingenuity "very seriously complicated the Louisiana question." As a result, there had emerged a "dissatisfied and uneasy feeling among their constituents" that made it difficult for Republicans in Congress to "look with any gratification upon the spectacle of a State Legislature organized under the protection of Federal bayonets." The "broader view of Southern matters" that the *Tribune* encouraged Republican leaders to take reflected a growing consensus in the North that the federal government was no longer the protector of its citizens, as Republicans had claimed in 1865. Now it was what citizens—white citizens, that is—needed protection from.[24]

No one understood the implications of the "banditti" fiasco better than Sheridan himself. Writing in early 1875, he predicted, "the next rebellion was to be fought under the stars and stripes and in the North as well as the South." Sheridan also believed that white southerners had learned an important lesson from the Civil War. "The mistake [Confederates made] in 1861," he mused, "was to have had their own flag."[25]

In 1876, as Americans celebrated a century of independence, the country seemed to teeter on the precipice of another revolution. South Carolina's warlike Redemption inspired Democrats nationwide to make preparations for the fall's presidential contest. Reports of rifle clubs being organized across the North worried Republican officials to the extent that President Grant issued a stern warning to anyone who planned to disrupt Rutherford B. Hayes's upcoming inauguration. That contested election, in which Hayes's Democratic opponent, Samuel J. Tilden, had won the popular vote, spurred "indignation" conventions across the North; Democrats called for armed resistance to Hayes, and the sergeant-at-arms of the House proposed to "deputize" a hundred thousand men to enforce Tilden's election. Drunk with revolutionary imagery, Joseph Pulitzer, editor of the *New York World*, declared his readiness to "bare his breast to the bullet of the tyrant and rush headlong upon his glittering steel."[26]

In a staggering political conversion, former abolitionist George Julian, a congressman from Indiana who had supported Radical Reconstruction, the Civil Rights Act, and suffrage for all African Americans and white women, had become a Tildenite. At a Democratic rally in Indianapolis, Julian fired up his audience with invocations of both 1776 and 1861, reminding the crowd that "a century ago, our fathers took up arms in defense of their right to a voice in the Government.... We assert that right now, when we ask that the will of the people be registered as the supreme law, and that whoever may defy it by overt acts shall receive the same treatment which the nation awarded to the men who appealed from the ballot to the bayonet in 1861." Furthermore, Julian promised, "millions of men would be found ready to offer their lives as hostages to the sacredness of the ballot as the palladiums of our liberty."[27] To a modern reader, these statements may read like hyperbole of the worst sort, but the crowds in Indianapolis, Columbus, and elsewhere, by all reports, lapped it up.

Grant and Hayes prepared for an onslaught that never came, but the threat remained real. The South's Redemption had tapped into a strain of revolutionary romanticism and disillusionment with the federal government that coalesced in the centennial year to highlight the centrality of violence to American national identity. Americans were a people at war—with the indigenous people of the continent, the labor movement, immigrants and racial "others," and a growing host of enemies within, but white southerners were no longer among them. Ironically, as George Julian pointed out, war had reconciled the nation.

NOTES

Portions of this chapter previously appeared in chapter 6 of *Beyond Redemption* by Carole Emberton (Chicago: University of Chicago Press, 2013).

1. Flannery O'Connor, *The Violent Bear It Away* (New York: Farrar, Straus and Giroux, 1960).

2. Thomas Jefferson to Marquis de Chastellux, June 7, 1785, in *The Papers of Thomas Jefferson* (Princeton, N.J.: Princeton University Press, 1953), 8:184–86.

3. William Faulkner, *Absalom, Absalom!* (New York: Viking, 1990), 217.

4. Newton B. Jones, "The Washington Light Infantry at the Bunker Hill Centennial," *South Carolina Historical Magazine* 65 (October 1964): 195–204; Richard Zucek, *State of Rebellion: South Carolina during Reconstruction* (Columbia: University of South Carolina Press, 1996).

5. *Charleston News and Courier*, June 12, 14, 18, and 19, 1875; *Boston Post*, June 17, 1875; Jones, "Washington Light Infantry," 197–99.

6. *Boston Post*, June 17, 1875.

7. John Hope Franklin, *The Militant South, 1800–1861* (1956; rpt., Urbana: University of Illinois Press, 2002).

8. Michel Foucault, *Discipline and Punish: The Birth of the Prison* (New York: Vintage, 1977).

9. James K. Hogue, *Uncivil War: Five New Orleans Street Battles and the Rise and Fall of Radical Reconstruction* (Baton Rouge: Louisiana State University Press, 2006), 116–43; Lawrence N. Powell, "Reinventing Tradition: Liberty Place, Historical Memory, and Silk-Stocking Vigilantism in New Orleans Politics," *Slavery and Abolition* 20, no. 1 (1999): 127–49; Joe Gray Taylor, *Louisiana Reconstructed, 1863–1877* (Baton Rouge: Louisiana State University Press, 1974), 291–96; Justin A. Nystrom, *New Orleans after the Civil War: Race, Politics, and a New Birth of Freedom* (Baltimore, Md.: Johns Hopkins University Press, 2010). Accounts by writers sympathetic to the CCWL include Frank L. Richardson, "My Recollections of the Battle of the Fourteenth of September, 1874," *Louisiana Historical Quarterly* 3 (1920): 498–501; W. O. Hart, "History of Events Leading Up to the Battle of Liberty Place," *Louisiana Historical Quarterly* 7 (1924): 571–95; Walter Prichard, "Origin and Activities of the 'White League' in New Orleans," *Louisiana Historical Quarterly*

(Spring 1940): 525–43; Stuart Omar Landry, *The Battle of Liberty Place: The Overthrow of Carpet-Bag Rule in New Orleans, September 14, 1874* (New Orleans, La.: Pelican, 1955).

10. [Signature unreadable] to Tom C. W. Ellis, September 18, 1874, Ellis Family Papers, Louisiana State University, Baton Rouge.

11. Primo Levi, *The Drowned and the Saved* (New York: Vintage, 1989), 106, 126.

12. 43rd Cong., 2nd sess., House of Representatives, 261, pt. 3, "Louisiana Affairs," 414.

13. Ibid., 771–72.

14. Ibid., 763, 760, 758, 761, 772, 765, 764, 382, 314.

15. John R. Lynch, *The Facts of Reconstruction* (New York: Arno, 1968), 119–22.

16. *Forest Register*, September 28, 1875; *Yazoo Democrat*, September 28, 1875; Charles Nordhoff, *The Cotton South in the Spring and Summer of 1875* (New York: Appleton, 1876), 77, 175–201.

17. 43rd Cong., 2nd sess., "Louisiana Affairs," 312, 314.

18. *Boston Post*, June 18 and 19, 1875.

19. 43rd Cong., 2nd sess., "Louisiana Affairs," 759; Alfred B. Williams, *Hampton and His Red Shirts: South Carolina's Deliverance in 1876* (Charleston, S.C.: Walker, Evans and Cogswell, 1935), 63.

20. Philip Sheridan to Secretary of War [William W.] Belknap, January 4, 1875, Philip H. Sheridan Papers, Library of Congress, Washington, D.C.

21. Ella Lonn, *Reconstruction in Louisiana after 1868* (New York: Putnam, 1918), 298–301; Joe Gray Taylor, *Louisiana Reconstructed, 1863–1877* (Baton Rouge: Louisiana State University Press, 1974), 306–7; *New York Times*, January 7, 1875.

22. See John Y. Simon, ed., *The Papers of Ulysses S. Grant*, vol. 26: *1875* (Carbondale: Southern Illinois University Press, 2003), 22, 25.

23. *New York Times*, January 7, 1875.

24. *Chicago Tribune*, January 9, 1875.

25. Philip Sheridan to Orville Babcock, January 24, 1875, Philip H. Sheridan Papers, Library of Congress, Washington, D.C.

26. Quoted in C. Vann Woodward, *Reunion and Reaction: The Compromise of 1877 and the End of Reconstruction* (New York: Oxford University Press, 1966), 110.

27. Ibid., 112.

"I Have Had to Pass through Blood and Fire"

Henry McNeal Turner and the Rhetorical Legacy of Reconstruction

ANDRE E. JOHNSON

In a letter to the editor in the *Christian Recorder* dated August 31, 1867, Henry McNeal Turner (1834–1915) of Georgia chronicled some of the experiences of being a minister and spokesperson. He wrote about being "depressed with so many cares, responsibilities, and anxieties," even more so than he had while serving as a "chaplain in the United States Army." He mentioned that he had "been away from my family so long, roaming over hills and through the valleys of this country" that his own children no longer recognized him. He wrote that his "encounters, cares, labors, travels, night studies and such other burdens had made my head as gray at thirty-four years, as my family of people generally are at fifty-four years." Nevertheless, he closed this part of the letter by writing, "should I live to see next March, I propose to present to Bishop [Alexander Walker] Wayman one of the finest Conferences in the African Methodist Episcopal Church [AME Church], composed of Georgia ministers. Then, having seen thy salvation, O Lord, I hope to retire in peace in the comfortable shades of my family circle, and to the more limited responsibilities of the pastoral work."[1]

Turner's desire for retirement if he could "see next March" is understandable when one examines the work that Turner did during Reconstruction. In a speech before the African Methodist Episcopal Conference, Turner reminded his audience that "to recount my labors would necessitate the writing of a volume, which I may do at some future day; but for the present, it must suffice to say that I have had to pass through blood and fire. No man can imagine what I have had to endure but one who has [been] through it." Turner "preach[ed] three times every Sabbath and every night in the week for months." After each sermon, he wrote, he had to "come out of the pulpit and explain the history, character, purpose, and object of the [AME] Church for hours to satisfy the colored [people] and whites." In one year alone, he had traveled "over 15,000 miles

The Reverend Henry McNeal Turner was a chaplain in the First U.S. Colored Regiment. *Harper's Weekly*, December 12, 1863. Prints and Photographs Division, Library of Congress, Washington, D.C.

in organizing and planting churches and superintending the work together and [he had] preached and spoke[n] over 500 times."[2]

Like many other black ministers of the period, Turner's work was not limited to the ecclesiastical realm. Turner bragged that outside of Colonel John E. Bryant, a prominent northern leader of the Georgia Republican Party, he had done "more work in the political field than any five men in the state." Turner organized the Republican Party in Georgia and wrote that he had "put more men in the field, made more speeches, organized more Union Leagues, Political Associations, Clubs, and have written more campaign documents that received larger circulation than any other man in the state." He continued by reminding his audience that much of his work had not been "performed amid sunshine and prosperity."

> I have been the constant target of Democratic abuse and venom, and white Republican jealousy. The newspapers have teemed with all kinds

of slander, accusing me of every crime in the catalogue of villainy. I have even been arrested and tried on some of the wildest charges, and most groundless accusations ever distilled from the laboratory of hell. Witnesses have been paid as high as four thousand dollars to swear me in the penitentiary; white preachers have sworn that I tried to get up insurrection, etc., a crime punishable with death, and all such deviltry has been resorted to for the purpose of breaking me down.[3]

For Turner, attacks against him and talk of violence were not hyperbole. In fact, for African Americans during Reconstruction, these burdens were an everyday part of life. One example of this type of violence happened in Memphis, Tennessee, from May 1 to 3, 1866. A congressional committee that investigated the Memphis Massacre concluded that 46 black people died, 285 people were injured, and more than a hundred houses and other property belonging to African Americans were burned. However, what may have shocked many who heard the testimony or read the report was the number of incidents of rape.

> The crowning acts of atrocity and diabolism committed during these terrible nights were the ravishing of five different colored women by these fiends in human shape, independent of other attempts at rape. The details of these outrages are of too shocking and disgusting character to be given at length in this report, and reference must be had to the testimony of the parties. It is a singular fact, that while this mob was breathing vengeance against the negroes and shooting them down like dogs, yet when they found unprotected colored women they at once "conquered their prejudices," and proceeded to violate them under circumstances of the most licentious brutality.[4]

In listing the atrocities that the white mob committed, the report concluded:

> Hardly any crime seems to have been omitted. There were burglary, robbery, arson, mayhem, rape, assassination, and murder, committed under circumstances of the most revolting atrocity, the details of which in every case are fully set out in the testimony. In many cases negroes were murdered, and their bodies remained on the ground for forty-eight hours and had reached [a] stage of decomposition before they were buried; the relatives and friends of the murdered parties being afraid to appear on the street to claim the dead bodies, and the authorities permitted them to remain longer than they would have permitted the body of [a] dead dog to remain on the street.[5]

While historians see the congressional investigation as a positive step that led the U.S. government to take "extraordinary measures to protect freed people,"⁶ violence against African Americans went unabated. Despite major reforms under congressional Reconstruction, white terrorism was still part of the everyday lives of African Americans. For instance, Turner shared with readers of the *Christian Recorder*, the official organ of the African Methodist Episcopal Church, an incident of violence that happened to one of the deacons of the church. During a visit by Turner to Opelika, Alabama, Deacon Robert Alexander informed him that on a Thursday evening, four white citizens broke into Alexander's room at midnight and assaulted him, beating and stabbing him nearly to death. When Turner first saw Alexander, he wrote that he looked like a "lump of curdled blood." When several African American women went "screaming" to the agent of the Freedmen's Bureau for help, he simply replied, "I can't do anything for you," and according to Turner, "he never got out of his bed."⁷

In another report published in the *Christian Recorder* on February 23, 1867, Turner reported that while visiting one of his ministers, Robert Cromley, in Warrentown, Georgia, he learned that "several whites" had threatened Turner's life if he ever returned to that place. Turner's life was only spared because fifteen African Americans "armed themselves to the teeth, with every conceivable weapon and remained by him till he got ready to leave."⁸

Testifying before a congressional committee on November 3, 1871, Turner explained that "in a dozen instances, if I had not secreted myself in houses at times, in the woods at other times, in a hollow log at another time, I would have been assassinated by a band of night-prowlers or rovers." When asked if he had seen any evidence of night marauders injuring other African Americans, Turner replied that he had witnessed "scores of them." He recounted the times he had seen "men who had their backs lacerated" and men "who had bullets in them." He had witnessed others with their "arms shot off; shot so badly that they had to be amputated" and others with their "legs shot off."⁹

Turner had established himself as a public figure during the Civil War as a correspondent for the *Christian Recorder*. He wrote on issues of the day, church life, and happenings in Washington, D.C., and while serving as a chaplain, his correspondence from the battlefield became must-reads.¹⁰ It was during Reconstruction, however, that Turner's public persona was elevated, and he established himself not only in the black community, but in the white community. While he preached and built the AME Church in Georgia, Turner served at Georgia's constitutional convention (1867), was elected to the Georgia House of Representatives (1868), became the customs inspector and postmaster general in Macon (1869), won reelection to the state House (1870), served as pastor of St. Philip AME Church in Savannah (1872–1876), became publications manager for the AME Church (1876–1880), and was elected bishop of the church (1880). He did this while finding time to write regularly for the *Christian Recorder* and for other newspapers, magazines, and journals.

Turner's Reconstruction-era writing focused on issues, problems, and concerns that were germane to African Americans navigating the treacherous waters of the period. Despite the violence and uncertainty besetting African Americans after the war, Turner started the year 1866 on an optimistic note, speaking before a packed house at Springfield Baptist Church on January 1 in Augusta, Georgia. Organizers called the day the First Anniversary of Freedom, celebrating the end of the Civil War and the ratification of the Thirteenth Amendment, which abolished chattel slavery. Many in the audience that day were ready to tackle the rebuilding of the South through Reconstruction efforts. With celebration in the air and moving forward on the minds of his audience, Turner ended his speech by charging black people to seek reconciliation. "Let us love the whites, and let bygones be bygones, neither taunt nor insult them for past grievances, respect them; honor them; work for them; but still let us be men. Let us show them we can be a people, respectable, virtuous, honest, and industrious, and soon their prejudice will melt away, and with God for our father, we will all be brothers."[11]

This optimism led Turner to assist in the Reconstruction efforts in the state of Georgia, and one of the first places he turned his attention was the colored convention movement.[12] Starting in 1830, these conventions gave African Americans space and place to voice their opinions and concerns about the issues and problems many faced on a daily basis. The convention delegates promoted the ideas of equal treatment under the law, suffrage, temperance, education, and moral reform. Historian Howard Bell argued that the conventions not only "mirrored progress, but influenced Negro opinion, and demonstrated to the American public that the man of color was ready to assume the full responsibilities of citizenship."[13]

Ten days after his 1866 emancipation address, Turner joined other African Americans to hold a freedmen's convention in Augusta, Georgia. Turner made his presence known throughout the meeting by advocating for the masses of newly freed delegates. When one delegate suggested that *Cushing's Manual* be adopted as the rules governing the convention, Turner objected because many of the participants were not used to this type of formality. Turner thought that a few simple rules would suffice, and after much discussion, his suggestion prevailed.[14]

From this convention, delegates created the Georgia Equal Rights Association, which met in April 1866. The convention's president, J. E. Bryant, named Turner to serve as one of the editors of the association's newspaper, the *Loyal Georgian*. The participants also named Turner as their delegate to Congress to represent the interest of the convention. At the Equal Rights and Educational Association convention in October 1866, delegates appointed Turner to a committee responsible for conferring with the rival Union League with the goal of "uniting all the friends of equal rights in one convention." He also served on the committee tasked with "Address[ing the] Condition of the Colored People in the State." As at previous conventions, the participants selected Turner to serve as the official Washington delegate on behalf of African Americans in Georgia, and he recommended that the leaders of the convention publish the proceedings from the meeting.[15]

Writing weeks later in the *Recorder*, Turner praised the work of the African American delegates: "The convention of colored men from all parts of the State, which was held here a few weeks since, did honor to our race, and exhibited a degree of progress intellectually, and highly commendable, in a people so recently freed. There was marked ability developed in their entire proceedings, the idea that colored men could not govern themselves, if permitted, is all a hoax. The addresses which they prepared and memorialized the legislature with, will stand as a monument of colored ability in Georgia for centuries."[16]

While working in the colored convention movement during this period of his career, Turner's rhetoric continued to be both hopeful and optimistic. In a speech to the Union League Association on April 29, 1867, he said that it "behooves both colors to cooperate, to join hands, and strive to the same goal." He called for a unified South and argued that the "Southern gentleman was the best and truest friend of the Negro."[17]

From his letters to the Union Republican congressional committee, we discover how formerly enslaved people received and disseminated political information. Turner explained that he and others participated in "dialogues" that instructed freedpeople about their rights. Structured in a call-and-response fashion, leaders like Turner would "read over the dialogues" to the audience, who would respond according to a prepared script. Leaders would then comment on the dialogues at "great length, so that no mistake might be entertained."[18] For example, in one dialogue, Turner acted as a freedperson, and his colleague and friend Tunis Campbell played the role of what Turner called the "true Republican." Then Turner, taking the part of the audience, asked questions about the new Reconstruction measures, and Campbell, as leader, answered in a "suitable voice, giving emphasis to the facts being related." "You ought to have seen the effect which it produced," remarked Turner. "When Campbell would read some of those pointed replies, the whole house would ring with shouts, and shake with the spasmodic motions and peculiar gestures of the audience." Turner suggested that this way of learning had double the effect on the uneducated masses, and he ordered the dialogues to continue until the people "[knew] them by heart" and could "relate them from memory." According to Turner, many of the recently emancipated people sought this information. While traveling, he would come upon "25–30 people sitting under a tree reading the Reconstruction dialogues."[19]

However, this did not stop opponents of Reconstruction, and Turner wrote about disappointments too. Commenting on strife between landowners and laborers, Turner lamented that politically, things were at a "boiling point." In an article for the *Christian Recorder* in August 1867, Turner described the contest between the "retrogressive" and "progressive" parties as "bitter." He noted how the opponents of Reconstruction were doing "all in their power to retard, if not thwart the measure." Additionally, he called out Confederate sympathizer and future U.S. senator Benjamin Hill as one of Reconstruction's leading opponents. "The Hon. Mr. Hill," wrote Turner, has produced "several very bitter articles, denouncing everybody but him and his, which from their venom and malignant epithets did much harm among the common whites. He wrote some fifteen or sixteen articles which have been copied by most of the conservative papers, notwithstanding they were devoid of reason or consistency."[20]

Nevertheless, grounded in his optimism and belief in democracy, Turner held out hope for the Reconstruction project. In an editorial published on August 31, 1867, while admitting there had been a "vast amount of ignorance here among all classes, relative to the state of the country," he "thanked God that all parties are to be elevated through the ordeal [Reconstruction] we are passing [through]." He believed that Reconstruction in the state of Georgia was inevitable. In addition, he had faith that few white Georgians would "vote to keep up civil commotion and political strife," which would follow opposition to Reconstruction.[21]

Turner's hard work on behalf of Reconstruction efforts did not go unnoticed. He served as a delegate to the Georgia constitutional convention, and remembering that South Carolina had not allowed him a formal education while he was young, he offered a resolution that the state provide an education for all its citizens. According to one historian, in the preamble of the resolution Turner pointed out that the "moral, intellectual, and physical greatness of [a] nation was dependent upon the literary status of the people who support it, and that it was the duty of a democratic government to provide for the education of its citizenry, especially when the vote of the masses determines the issues, laws, and directors of the nation's destiny." When Turner's resolution was referred to the Committee on Education, however, the committee refused to report or comment on it.[22]

Because of his commitment and hard work on behalf of the Republican Party, in June 1868 the people of Bibb County, Georgia, elected Henry McNeal Turner to the Georgia House of Representatives. However, two months later, white legislators introduced a bill that denied elected African Americans the right to serve in the legislature because the newly adopted state constitution did not explicitly give African Americans the right to hold office.

After much debate on the measure to expel African American members, Turner addressed the body on September 3, 1868. Understanding that expulsion was a foregone conclusion, Turner proclaimed, "You may expel *us*, gentlemen, by *your* votes, today; but, while *you* do it, remember that there is a just God in heaven, whose All-seeing Eye beholds alike the acts of the oppressor and the oppressed, and who despite the machinations of the wicked, never fails to vindicate the cause of Justice, and the sanctity of His own handiwork."[23]

Despite his expulsion from office, Turner maintained hope that Reconstruction would work. In 1870, the states ratified the Fifteenth Amendment. Writing for the *Recorder* in May 1869, Turner had wondered if the amendment would lead to full equality. He called the amendment "incomplete" at that time because he feared that states would not ratify it, and he subscribed to the adage "a half [a] loaf is better than nothing at all." Turner also believed Congress had been too cautious and conservative with the amendment. Legislators had struck clauses that guaranteed all citizens the right to hold office and be jurors. Turner argued that the American people would have supported the amendment in its more complete form and that Congress risked compromising American ideals. Turner wrote, "Besides, a mere voter, or making a man a mere political Jack Ass is not an American idea of an elector, nor has it ever been, from the establishment of our government."[24]

However, when the states ratified the amendment, Turner celebrated its passing. "The ratification of the Fifteenth Amendment to the Constitution is the finish of our national fabric; it is the headstone of the world's asylum; the crowning event of the nineteenth century; the brightest glare of glory that overhung land or sea. Hereafter, the oppressed children of all countries can find a temple founded upon gratitude and religious equity, ample enough to accommodate them all." With the grandest of eloquence, Turner further proclaimed:

> This Amendment is an ensign of our citizenship, the prompter of our patriotism, the bandage that is to blindfold Justice while his sturdy hand holds the scales and weighs out impartial equity to all, regardless of popular favor or censure. It is the ascending ladder for the obscure and ignoble to rise to glory and renown, the well of living water never to run dry, the glaring pillar of fire in the night of public commotion, and the mantling pillar of cloud by day to repel the scorching rays of wicked prejudice. . . . It is a national guarantee, as fair as the moon, clear as the sun, and terrible as an army with banners. . . . The Fifteenth Amendment is

the shining robe covering in immaculate grandeur the nude and exposed parts of our country, which hitherto made her fragile and vulnerable before enemies.[25]

Turner's second reason for hope during Reconstruction was the passage of the 1875 Civil Rights Act. The bill explicitly banned discrimination from public places and was one of the last major reforms of Congress during this period. Drawing on his relationships with senators and representatives formed during his time in Washington, D.C., Turner lobbied, argued, and helped promote the passage of this bill. In a letter entitled "President and Civil Rights" published in the *Recorder* on November 26, 1874, Turner had criticized President Ulysses S. Grant when reports began to circulate that Grant, who was an early supporter of the bill, began to waver. Turner argued that Grant had "lost some of his ardor, and grown somewhat indifferent in regard to this all-important measure." Understanding that he was attacking a president popular with African Americans, Turner warned that no one, including the people who held "positions under [Grant]" and the ones who simply have the "good of the party at stake, should be silent." For Turner, there was "no party" when politicians were fighting over "his rights." He thought that every person "should measure their party's allegiance" as that party measured out their personhood.[26]

Turner saw the Civil Rights Act as the culmination of the Reconstruction measures. "Its failure is our failure. Its success is our success. Indeed, it holds in its grasp our destiny as a race. We stand or fall in that Bill." He continued: "Should it fail, I shall regard it as the indignant proclamation of heaven, saying *arise and depart, for this is not your home. This is a White Man's Government*. But if it succeeds, then it may be interpreted as the voice of God; saying to the Negro, 'Awake from your lethargy, and build schools, churches, houses, and prepare to run the race of life where you are.'"[27]

Despite Turner's optimism and high hopes for radical change during Reconstruction, the 1876 elections told a different story. Though the Constitution enfranchised black men, Turner noted that southern white conservatives had regained electoral power through intimidation, violence, and murder. In a letter to the *Recorder* published on December 14, 1876, Turner criticized the government and especially those in the North for not doing enough to protect the lives, property, and franchise of African Americans. For Turner, the nation was bound by every consideration to secure for its citizens the "protection of life and person." Instead, African Americans were hurled into a "vortex of a new revolution which would have taxed the skill and energies of the most enlightened people on earth." Accordingly, "the meanness of this nation towards the negro, will never be known until it is read in the glare of eternity." Further, he wrote:

When they say, "we have done everything we could for the colored people of the South" they utter a thousand falsehoods in one breath; and there is not a negro whose blood has been shed, that does not crimson the garments of every white man in the North. The best that can be said for this country is that it is a nation of murderers. The North has been killing Southern negroes as virtually as the Ku-Klux and White Leagues have, and every white statesman, orator, minister of the Gospel, merchant, doctor, and private citizen in this whole nation, who has not fought these massacres (for holding your mouth is no excuse) and the injustice perpetrated [on] the blacks, the nation's wards are guilty before God. And if they ever get to heaven at all, they will have to swim there through the blood of forty-six thousand negroes, which it is reported in Washington have been killed since January 1866.[28]

"May God slash this nation; may it writhe; may it groan and sigh; and may it bleed or die, or else learn wisdom; learn humanity black or white, brown or red," Turner concluded.[29]

Seeing the gains African Americans had made since the end of the war begin to erode, Turner, like many other black southerners, turned his attention to Africa. Turner became a staunch supporter and defender of African emigration, but his support of the primary engine of emigration—the American Colonization Society—elicited expressions of surprise. The ACS, after all, had been created by earlier generations of white supremacists, men determined to rid the nation of black people through a whole-scale resettlement to Africa. Thus, when word spread that the ACS had made Turner an honorary vice president, many African Americans issued strong warnings to him about working with the society. In a letter published in the *Savannah Colored Tribune* on February 19, 1876, Turner explained his reasoning, arguing that the only prospect for what he heralded as a "Negro nationality" lay overseas: "Don't you see it's a white man's Government? And don't you see they mean at all hazards to keep the Negro down? And don't you see the Negro does not intend to stay down, without a fuss and an interminable broil? Then why waste our time in trying to stay here?"[30]

In another letter published in the *Savannah Colored Tribune* on March 18, 1876, Turner again defended his emigration position:

> I am called a fanatic, a fool, an aspirant for royal honors, the would be king, etc. How long can the Negro race last in this country at such a ratio of murdering as is now in process of operation in this state[?] . . . No white man has been or will be arrested if he kills forty Negroes (I judge

the present by the past.). So you anti-emigrationists must now come up with your life preservers, or tell us how long the Negro race can exist at this rate before he will become exterminated. I am not complaining about it; I used to complain, but I have to quit; it used to be the fault of white men—but it is now the fault of Negro men. We all know our lives are not worth a cent.[31]

Henry McNeal Turner eventually left the Republican Party that he had helped to build in the state of Georgia. After a stint in the Prohibition Party, he did the unthinkable by supporting and openly campaigning for Democrat William Jennings Bryan in the 1900 presidential election against William McKinley.

In one of his best-titled editorials, "McKinley the God of Fool Negroes, Re-Elected," Turner connected his support for Bryan to the earlier days of Reconstruction. He noted that there was a major difference between the Republicans of the days of Reconstruction and those of the later era. The former he called the "grand galaxy of reformers" and suggested, "no grander men ever lived." But the latter were "deceptive pimps who are trying to palm themselves off as Republican benefactors." For Henry McNeal Turner, Reconstruction was where the United States first got it right—but eventually got it wrong.

NOTES

1. Henry McNeal Turner, "Letter from Rev. H. M. Turner," *Christian Recorder*, August 31, 1867.

2. Henry McNeal Turner, *Speech before the Conference: The Quarto-Centennial of Bishop Henry M. Turner* (Philadelphia, 1905), 113–18.

3. Ibid.

4. "Memphis Riots and Massacres," *U.S. Serial Set*, no. 1274, House Report 101, 39th Cong., 1st sess., 13.

5. Ibid., 22.

6. Stephen V. Ash, *A Massacre in Memphis: The Race Riot That Shook the Nation One Year after the Civil War* (New York: Hill and Wang, 2013), 187.

7. Andre E. Johnson, *An African American Pastor during Reconstruction, 1866–1880* (Lewiston, N.Y.: Mellen, 2013), 3:14.

8. "A Minister's Life in Danger," *Christian Recorder*, February 23, 1867.

9. Johnson, *African American Pastor*, 3:206, 209.

10. See Andre E. Johnson, *The Forgotten Prophet: Bishop Henry McNeal Turner and the African American Prophetic Tradition* (New York: Lexington, 2012), 27–30; "The Chaplain Letters," in Johnson, *An African American Pastor before and after the American Civil War*, vol. 2 (Lewiston, N.Y.: Mellen, 2012); and Jean Lee Cole, *Freedom's Witness: The Civil War Correspondence of Henry McNeal Turner* (Morgantown: West Virginia University Press, 2013).

11. Henry McNeal Turner, *Celebration of the First Anniversary of Freedom* (Augusta, Ga., 1866), 14.

12. Andre Johnson, "'Further Silence upon Our Part Would Be an Outrage': Bishop Henry McNeal Turner and the Colored Convention Movement," in *Colored Conventions in the Nineteenth Century and the Digital Age*, ed. Gabrielle Foreman (Durham, N.C.: Duke University Press, 2019).

13. Howard Bell, *A Survey of the Negro Convention Movement, 1830–1861* (New York: Arno, 1969), 13–14.

14. *Proceedings of the Freedmen's Convention of Georgia* (Augusta, Ga., 1866), 4–5, http://coloredconventions.org/items/show/524.

15. *Proceedings of the Council of the Georgia Equal Rights Association Assembled at Augusta, Ga. April 4th 1866* (Augusta, Ga., 1866), 4–5, http://coloredconventions.org/items/show/1193; *Proceedings of the Convention of the Equal Rights and Educational Association of Georgia* (Augusta, Ga., 1866), 2–3, http://coloredconventions.org/items/show/525.

16. Johnson, *African American Pastor*, 3:25.

17. "Affairs in South Carolina," *New York Times*, May 5, 1867.

18. Johnson, *African American Pastor*, 3:151.

19. Ibid.

20. Ibid., 3:41.

21. Ibid., 3:44–45.

22. Paul Lawrence Sanford, "The Negro in the Political Reconstruction of Georgia, 1866–1872" (MA thesis, Atlanta University, 1947), 18.

23. Ethel Maude Christler, "On the Eligibility of Colored Members, in Participation of Negroes in the Government of Georgia, 1867–1870" (MA thesis, Atlanta University, 1932), 96.

24. Johnson, *African American Pastor*, 3:58.

25. Henry McNeal Turner, *A Speech on the Benefits Accruing from the Ratification of the Fifteenth Amendment and Its Incorporation into the United States of America* (Atlanta, Ga.: New Era Printing, 1870), 13.

26. Johnson, *African American Pastor*, 3:91.

27. Ibid., 3:92.

28. Ibid., 3:111.

29. Ibid., 3:111–12.

30. Ibid., 3:99.

31. Ibid., 3:105.

Memory Battles

History, Memory, and the Meanings of Reconstruction

K. STEPHEN PRINCE

On a muggy late summer afternoon in 1874, the elite white men of New Orleans overthrew the state government of Louisiana. For weeks, the leadership of the Crescent City White League—equal parts social club, political movement, and white supremacist militia—had circulated false news stories about an imminent African American takeover of the city. On September 14, the highly organized companies of the White League met the city's integrated Metropolitan Police in a battle on Canal Street. It was a rout. More than eight thousand White Leaguers—many of them Confederate veterans—easily dispatched the Metropolitans and their allies, who numbered fewer than four thousand. With the northern-born Republican governor of Louisiana, William Pitt Kellogg, in hiding in the federal custom house, the White League installed its own governor. The White League held control for four days before federal troops arrived to restore Kellogg to power. Sixteen members of the White League and thirteen Metropolitan policemen died in the fighting. Initially, the skirmish was simply called the Battle of September Fourteenth. Over time, however, it earned a somewhat grander name: the Battle of Liberty Place.[1]

In the years after 1874, Liberty Place became a touchstone of white identity in New Orleans. On the third anniversary of the battle, the white residents of the city staged an elaborate memorial ceremony. After an early morning mass at St. Louis Cathedral, the leaders of the White League led a procession to the graves of its members killed in the battle, placing a white ribbon on each. An afternoon parade retraced the path that the White League companies had followed in 1874. The events culminated in a ceremony and a twenty-one-gun salute near the site of the battle. These elaborate rituals were repeated annually for several years.[2] In September 1891, a twenty-foot-tall obelisk commemorating the battle was erected on Canal Street. "No fitter spot could be chosen for a monument to celebrate the uprising of a whole people," wrote one of the city's papers. After a procession and a number of speeches, the statue was dedicated, and "the history of the Fourteenth of September was signed and sealed in stone."[3] Into the twentieth century, the city's newspapers celebrated the anniversary with effusive tributes to the "heroes of the fourteenth," whose deaths secured "liberty for the citizens of this state."[4]

From a historian's perspective, the immediate effects of the battle were actually somewhat limited. After all, Kellogg was restored to the governor's office in less than a week. The Republicans retained power in Louisiana for two more years, until the contested election of 1876 restored Democratic control. But none of this mattered in the realm of memory. After the fact, White League veterans and their supporters imbued the Battle of Liberty Place with extraordinary symbolic significance. In popular memory, the battle came to represent the victory of local control over federal despotism, elite rule over class confusion, and white supremacy over racial admixture. In the midst of Reconstruction—a period in which white southerners saw their world turned upside down—the victory of the White League was a reaffirmation of hierarchy and order. It is important to recognize, moreover, that commemorations of Liberty Place were never exclusively or even primarily about the past. To celebrate the events of September 14 was to employ the history of the city to make a claim on the present. The Battle of Liberty Place buttressed elite notions of status, belonging, and whiteness well into the twentieth century. White New Orleanians used the memory of Liberty Place to justify their continued control of the city.[5]

To study popular memory is to recognize a simple truth: historians are not the only ones with access to stories of the past. Other people turn to the past as well. Just as individuals' memories structure their behavior in the present, societies organize themselves with reference to shared ideas about the past. Unlike the professional study of history, however, popular memory does not aim for accuracy or objectivity. Memory does not need to be true to life; it simply needs to be useful. This point leads to two conclusions. First, popular memory tells us very little about the event being remembered and a great deal about the society doing the remembering. In other words, the 1891 dedication of the Liberty Place monument is better understood with reference to the 1890s than to the 1870s. Second, since memory is endlessly malleable, disagreement and divergent points of view are to be expected. Though some perspectives gain a wider hearing than others, historians of memory must be attuned to evidence of disagreement and to the existence of oppositional countermemories.[6]

So why does a chapter in a volume dedicated to the Memphis Massacre open with a discussion of an event that took place in New Orleans? This slight detour should serve as a reminder that many of the issues addressed in this volume are applicable far beyond Memphis. Reconstruction was a national project whose legacies were felt throughout the United States. Memphians were not alone in using the history of Reconstruction to shape their future. New Orleanians did it too, as did other Americans—northern and southern, black and white. Throughout the late nineteenth century and well into the twentieth, discussions of Reconstruction appeared with extraordinary frequency in political debates, popular literature and film, and works of history. On the one hand, the story of Reconstruction proved to be a potent weapon in the service of white supremacy. As they set about building white supremacy into the landscape and political structures of the region, late nineteenth- and early twentieth-century white southerners relied on a stylized and partisan narrative of Reconstruction. Reconstruction served as a cautionary tale, the ultimate example of the dangers posed by African American enfranchisement and political participation. At the same time, African Americans told their own stories about the post–Civil War years, keeping alive a narrative of Reconstruction focused on emancipation, enfranchisement, and black accomplishments. While white narratives of Reconstruction tended to minimize the period's extreme racial violence, black countermemories refused to remain silent or forgotten. Well into the twentieth century in Memphis, New Orleans, and beyond, the memory of Reconstruction remained immediate, relevant, and powerful.[7]

The most frequently cited end point of Reconstruction is 1877, when the ousting of Republican regimes in South Carolina, Louisiana, and Florida completed the Democratic Redemption of the South. Even before that date, however, white southerners cast Reconstruction as an unnatural and dangerous aberration in U.S. history. By rhetorically setting Reconstruction apart from the main currents of the nation's history, white southern opinion makers hoped to invalidate and delegitimize the period's legislative accomplishments. An 1874 speech by Mississippi representative Lucius Q. C. Lamar provides a case in point. The erstwhile topic of Lamar's speech was a contested gubernatorial election in Louisiana, but the oration actually served as a broadside attack on the course and conduct of Republican Reconstruction in the South. Lamar criticized the "pitiless provisions" of federal Reconstruction and accused congressional Republicans of pursuing a "policy that works the degradation, humiliation, wretchedness, and torture, for its own sake, of the Southern people." Lamar claimed that the "results of the war" had long since been secured.[8] White southerners had accepted the outcome of the war and the validity of the Reconstruction amendments, meaning that continued federal support of corrupt Republican regimes in the South was "undisguised tyranny."[9] He insisted that the Reconstruction experiment must be brought to a close in the interest of national unity and reunion. The central arguments that Lamar advanced in this speech, particularly the charges of federal overreach and a needlessly punitive Reconstruction, would be reiterated and recycled in much subsequent white southern memory work.

In 1890, Massachusetts senator Henry Cabot Lodge proposed a law that would have allowed federal oversight of certain southern elections. The Lodge Federal Elections Bill—white southerners called it the Force Bill—signaled a resurgence of the Republican Party's interest in African American voting rights, which had flagged after 1877. Largely in response to the Lodge bill, Alabama congressman Hilary Herbert organized a volume titled *Why the Solid South?* The phrase "Solid South" referred to the Democratic Party's electoral stranglehold on the region, and the answer to the question posed in the book's title was simple: Reconstruction. Herbert asked each of the contributors to write a history of Reconstruction in his own state. The essays faithfully reiterated the volume's main theme: federal control of southern racial affairs during Reconstruction had ushered in an era of bad government, financial mismanagement, and racial antagonism. Reconstruction served here as a warning, a bold example of the dangers to be avoided in the present controversy. Though the book was presented as an objective history of Reconstruction, it was, in fact, a thinly veiled attempt to forestall further federal involvement in southern elections.[10] Congress failed to pass Lodge's bill. The political efficacy of Reconstruction memory, however, was a lesson that would not soon be forgotten.

By the turn of the twentieth century, a more stridently white supremacist depiction of Reconstruction took hold. The timing was not coincidental. In the last decade of the nineteenth century and the first decade of the twentieth, white southerners had set about eradicating the last vestiges of black civil equality and political participation. The resulting system of racial inequality, known as Jim Crow, would last until the post–World War II decades. Turn-of-the-century black southerners endured a three-pronged attack on their civil and political rights. Disfranchisement statutes stripped most African Americans of the right to vote. Segregation separated the public spaces of the South into black and white spheres, with the best and most modern amenities invariably reserved for whites. Above it all loomed the horrific specter of mob violence and lynching, the ultimate punishment for those who resisted the racial order or stepped out of line. Jim Crow was not born overnight. The system grew from years of legislation, agitation, and organization. This political work of Jim Crow benefited from—and helped to create—a white supremacist memory of Reconstruction.[11]

Few southern politicians in the Jim Crow era were more adept at using the memory of Reconstruction than Benjamin R. Tillman. As a young man in South Carolina, Tillman had joined the Red Shirts, a group of white supremacist vigilantes who were largely responsible for the overthrow of Republican rule in the state. Years later, while serving as South Carolina's governor and then senator, Tillman frequently used the story of Reconstruction to advance the cause of white supremacy. In a 1907 speech on the floor of the Senate, Tillman was characteristically outspoken, recalling his involvement in the Red Shirts:

> It was in 1876, thirty years ago, and the people of South Carolina had been living under negro rule for eight years. There was a condition bordering on anarchy. Misrule, robbery, and murder were holding high carnival. The people's substance was being stolen, and there was no incentive to labor. Our legislature was composed of a majority of negroes, most of whom could neither read nor write.... We felt the very foundations of our civilization crumbling beneath our feet, that we were sure to be engulfed by the black flood of barbarians who were surrounding us.[12]

This condition of affairs, Tillman explained, grew intolerable, forcing the white people of the state to take action: "It was then that 'we shot them'; it was then that 'we killed them'; it was then that 'we stuffed ballot boxes.'" Noting that 1876 was the centennial of the American Revolution, Tillman declared that "the action of the white men of South Carolina in taking the State away from the negroes we regard as a second declaration of independence by the Caucasian from African barbarism."[13] As South Carolina and the rest of the South passed legislation that systematically stripped African Americans of their political and civil rights, the story of Reconstruction (or a version of it) proved exceedingly useful. Invoking the crisis of the 1876 election allowed Tillman to prove the necessity of Jim Crow legislation in 1906. White supremacy, he insisted, was a matter of self-defense. The history of Reconstruction showed as much.

Contemporary fiction also registered this white supremacist turn. Though Reconstruction-themed novels by the popular southern authors Thomas Nelson Page and Joel Chandler Harris were significant, it was the work of Thomas Dixon that best captured the prevailing literary and political mood. In *The Leopard's Spots* (1902) and *The Clansman* (1905), Dixon rewrote the history of Reconstruction to serve the needs of turn-of-the-century white supremacy.[14] Throughout the novels, Dixon argued that black political engagement constituted a direct threat to white southern well-being. This threat was often rendered sexually: black-on-white rape plays a central role in both books despite the fact that, as African American anti-lynching activist Ida B. Wells-Barnett forcefully argued, the vast majority of rapes across the color line were committed on black women by white perpetrators.[15] The specter of black-on-white rape proved extraordinarily powerful in justifying the violence of lynching and the injustice of Jim Crow. In his fiction, Dixon recast Reconstruction as a gendered melodrama. At the heart of his stories stood the white womanhood of the South living in constant fear of sexual violence at the hands of enfranchised and empowered black men—and the white men who would protect them by any means necessary. It bears repeating that Dixon's novels had much more to do with the political needs of the early twentieth century than with the actual facts of Reconstruction. Even so, Reconstruction proved ideal historical fodder for the defenders of Jim Crow.

While Dixon's novels were popular, their most lasting contribution to the diffusion of a white supremacist memory of Reconstruction was as inspiration for director D. W. Griffith's *The Birth of a Nation* (1915). More than three hours long, the film was a sensation. It took the Civil War and Reconstruction as its subject, and large portions of the plot were lifted directly from Dixon's *The Clansman*. Following Dixon, the film casts the Ku Klux Klan as heroes and the saviors of the white South. In the climactic sequence, the riders of the Ku Klux Klan free a white woman from the clutches of a black legislator, clear the streets of an unruly black mob, and scatter a group of black soldiers laying siege to a cabin full of white people. In the following scene, armed Klansmen effectively end Reconstruction by denying African Americans the right to vote in the next election. Though the National Association for the Advancement of Colored People (founded in 1909) led a nationwide protest, the film was extraordinarily popular in both the North and South. Marrying a now-familiar narrative of Reconstruction to the relatively new medium of cinema, *The Birth of a Nation* was the capstone of a generation of white supremacist memory.[16]

Though popular memory and academic history are best understood as distinct, if not contradictory, approaches to the past, a group of professional historians played a powerful and unique role in legitimizing prevailing white supremacist notions of Reconstruction. From the 1890s to the 1910s, William Archibald Dunning of Columbia University trained a generation of historians, who authored the first state-level studies of Reconstruction. Though they were less overtly political than Benjamin Tillman or Thomas Dixon, the so-called Dunning School was deeply critical of northern Republicans, suspicious of the capabilities of southern African Americans, and generally inclined to sympathize with the white South. They were also extraordinarily influential. On Dunning's death in 1922, the New York magazine *Independent* wrote, "No other American has ever so exhaustively studied the period of reconstruction as professor Dunning did, and no other writer, historian or publicist, has so deeply or sanely influenced later American thinking upon the rights and wrongs of that unhappy time."[17] The general outlines of the Dunning School's vision of Reconstruction reigned as academic orthodoxy until the post–World War II era.

By the mid-twentieth century, with the passage of years and the solidification of the Jim Crow system, the memory of Reconstruction ceased to be as central to the South's political ideology as it had been at the turn of the century. Even so, white southern politicians still made semiregular references to the period. During the New Deal, opponents of Franklin Delano Roosevelt mobilized the specter of Reconstruction in an attempt to discredit Roosevelt's expansive economic agenda. Roosevelt's allies became "carpetbaggers"—a Reconstruction-era epithet for northern politicians in the South—while New Deal programs and regulations prompted invidious comparisons to the overreach of the Radical Republicans. Attempts during the New Deal era to outlaw poll taxes and pass anti-lynching legislation prompted predictable references to the racial horrors of Reconstruction.[18] Few southern politicians took these comparisons as far as South Carolina's Ellison "Cotton Ed" Smith. In the run-up to the 1938 election, Smith's followers donned red shirts in a conscious imitation of their white supremacist forebears. Smith's victory speech, delivered beside a monument to Redeemer governor Wade Hampton, featured a pledge to resist "the mongrel breed who would take us back to the horrid days of Reconstruction."[19] More than sixty years after the close of Republican Reconstruction in South Carolina, such rhetoric retained its power.

It should come as no surprise that the memory of Reconstruction made something of a comeback in the post–World War II years, as the civil rights movement began to dismantle the structures of Jim Crow that had governed southern race relations for decades. Historian C. Vann Woodward, a liberal white southerner, dubbed the period "the second Reconstruction," but the sentiment extended far beyond academia.[20] Once again, conservative white southerners, now engaged in a campaign of massive resistance to Supreme Court–ordered desegregation after the 1954 *Brown v. Board of Education* case, decried federal involvement in the region's race relations. Though the civil rights movement did not offer the final word on popular memories of Reconstruction, the 1964 Civil Rights Act, which marked the first federal attempt to protect civil rights since the 1870s, offers a useful bookend to this survey of white southern memory. In a fitting irony, it was President Lyndon B. Johnson, a white southerner, whose signature turned the Civil Rights Act into law.[21]

Of course, white southerners did not remember Reconstruction in a vacuum. A black memorial tradition coexisted and competed with white accounts of Reconstruction, although vast differences in power and access meant that the white (and white supremacist) stories of Reconstruction received a much wider hearing in the South and in the nation. This does not mean that African Americans accepted the prevailing white narrative of Reconstruction. In their writings, speeches, and creative works, black activists and intellectuals kept alive an alternative version of this history. Where white southern treatments of Reconstruction focused on federal overreach, chronic misgovernment, and black incapacity, African Americans' memory work emphasized the successes and accomplishments of the era. Refusing to accept white supremacist misrepresentations, black memory resolutely insisted that emancipation, civil rights, and political rights were the most important legacies of the Civil War and its aftermath. The memory of Reconstruction could be a powerful tool of oppression, but it also served as a seedbed of resistance.

In the early postwar years, Emancipation Day celebrations offered the means through which average black southerners were most likely to participate in the commemoration of Reconstruction. From the immediate postwar years on, local communities regularly held ceremonies, parades, and other events devoted to emancipation. One of the first commemorations, held in Charleston in 1865, featured a mock funeral for the institution of slavery, featuring fifty female mourners dressed in black "but with joyous faces."[22] These commemorations allowed newly emancipated people, long denied a history, to act as curators of their own past. In addition, these ceremonies allowed African Americans to make a powerful claim on inclusion by, quite literally, taking to the streets. Though the contents of these celebrations and the dates on which they happened varied widely across the South, African American emancipation celebrations were a regular occurrence for decades after the Civil War. By the early twentieth century, as the Jim Crow regime foreclosed the relative openness of the Reconstruction era, the more overtly political content of these parades had to be carefully managed. Even so, their larger significance remains clear. In public emancipation celebrations, African Americans told their own stories of the southern past, celebrating emancipation as they laid claim to the public spaces of the region.[23]

Throughout the late nineteenth century and early twentieth, African American intellectuals regularly turned to the history of Reconstruction. For example, the shifting currents of popular memory proved a matter of pressing concern for Frederick Douglass. Born enslaved in Maryland, Douglass made his name as an abolitionist speaker and author before the Civil War. In 1876, as Reconstruction wound down and the nation celebrated its centennial, Douglass worried about the rising tide of sectional reunion between North and South. "If war among the whites brought peace and liberty to blacks," he asked, "what will peace among the whites bring?"[24] Douglass worried that an overly hasty reunion between the former combatants would result in a betrayal of emancipation and Reconstruction. He insisted that the failure of Reconstruction was rooted not in federal overreach or black incompetence, but in white southern violence and the Republican Party's flagging commitment to its African American allies. Until the end of his life, Douglass claimed that Reconstruction was just and that emancipation was the most sacred legacy of the Civil War era. More than this, he insisted that memory—the way that Americans understood the tumultuous events of the 1860s and 1870s—mattered deeply.[25]

Douglass was not alone. Around the turn of the century, a number of other African American authors undertook a defense of the Reconstruction project.

T. Thomas Fortune, editor of the *New York Age* and one of the foremost black radicals of the era, presented a profound reconsideration of Reconstruction in his 1884 book, *Black and White*. Fortune's economic interpretation of the postwar era offered a direct challenge to the sort of racial melodrama that passed as popular memory among southern whites.[26] In two pamphlets, "Southern Horrors" (1892) and "A Red Record" (1895), Ida B. Wells traced the region's lynching epidemic to the white South's attempt to reassert control in the aftermath of the Civil War and Reconstruction.[27] In his 1905 book, *The Aftermath of Slavery*, William A. Sinclair defended the policies of the Radical Republicans and roundly criticized white southerners for a wave of violence that had turned the South into a "charnel-house and chamber of horrors."[28] A number of other African American thinkers at the turn of the century, including Bishop Henry McNeal Turner and educator Booker T. Washington, also reflected on the significance of emancipation and Reconstruction in their speeches and writings.[29]

The most influential black intellectual of the early twentieth century was W. E. B. Du Bois, who explored Reconstruction at great length in his classic *The Souls of Black Folk* (1903). The book's second chapter, "Of the Dawn of Freedom," offers a reinterpretation of the history of Reconstruction. Du Bois, who had earned a PhD from Harvard University, denied the dominant, white supremacist narrative of the period, casting Reconstruction as an experiment in racial justice left tragically incomplete.[30] More than three decades later, Du Bois returned to the history of the postwar era in his magisterial *Black Reconstruction in America* (1935). Though the volume is justly famous for its nuanced and extraordinarily detailed analysis of postwar labor relations, the most significant aspect of *Black Reconstruction* may be its treatment of history writing and popular memory. In the book's last chapter, "The Propaganda of History," Du Bois engaged with the falsehoods that had come to pass as the history of Reconstruction. Focusing particularly on the legacy of the Dunning School, Du Bois offered a defense of Reconstruction and a powerful reflection on the uses and misuses of history.[31]

Fine art also shaped popular memories of Reconstruction. In 1934, African American painter Aaron Douglas, a native of Kansas who was deeply involved in the artistic and cultural movement known as the Harlem Renaissance, completed a series of four paintings called "Aspects of Negro Life." The second of the series, *From Slavery to Reconstruction*, highlights the promise and betrayal of Reconstruction. The image explores the dawning of freedom. Responding to the reading of the Emancipation Proclamation, the formerly enslaved people arise while a trumpet blows "jubilee," a term used to denote the coming of freedom. The central portion of the image highlights the birth of black politics during Reconstruction. The painting's central figure, armed with a ballot, points to the capitol building in the distance as his followers turn from the work of picking cotton to embrace the political realm. The painting also dramatizes the retreat from Reconstruction. As Union soldiers march out of the South, the riders of the Ku Klux Klan make their appearance, forcing the freedpeople to return to the soil. Much like the actual history it depicts, the resolution of Douglas's imagined Reconstruction is decidedly mixed.[32]

During the civil rights era, movement supporters found inspiration and lessons by studying the post–Civil War era. Though Martin Luther King Jr.'s "I Have a Dream" speech, which he delivered in 1963 at the March on Washington for Jobs and Freedom, is justly remembered as a touchstone in the civil rights struggle, it is also worth considering the speech as a statement on the legacies of Reconstruction. King's "I have a dream" refrain, the most famous portion of the speech, occurred near the end of the address. Before that, however, he used his surroundings to reflect on the meaning of freedom. The speech was delivered on the steps of the Lincoln Memorial. Describing Abraham Lincoln's Emancipation Proclamation as "a great beacon light of hope to millions of negro slaves," King insisted that the promise of emancipation had not been fulfilled. "One hundred years later, the Negro is still not free," he claimed. "One hundred years later the life of the Negro is still sadly crippled by the manacles of segregation and the chains of discrimination." Left unspoken in King's formulation was the betrayal of Reconstruction. Indeed, Reconstruction was the historical ghost haunting King's address. The incomplete revolution of the 1860s and 1870s functioned as the tie connecting the promises of the past to the "shameful condition" of the present. It was the failure of the first Reconstruction that prompted demands for a second. By the same token, the lingering promise of emancipation and Reconstruction provided King with hope for a brighter, more just future.[33]

History is not simply the study of events. It is also the study of the ways that people have understood those events and used them to guide further action. History is layered. Though we tend to divide the past into discrete and finite eras, the lived experience of individuals is never so neat and tidy. Even after 1877, the struggles of Reconstruction remained deeply relevant. The memory of Reconstruction was hotly contested precisely because the period itself was so momentous, violent, and transformational. The issues at stake—the rights of citizenship, the bounds of the nation, the power of the federal government, the legacies of race in the United States—all but guaranteed that the battles of Reconstruction would be fought again and again in the realm of memory. Indeed, these issues remain vexing to the present day.

To conclude, I return to New Orleans and the Battle of Liberty Place. The Liberty Place monument stood on Canal Street, the city's main business thoroughfare, for decades. Generations of New Orleanians, black and white, could not help but engage with the history of Reconstruction whenever they passed

Erected in 1905, a bronze representation of Nathan Bedford Forrest in his Confederate uniform reigned over downtown Memphis for more than a century. It was removed in December 2017, one year and seven months after the unveiling of the Memphis Massacre marker. Detroit Publishing Company Photograph Collection, Prints and Photographs Division, Library of Congress, Washington, D.C.

by. By the late twentieth century, however, the prevailing currents of memory had shifted significantly. A violent white supremacist coup no longer seemed a point of pride in a post–civil rights New Orleans. In the 1980s, repairs to Canal Street offered the city an opportunity to place the statue in storage. Several years later, local groups sued to bring the statue back. After an extensive debate, the monument was placed in an inconspicuous spot off Canal Street. For another twenty-five years, the Liberty Place monument stood within a stone's throw of Canal Street but out of sight, wedged between an electrical transformer, a retaining wall, and a parking garage. Then, in 2015 a white supremacist shot nine black parishioners at the Emanuel African Methodist Episcopal Church in Charleston, South Carolina. In response, New Orleans mayor Mitch Landrieu vowed to remove Confederate and white supremacist symbolism from the memorial landscape of his city. He specifically targeted three monuments dedicated to leading Confederates—Robert E. Lee, Jefferson Davis, and P. G. T. Beauregard—and the obelisk commemorating the Battle of Liberty Place. More than a century after its dedication, the Liberty Place monument was removed in April 2017.[34]

Does Landrieu's act signify the last word on Reconstruction memory? Not likely. One specific monument to white liberty in New Orleans no longer stands, but the legacies of Reconstruction run much deeper.

NOTES

1. Justin A. Nystrom, *New Orleans after the Civil War: Race, Politics, and a New Birth of Freedom* (Baltimore, Md.: Johns Hopkins University Press, 2010), 160–85; and James Hogue, *Uncivil War: Five New Orleans Street Battles and the Rise and Fall of Radical Reconstruction* (Baton Rouge: Louisiana State University Press, 2006), 116–43.

2. Lawrence Powell, "Reinventing Tradition: Liberty Place, Historical Memory, and Silk-Stocking Vigilantism in New Orleans Politics," *Slavery and Abolition* 20, no. 1 (1999): 127–49. Powell's account is the only scholarly exploration of popular memories of Liberty Place.

3. "Remembered," *Daily Picayune* (New Orleans), September 15, 1891, 1.

4. Unidentified newspaper clipping in scrapbook, MSS 422, box 2, Frederick Nash Ogden Papers, Louisiana Research Collection, Tulane University, New Orleans (first quote); "Lesson of the Fourteenth of September," *Times-Picayune* (New Orleans), September 14, 1915, 14 (second quote).

5. Powell, "Reinventing Tradition."

6. Barbie Zelizer, "Reading the Past against the Grain: The Shape of Memory Studies," *Critical Studies in Mass Communication* 12 (June 1995): 214–39. See also Jeffrey K. Olick, Vered Venitzky-Seroussi, and Daniel Levy, eds., *The Collective Memory Reader* (New York: Oxford University Press, 2011). For memory in the American South, see W. Fitzhugh Brundage, ed., *Where These Memories Grow: History, Memory, and Southern Identity* (Chapel Hill: University of North Carolina Press, 2000); and Brundage, *The Southern Past: A Clash of Race and Memory* (Cambridge, Mass.: Harvard University Press, 2005).

7. Bruce E. Baker, *What Reconstruction Meant: Historical Memory in the American South* (Charlottesville: University of Virginia Press, 2007); and Carole Emberton and Bruce E. Baker, eds., *Remembering Reconstruction: Struggles over the Meaning of America's Most Turbulent Era* (Baton Rouge: Louisiana State University Press, 2017).

8. "Louisiana Contested Election, Speech of Hon. L. Q. C. Lamar of Mississippi, in the House of Representatives, June 8, 1874," *Congressional Record*, 43rd Cong., 1st sess., 428.

9. Ibid., 431.

10. Hilary Herbert et al., eds., *Why the Solid South? or, Reconstruction and Its Results* (Baltimore, Md.: R. H. Woodward, 1890); Baker, *What Reconstruction Meant*, 22–25.

11. Leon F. Litwack, *Trouble in Mind: Black Southerners in the Age of Jim Crow* (New York: Vintage, 1999); Grace Hale, *Making Whiteness: The Culture of Segregation in the South* (New York: Pantheon, 1998); Michael Perman, *Struggle for Mastery: Disfranchisement in the South, 1888–1908* (Chapel Hill: University of North Carolina Press, 2001).

12. Benjamin R. Tillman, speech in the U.S. Senate, January 21, 1907, *Congressional Record*, 59th Cong., 2nd sess., 1440.

13. Ibid. See also Stephen Kantrowitz, *Ben Tillman and the Reconstruction of White Supremacy* (Chapel Hill: University of North Carolina Press, 2000).

14. Thomas Dixon Jr., *The Leopard's Spots: A Romance of the White Man's Burden, 1865–1900* (New York: Doubleday, Page, 1902); Dixon, *The Clansman* (New York: Doubleday, Page, 1905).

15. Jacqueline Jones Royster, *Southern Horrors and Other Writings: The Anti-Lynching Campaign of Ida B. Wells, 1892–1900*, 2nd ed. (New York: Bedford/St. Martin's, 2016).

16. Thomas Cripps, *Slow Fade to Black: The Negro in American Film, 1900–1942* (New York: Oxford University Press, 1977), 41–69.

17. Quoted in John David Smith, "Introduction," in *The Dunning School: Historians, Race, and the Meaning of Reconstruction*, ed. John David Smith and J. Vincent Lowery (Lexington: University of Kentucky Press, 2013), 1.

18. Baker, *What Reconstruction Meant*, 89–109; and Jason Ward, "Remembering and Refighting Reconstruction in the Roosevelt Era," in Emberton and Baker, *Remembering Reconstruction*, 35–56.

19. Quoted in Baker, *What Reconstruction Meant*, 102.

20. C. Vann Woodward, *The Strange Career of Jim Crow* (1955; rpt., New York: Oxford University Press, 1994), 8.

21. Baker, *What Reconstruction Meant*, 145–62.

22. Kathleen Clark, "Celebrating Freedom: Emancipation Day Celebrations and African American Memory in the Early Reconstruction South," in Brundage, *Where These Memories Grow*, 118.

23. Kathleen Clark, *Defining Moments: African American Commemoration and Political Culture in the South, 1863–1913* (Chapel Hill: University of North Carolina Press, 2005); and Mitch Kachun, *Festivals of Freedom: Memory and Meaning in African American Emancipation Celebrations, 1808–1915* (Amherst: University of Massachusetts Press, 2003).

24. Quoted in David W. Blight, *Race and Reunion: The Civil War in American Memory* (Cambridge, Mass.: Belknap, 2001), 132.

25. David W. Blight, *Frederick Douglass's Civil War: Keeping Faith in Jubilee* (Baton Rouge: Louisiana State University Press, 1989).

26. T. Thomas Fortune, *Black and White: Land, Labor, and Politics in the South* (1884; rpt., New York: Washington Square Press, 2007).

27. Royster, *Southern Horrors and Other Writings*.

28. William A. Sinclair, *The Aftermath of Slavery: A Study of the Condition and Environment of the American Negro* (New York: Small, Maynard, 1905), 97.

29. Andre E. Johnson, *The Forgotten Prophet: Bishop Henry McNeal Turner and the African American Prophetic Tradition* (New York: Lexington, 2012); Robert J. Norrell, *Up from History: The Life of Booker T. Washington* (Cambridge, Mass.: Harvard University Press, 2009).

30. W. E. B. Du Bois, *The Souls of Black Folk*, ed. David W. Blight and Robert Gooding Williams (1903; rpt., Boston: Bedford/St. Martin's, 1997).

31. W. E. B. Du Bois, *Black Reconstruction in America, 1860–1880* (1935; rpt., New York:

Free Press, 1998), 711–30. See also David Levering Lewis, *W. E. B. Du Bois: A Biography* (New York: Henry Holt, 2009), 576–94.

32. See Susan Earle, ed., *Aaron Douglas: African American Modernist* (New Haven, Conn.: Yale University Press, 2007).

33. Clayborne Carson and Kris Shepard, eds., *A Call to Conscience: The Landmark Speeches of Dr. Martin Luther King, Jr.* (New York: Grand Central Publishing, 2001), 81–87, 81 (quotations).

34. Kevin Litten, "New Orleans Officials Can Remove Liberty Place Monument, Federal Judge Rules," NOLA.com, March 9, 2017, http://www.nola.com/politics/index.ssf/2017/03/new_orleans_officials_can_remo.html; Beau Evans, "Removal of the First of Four New Orleans Confederate Monuments Begins with Liberty Place," NOLA.com, April 24, 2017, http://www.nola.com/politics/index.ssf/2017/04/monuments_removed_new_orleans.html.

ACKNOWLEDGMENTS

The Memphis Massacre Project has been deliberately collective from its conception, and the people to whom we're indebted reflect that inclusivity. Indeed, the project was born of conversations with others, first with Gregory P. Downs when he planted the seed for a public commemoration timed for the sesquicentennial of the Memphis Massacre, and then shortly thereafter with Timothy Good, the superintendent of the Ulysses S. Grant National Historic Site. From there, our community grew.

Recognizing that the Memphis Massacre is a part of every American's history, we sought the institutional, intellectual, and financial support of a broad group of partners. Much-needed financial support came from the University of Memphis's Department of History, African and African American Studies Program, Department of Communication, the Benjamin L. Hooks Institute for Social Change, the Marcus Orr Center for the Humanities, and the College of Arts and Sciences. The Rhodes College History Department and Communities for Conversation, the West Tennessee Historical Society, the Tennessee Civil War National Heritage Area, the National Park Service, Humanities Tennessee, the Second Congregational Church of Memphis, and private donors Ronald and Marianne Walter and Dr. Charles Crawford contributed additional support and funding. Their generosity underwrote six months of public programming, paid for our capstone symposium, and helped underwrite this volume.

Equally as important, we have been supported in less tangible ways by our community partners. LeMoyne-Owen College, the Pink Palace–Memphis Museums, the Memphis Public Library, the University of Memphis Libraries, the National Civil Rights Museum, the Orange Mound Community Center, the Orange Mound Gallery, and Southwest Tennessee Community College provided space for public lectures, book talks, teachers workshops, and exhibits, enabling us to reach out to and draw in a deep and diverse audience who, in turn, repaid us with energy, intellect, and question after probing question. The synergy was amazing.

The Memphis branch of the NAACP deserves special recognition. Unwaveringly committed to the erection of a physical marker recognizing the Memphis Massacre, Phyllis Aluko (the first African American woman to be appointed as the chief public defender of Shelby County) and Madeline Cooper Taylor (executive director of the Memphis NAACP) worked in partnership with the National Park Service to give the nation its first ever marker recognizing any aspect of

Reconstruction's violent history. Their battle to place the Memphis Massacre marker deserves a book of its own. It is a tale of twenty-first-century race politics and what occurs when history-as-it-happened collides with history-as-imagined.

This book would not have been possible without the help of everyone who participated in the symposium on which it rests. In addition to the contributors to this volume, we thank our hard-working graduate students; Karen L. Bradley, whose administrative magic kept us out of the red; and an audience that gave up two lovely days to grapple with the history of three days of terror. We also thank Femi Ajanaku, Stephen V. Ash, the Honorable Bernice B. Donald, Peter Gathje, Aram Goudsouzian, Max Grivno, Bobby Lovett, the Honorable Mark Luttrell, Steve Masler, Charles McKinney, Ladrica Menson-Furr, Thomas Nenon, Cecelia O'Leary, Robert K. Sutton, Madeline C. Taylor, Ronald Walter, Karen Weddle-West, and Antoinette Van Zelm for their thoughtful commentaries on and contributions to the Memphis Massacre Project. Together, they enriched our initiative by anchoring Reconstruction in our history and in our city.

Our deepest appreciation goes to our then-dean, Thomas Nenon, and Aram Goudsouzian, chair of the History Department. Neither wavered in their support of us and our project, even when we came to them, hat in hand, looking for money.

We thank Mick Gusinde-Duffy, Bethany Snead, and the rest of the staff at the University of Georgia Press for their enthusiasm and for recognizing the need to bring Reconstruction history to a much bigger audience. Likewise, we thank the anonymous readers and editor Merryl A. Sloane, whose careful readings and considerable wisdom made this a much better volume.

Finally, we thank our daughters, who assumed the daunting job of making us look better and sound better: graphic designer Katy O'Donovan Peterson prepared the art for our promotional materials and the Memphis Massacre website, and copyeditor Julia Bond Ellingboe saved us from any number of embarrassing howlers and infelicitous phrases as we turned a conference into a book. Our project and this volume are the better for their contributions.

CONTRIBUTORS

BEVERLY GREENE BOND is a professor of history at the University of Memphis. In addition to being the author of essays on Memphis history and African American women in Memphis and Tennessee, Bond is the coeditor of the two-volume *Tennessee Women: Their Lives and Times* and coauthor of *Memphis in Black and White*, *Beale Street*, and two books on the history of the University of Memphis. Bond is also codirector of the Memphis Massacre Project.

GREGORY P. DOWNS is a professor of history at the University of California, Davis. He is the author of *After Appomattox: Military Occupation and the Ends of War*, *Declarations of Dependence: The Long Reconstruction of Popular Politics in the South*, and *The Second American Revolution: The Civil War Era Struggle over Cuba and the Rebirth of the American Republic*. With Kate Masur, he cowrote the National Park Service's theme study on Reconstruction and helped edit the park service's handbook on Reconstruction. With Scott Nesbit, he developed the digital site Mapping Occupation.

JIM DOWNS is a professor of history and the director of American studies at Connecticut College. He is the author of *Sick from Freedom: African American Illness and Suffering during the Civil War and Reconstruction* and is coeditor with David Blight of *Beyond Freedom: Disrupting the History of Emancipation*.

CAROLE EMBERTON is an associate professor of history at the University at Buffalo. Her first book, *Beyond Redemption: Race, Violence, and the American South after the Civil War*, won the Willie Lee Rose Prize for best book on southern history from the Southern Association of Women Historians.

TIMOTHY S. HUEBNER is the Sternberg Professor of History at Rhodes College in Memphis. He is the author of *Liberty and Union: The Civil War Era and American Constitutionalism*, *The Taney Court: Justices, Rulings, and Legacy*, and *The Southern Judicial Tradition: State Judges and Sectional Distinctiveness, 1790–1890*. He is the coeditor with Kermit L. Hall of the second edition of *Major Problems in American Constitutional History*. Huebner also serves as the coeditor of the Southern Legal Studies series for the University of Georgia Press and as an associate editor of the *Journal of Supreme Court History*.

ELIZABETH L. JEMISON is an assistant professor of religion at Clemson University. She is the author of *Christian Citizens: Race and Belonging in the Post-Emancipation South*. Jemison was recognized in the 2016–2017 cohort of the Young Scholars in American Religion program.

ANDRE E. JOHNSON is an associate professor in the Department of Communication at the University of Memphis. He is the author of *The Forgotten Prophet: Bishop Henry McNeal Turner and the African American Prophetic Tradition*, which won the National Communication Association's African American Communication and Culture Division Outstanding Book Award in 2013. He is the coauthor with Amanda Nell Edgar of *The Struggle over Black Lives Matter and All Lives Matter*, and he is the author of *No Future in This Country: The Prophetic Pessimism of Bishop Henry McNeal Turner*.

KATE MASUR is an associate professor of history at Northwestern University. She is the author of *An Example for All the Land: Emancipation and the Struggle over Equality in Washington, D.C.*, the editor of a new edition of John E. Washington's *They Knew Lincoln*, and the coeditor with Gregory P. Downs of *The World the Civil War Made*.

SUSAN EVA O'DONOVAN is an associate professor of history at the University of Memphis and the codirector of the Memphis Massacre Project. She is a former editor with the Freedmen and Southern Society Project, the coeditor of two volumes of *Freedom: A Documentary History of Emancipation, 1861–1867*, and the author of *Becoming Free in the Cotton South*. An OAH Distinguished Lecturer, she has been the recipient of several awards, including the James A. Rawley Prize from the OAH and fellowships at the Newberry Library and the Gilder Lehrman Center for the Study of Slavery, Resistance, and Abolition.

K. STEPHEN PRINCE is an associate professor of history at the University of South Florida. He is the author of *Stories of the South: Race and the Reconstruction of Southern Identity, 1865–1915* and *Radical Reconstruction: A Brief History with Documents*.

JOSEPH P. REIDY is an emeritus professor at Howard University. With Ira Berlin, Leslie S. Rowland, and others, he coedited the first four volumes of *Freedom: A Documentary History of Emancipation, 1861–1867* and *Free at Last: A Documentary History of Slavery, Freedom, and the Civil War*, which won the Lincoln Prize in 1994. His other works include *From Slavery to Agrarian Capitalism in the Cotton Plantation South: Central Georgia, 1800–1880* and *Illusions of Emancipation: The Pursuit of Freedom and Equality in the Twilight of Slavery*.

JOHN C. RODRIGUE is the Lawrence and Theresa Salameno Professor in the Department of History at Stonehill College. He is the author of *Lincoln and Reconstruction* and *Reconstruction in the Cane Fields: From Slavery to Free Labor in Louisiana's Sugar Parishes, 1862–1880*. He has been an editor on the Freedmen and Southern Society Project at the University of Maryland, and he is a coeditor of the 1865 volume of *Freedom: A Documentary History of Emancipation*.

HANNAH ROSEN is an associate professor of history and American studies at William and Mary. She is the author of *Terror in the Heart of Freedom: Citizenship, Sexual*

Violence, and the Meaning of Race in the Postemancipation South. She is also the codirector with Martha Jones of the Celia Project: The History and Memory of Slavery and Sexual Violence, a collaborative, interdisciplinary research endeavor.

JOSHUA D. ROTHMAN is a professor of history and chair of the Department of History at the University of Alabama. He is the author of several books, including *Flush Times and Fever Dreams: A Story of Capitalism and Slavery in the Age of Jackson*, which won the Frank L. and Harriet C. Owsley Award from the Southern Historical Association for the best book in southern history.

JULIE SAVILLE is an associate professor emerita at the University of Chicago. She is the author of *The Work of Reconstruction: From Slave to Wage Laborer in South Carolina*; coeditor of *The Wartime Genesis of Free Labor: The Lower South* (part of the documentary history *Freedom: A Documentary History of Emancipation in the United States*), and assistant editor of two volumes of *The Papers of Frederick Douglass*.

CALVIN SCHERMERHORN is a professor of history at Arizona State University. He is the author of *Unrequited Toil: A History of United States Slavery*, *The Business of Slavery and the Rise of American Capitalism, 1815–1860*, and *Money over Mastery, Family over Freedom: Slavery in the Antebellum Upper South*. He is also the coeditor of *Rambles of a Runaway from Southern Slavery* by Henry Goings.

ANDREW L. SLAP is a professor of history at East Tennessee State University. He is the author of *The Doom of Reconstruction: The Liberal Republicans in the Civil War Era* and *African American Communities during Slavery, War, and Peace: Memphis in the Nineteenth Century*, the editor of *Reconstructing Appalachia: The Civil War's Aftermath*, and the coeditor of *This Distracted and Anarchical People: New Answers for Old Questions about the Civil War Era North* and *Confederate Cities: The Urban South during the Civil War Era*. He is currently editing the *Oxford Reconstruction Handbook*.

INDEX

Italicized page numbers indicate illustrations.

abolition movement, 14–15, 33, 53–66, 161n5
Adams, John, 14–15
African Americans: Christianity of, 89–91; labor unions of, 85; legal restraints on, 80, 85, 104, 115n11; military service of, 6, 37–49, 69, 78, 120–30, 156; organizing traditions of, 135–46; orphanages for, *105*; as police officers, 84; political power of, 83–85; rape testimony of, 102–13; "Trail of Tears" of, 9, 27–34
African Methodist Episcopal (AME) Church, 91, 92, 178, 181, 200. *See also* Methodists
Agnew, Samuel, 95–96
Alexander, John, 122
Alexander, Lucretia, 90
Alexander, Robert, 181
American Colonization Societies, 155, 187
American Indians. *See* Native Americans
Anaconda Plan, 39
Armour, Harriet, 108, *109*, 110–11, 113
Ash, Stephen, 117n36
Attucks, Crispus, 153

Bacon, Jacqueline, 161n5
Baker, Ella, 121–22
Baker, York, 121
Baltimore, Md., 4, 27
Bankel, Henry, 126
Baptists, 90, 92, 96, 182
Bates, Edward, 157
Beaumont, Henry, 127
Beauregard, P. G. T., 200
Belz, Herman, 59, 162n10
Birth of a Nation (film), 2, 195
Black Codes, 159
"black constitutionalism," 149–61
Black History Month, 8

Black Lives Matter movement, 4, 9
Bloom, Peter, 102
Bloom, Rebecca Ann, 102, 109, 110, 113
Boudar, Thomas, 31
Bowers, Claude G., 2
Bowman, Stephen, 126
Brooks, Preston, 168
Brown, William J., 40–41
Brown, William Wells, 153
Brown v. Board of Education (1954), 196
Brownlow, William G. "Parson," 56, 61–65
Bryan, William Jennings, 188
Bryant, John E., 179, 182
Buckner, Jack, 124
Burns, Ken, 4
Butler, Benjamin, 70, 156

Callahan, John, 48
Campbell, B. M., 27–28
Campbell, Tunis, 183
Campbell, William B., 56, 58, 61, 62
Carruthers, George, 94
Chamberlain, Daniel, 167
Charleston, S.C., 4, 156; racial violence in, 82, 83
Chase, Salmon P., 163n28
Cherokee people, 28
Cherry, Tony, 47–48
Choctaw people, 16–17, 22, 28
Christianity, 89–99
citizenship, 41, 96, 149–50; birthright, x, 157; *Dred Scott* decision and, 150–55; enfranchisement and, 105–6, 156–61, 168–69; Fifteenth Amendment on, 185–86; Native Americans and, 153. *See also* suffrage
Civil Rights Act (1866), 82, 105, 159
Civil Rights Act (1875), 186

Civil Rights Act (1964), 9, 196
Clark, William, 123–24
Coe, William, 34, 45
Colfax Massacre (La.), 171–73
Compromise of 1850, 22
Compromise of 1877, 112
Constitution, on slavery, 12–13, 24n6, 149–61. *See also specific amendments*
"contrabands," 70, 79, 156
cotton economy, 5–6, 11–22, 31–32
Cox, Samuel S. "Sunset," 59
Creek Nation, 16, 28
Crescent City White League (CCWL), 169–70, 190–91. *See also* white supremacist organizations
Cromley, Robert, 181
Cromwell, Oliver, 174
Crutchfield, George, 125
Curtis, Benjamin, 151, 153

"damnesty oath," 59–61
Daniel, Peter V., 151
Davis, Angela, 132
Davis, Jefferson, x, 4, 9, 200
Declaration of Independence, 150–52, 154, 158, 161
Delany, Martin, 162n6
deserters, 122–23, 130n5
Dixon, Thomas, 194–95
Douglas, Aaron, 198, 199
Douglas, Stephen, 153
Douglass, Frederick, 90, 150, 152, 156, 157, 197
Downing, George T., 154
Dred Scott v. Sandford (1857), 96, 149–55, 157, 161
Du Bois, W. E. B., xi, 8, 198
Dunlap family, 123
Dunning, William Archibald, 195

Eaton, John, Jr., 49n9, 72–74
Egerton, Douglas, 135
Emancipation Proclamation, 37, 40, 55–57, 78, 93, 158; black citizenship and, 157; commemorations of, 41; exemptions to, 41, 57, 64–65, 158; King on, 199; military's role in, 54–60. *See also* abolition movement
Episcopalians, 93, 101n19
Equal Justice Initiative, xiii
Equal Rights and Educational Association, 182–83
Etheridge, Emerson, 58–59, 62
Ex parte Milligan, ix–x

Faulkner, William, 166
Fields, Barbara J., 72
Fifteenth Amendment, 2, 185–86
Finch, Adam, 143
Fisk, Clinton B., 44, 45
Fisk University, 85
Foner, Eric, xi, 4
Forrest, Nathan Bedford, x, 31; statue of, 4, 9, 200
Fort Pickering, Tenn., xi, 37, 40–41, 44; freedpeople of, 68–75, 98, 120–30
Fortune, T. Thomas, 140–41, 198
"forty acres and a mule," 137–38
Foster, Catherine "Kate" Olivia, 95
Foucault, Michel, 168
Fourteenth Amendment, 149–61; ratification of, 2, 96; Stevens on, ix, x
Franklin, John Hope, 8, 168
Frazier, Frank, 133
Freedmen's Bureau, 37, 44–48, 81, 97, 106; creation of, 44; Memphis Massacre inquiry by, 102
freedpeople, 68–75, 77–78, 79; Christianity of, 89–99; as "contraband," 70, 79, 156; hospitals for, 72–73; as "refugees," 70–71, 104–6, *105*
Fugitive Slave Act (1850), 150, 155, 156

Gabriel's Rebellion (1800), 15
Galloway, Abraham, 157, 158
Galtung, Johan, 68
Garnett, Henry Highland, 162n6
Garrison, William Lloyd, 149, 152
George, Ann, 43

Georgia Equal Rights Association, 182
Glory (film), 4
Grant, Ulysses S., ix, 41, 58, 95, 170–71; on civil rights, 186; Sheridan and, 174, 175
Griffing, J. B., 32
Griffith, D. W., 2, 195
Grimes, Frank, 128
Grimes, Lottie, 127–28
Guadeloupe, 134
guerrilla warfare, 71, 75

Hahn, Steven, xi, 135
Haitian Revolution, 15, 134, 157
Hampton, Wade, 167, 174, 196
Harlem Renaissance, 198
Harris, Albert, 29–34, 45
Harris, Joel Chandler, 194
Harris, Ransom, 62
Hart, Henry, 126
Hayden, Lewis, 153
Hayes, Molly, 108
Hayes, Rutherford B., 175–76
Hill, Benjamin, 184
Hirschman, A. O., 145
hospitals, 72–74, 112, 123
Howard, Oliver Otis, 44
Howard University, 85
Howley, Mathilda, 33
Hughes, Louis, 42–43
Hunt, Lucy, 44
Hunt, Neely, 107, 117n25

infectious diseases, 73, 79, 127
Ingraham, Joseph Holt, 11, 22
Irish immigrants, 37, 46–47, 51n31

Jackson, Andrew, 16
Jamaica, ix, 134
Jefferson, Thomas, 12, 150, 166; Louisiana Purchase by, 15–16
Jim Crow laws, x, 3, 6, 193–97
Johnson, Andrew, 47–48, 53, 159–60; on black suffrage, 64; on Memphis Massacre, ix–x;

as military governor, 56–66; Reconstruction policies of, 2, 57, 140; slavery views of, 56, 63–64; thanksgiving proclamation of, 96–97
Johnson, Lyndon B., 196
Johnson, Mary, 125–26
Jones, Alex, 125, 126
Jones, Jacqueline, 116n16
Jones, John G., 97
Jones, Robert, 126
Jones, Welland, 33
Jordan, Mary, 28–29, 32, 34
Jordan, Tony, 125–26
Julian, George, 175, 176

Kantrowitz, Stephen, 161n3
Kellogg, William Pitt, 190–91
King, Martin Luther, Jr., x, 199
Kinsley, Edward, 157
Knight, Isham, 123
Ku Klux Klan, 34, 169, 187, 195

Lamar, Lucius Q. C., 192
Landrieu, Mitch, 200
Lane, Isaac, 93
Lee, Fitzhugh, 167
Lee, Robert E., 95, 133, 200
LeMoyne Normal and Commercial School, 85
LeMoyne-Owen College, 5
Levi, Primo, 170
Lewis, Simon, 127
Liberia, 18
Liberty Place, Battle of, 190–91, 199–200
Lincoln, Abraham, 155–57, 168; assassination of, 95; Douglas debates of, 153; on *Dred Scott* decision, 153–54; election of, 39; Reconstruction plans of, 57–59. *See also* Emancipation Proclamation
Lipford, David, 123
Lodge, Henry Cabot, 193
Louisiana Purchase, 15–16
Lynch, James D., 159

Lynch, John R., 172
lynchings, xii–xiii

Madison, Warner, 45–46
Mageveny, John, 124
Maxwell, Henry J., 159
Maynard, Horace, 56
McCannon, Shreve, 166
McCargo (or Mack), Sidney, 121–22
McClellan, George B., 61, 62
McDorman, Todd F., 163n18
McKenney, Henrietta, 126
McKinley, William, 188
Memphis, 85; black churches of, 89, 96, 98–99; demographics of, 38, 115n12, 116n16; illustrations of, *18*, *55*; Irish immigrants of, 38, 46–47, 51n31; orphanage in, *105*; slavery in, 31, 69, 104
Memphis Massacre (1866), ix–xiii, 1–8, *103*; causes of, 7; historical marker of, xii, *3*, *9*; humanitarian crisis before, 68–75; sexual violence during, 102
Memphis Massacre Project, 4–5
Meriwether, Elizabeth, 118n46
Methodists, 90, 92, 96–97. *See also* African Methodist Episcopal Church
Middle Passage, 27
Minter, Andrew, 40, 45, 48
Mitchell, Margaret, 2
Motley, Anthony, 46

National Association of the Advancement of Colored People (NAACP), *3*, 8, 9, 195
National Civil Rights Museum, 5
National Equal Rights League (NERL), 62, 64, 159, 160
Native Americans, 16–17, 22, 28, 33; citizenship of, 153
Nell, William, 152–53
Nelson, Thomas A. R., 56
New Orleans, 15–16, 70; police force of, 84, 168–69, 190; racial violence of 1900 in, 86; school desegregation in, 85; slave market of, 31; White League of, 169–70, 190–91
New Orleans Massacre (1866), ix–xiii, 93
Northup, Solomon, 29
Northwest Ordinance (1787), 14, 154

O'Connor, Flannery, 166
Odd Fellows' Benevolent Society, 41
Olden, Amanda, 108
organizing traditions, 6, 135–46
orphanages, *105*

Page, Thomas Nelson, 194
Peace Democrats, 61
People's Party, 172
Pharr, James, 123
Piles, Robert, 126, 127
Pine Bluff, Ark., lynchings, xii–xiii
Pinkston, Eliza, 141–44
Pinkston, Henry, 143–44
police officers. *See* urban police
Porter, David D., 40
Presbyterians, 93, 95–96
Prichard, Raymond, 144
prison system, 117n25, 132
Prohibition Party, 188
prostitution, 107–8, 113
Pryor, Hubbard, 41, 42, 43
Pulitzer, Joseph, 175

Raboteau, Albert, 90–91
Rael, Patrick, 161n2
rape, 76n22, 86, 102–13
Rawson, Robert, 126
Reconstruction Acts (1867), 83, 141, 145
Red Shirts (paramilitary organization), 167, 174, 193–94
Remond, Charles Lenox, 152, 153, 163n18
Rhodes College, 5
Roach, David, 124
Robinson, Hannah, 27–28, 32, 34
Robinson, Peter, 124

Rock, John, 156
Rodney, Walter, 134
Roosevelt, Franklin Delano, 195–96

school desegregation, 85, 196
Scott, Rebecca, 145
Scott, Winfield, 39
Seminole people, 16, 28
Shelton, Jerry, 122
Sheridan, Philip, 174–75
Sherman, William T., 41
Sikes, William, 126
Sinclair, William A., 198
slave trade, 78; domestic, 19–22, 27–34; international ban of, 13
slavery, 90–91; Constitution on, 12–13, 24n6, 149–61; cotton economy and, 5–6, 11–22, 31–32; demographics of, 11–12, 20–21; in Guadeloupe, 134; "second," 12, 23n3; Wesley on, 90
smallpox, 73, 79, 126
Smith, Ellison "Cotton Ed," 196
Smith, Lucy, 68, 109, 110, 117n36
Smith, Richard, 123–24
Sons and Daughters of Ham (organization), 41
Spivak, Gayatri, 70
Stanton, Henry, 33, 41
Stevens, Thaddeus, 160; on Fourteenth Amendment, ix, x; on Pine Bluff lynchings, xii–xiii
Stevenson, Bryan, xiii
Stoneman, George, 98
streetcars, segregation on, 85
suffrage, 41, 48, 59, 141, 142; enfranchisement and, 105–6, 149–55, 168–69; Andrew Johnson's view of, 64; voter registration and, 9, 84. *See also* citizenship
Sumner, Charles, 168

Tade, Ewing O., 89
Tait, Bacon, 29
Taney, Roger B., 150–55

Taylor, Zachary, 28
Thirteenth Amendment, 54, 96; commemoration of, 182; provisions of, 158; ratification of, 6, 37, 53, 64, 134
Thomas, George H., 41
Thompson, Frances, 109, 110, 112–13, 117n36, 118n46, 119n51
Thurman, Howard, 91
Tibbs, Lucy, 110
Tidwell, Charles, 143–44
Tidwell, David, 143, 144
Tilden, Samuel J., 175
Tillman, Benjamin R., 193–94, 195
Tillson, Davis, 45
tobacco production, 11
Tourgée, Albion, xi
Townsend, Cynthia, 103, 125
transgender people, 112–13, 118n46, 119n51
Truth, Sojourner, 136
Turner, Henry McNeal, 8, 79–80, 178–88, 179, 198
Turner, Nat, 91

Union Leagues, 179, 183
University of Memphis, 5
urban police, 81–82, 104, 106, 120–30; in New Orleans, 84, 168–69, 190

Vesey, Denmark, 91
Vicksburg, siege of, 39, 40
violence, 120–30, 166–76; "epistemic," 70; sexual, 76n22, 86, 102–13; structural, 68–75; "useless," 170
Vorenberg, Michael, 54
voting registration, 9, 84. *See also* suffrage

Waldrep, Christopher, 161n2
War of 1812, 16
Warrington, David, 127–29, 129
Warrington, Diana, 127–29
Washington, Booker T., 198
Wayman, Alexander Walker, 178

Webb, William, 38–39
Welles, Gideon, 40
Wells, Ida B., 198
Wells-Barnett, Ida B., 194
Wesley, John, 90
Weston, Mary Anne, 127
White Man's Party, 172
white supremacist organizations, 34, 166–74, 171, 181, 187, 190

Whitney, Eli, 17
Woodson, Carter G., 8
Woodward, C. Vann, 196
World War I veterans, 86
Wyatt, Bayley, 137

Yeatman, James, 39
yellow fever, 127

www.ingramcontent.com/pod-product-compliance
Lightning Source LLC
Chambersburg PA
CBHW012231230426
43666CB00039B/2898